Praise for The Dream Visitor

"A compelling memoir of a model and actress who is drawn into investigating psychic phenomena and UFOs, and then encounters an alien in a vivid dream that gives her instructions on how to build a telepathic communications device. Daniela Giordano includes an American President, movies stars, celebrated psychics, and a design for a futuristic (or possibly an ancient) technology that through sheer determination she builds herself. Giordano's life sounds like the plot of a science fiction movie, except it's the real deal. What makes her life especially notable is that subsequent research on her alien dream device has confirmed that it apparently does have surprising properties. A remarkable memoir worth reading!" — Dr. Dean Radin, PhD, Chief Scientist at Institute of Noetic Sciences (IONS) Associated Distinguished Professor of Integral and Transpersonal Psychology at California Institute of Integral Studies (CIIS), Distinguished Professor, California Institute of Integral Studies Co-Editor-in-Chief, ExploreBoard Chair, Cognigenics

"*The Dream Visitor* is the unexpected journey of an Italian beauty queen turned actress into the realm of New Age science. As unbelievable as it may seem, Daniela Giordano's story is real and thought-provoking. At first, a curse, her lack of formal scientific training becomes a blessing as she follows her intuition from early experiments with Kirlian photography into the world of consciousness research and extrasensory/telekinetic phenomena. A UFO encounter leaves Daniela with a vision of a pyramid machine, a machine that she must build. But how? Spanning more than five decades, we learn how she uses her film career as the means to support her research and eventually make the machine. But does it work? Read it and find out, but be forwarned—*The Dream Visitor* may leave you with more questions than answers." — Dr. Mark Carlotto, Aerospace Engineer, Independent Scientist, and Author *Not of This World: An Emerging Picture of the UFO Phenomenon, Before Atlantis: New Evidence of Previous Technological Civilizations,* and *Martian Enigmas: A Closer Look*

THE DREAM VISITOR

THE DREAM VISITOR

THE LIFE OF AN
UNUSUAL WOMAN
CHANGED BY
ENCOUNTERS WITH
THE IMPOSSIBLE

DANIELA GIORDANO

EDITED BY KARYN LANGHORNE FOLAN

Bink Books
Bedazzled Ink Publishing Company • Fairfield, California

© 2021 Daniela Giordano

All rights reserved. No part of this publication may be reproduced or transmitted in any means, electronic or mechanical, without permission in writing from the publisher.

paperback 978-1-949290-69-1

Cover Design
by

Bink Books
a division of
Bedazzled Ink Publishing, LLC
Fairfield, California
http://www.bedazzledink.com

To Emilio

and . . . anyone who might be interested

ACKNOWLEDGMENTS

I send all my love to the Bedazzled Ink Publishing team. Their professionalism and affection followed me throughout the preparation of this book. A special thanks to Claudia Wilde, owner and publisher, who immediately loved my story; to Liz Gibson, Acquisitions Editor and Author Liaison, with whom a sincere friendship developed right from the start; and to Casey who worked her magic doing final edits on the manuscript. I couldn't find a better home for my book.

A thank you also goes to the Italian publisher Gordiano Lupi, of the Cultural Association IL FOGLIO, who, published my first book, entitled *Io, Daniela*, focusing on my professional career.

I wish to also thank the Italian publisher Enrico Baccarini, of Enigma Edizioni, who believed in me and this mad literary journey of mine publishing this book in Italian.

All my esteem and admiration goes to Dr. Dean Radin, PhD, Chief Scientist at the Institute of Noetic Sciences (IONS) and Associated Distinguished Professor of Integral and Transpersonal Psychology at the California Institute of Integral Studies (CIIS), who believed in me and honored me with his endorsement and support. Dean Radin has always devoted himself to probing the boundaries of consciousness, mainly psi phenomena, using the tools and techniques of science. He has held positions at AT&T Bell Labs, Princeton University, University of Edinburgh and at SRI International (Stanford Research Institute). So far his books have been translated into fourteen foreign languages. His support has been fundamental to me.

Many thanks go to Dr. Marc Carlotto for his immediate trust in my story. I knew of his work on the Mars surface from 1983/1984. I read about him when I bought *"Unusual Mars Surface Features"*, fourth edition, published by Mars Research, Glenn Dale, Maryland. It was there that I saw his name for the first time—and I have more or less followed his research during the following years.

I owe much to James Hansen, of Nota Diplomatica, former vice-consul in Italy and now a great communicator for companies, who helped me with advice, suggestions and actions.

I also thank Roberto Volterri, a university archaeologist, and author of many publications, whose long friendship dates back to the times I lived in Rome, and we had crazy joint projects. Without his encouragement, it is possible I would not have overcome difficult moments and finished this book.

A lot of affection also to Stefano Iachetti, Experimental Center of Cinematography in Rome, portrait photographer and author of books on the Stars of the seventies, who provided me with the professional competence to present this book to various publishers.

Special thanks to Hugo Santos, from New York, first just a fan and then a sincere friend, who has the ability to find my old photos in the most incredible places.

I also thank Robert Speight, of Twickenham, Middlesex, England, for his helpfulness and kind cooperation.

And I cannot forget Pierriccardo Ferreri, a longtime friend, always present and available when news and digital images that are difficult to find are needed.

Nor do I forget Giovanni Giordano, my cousin, who thanks to his profession as a television journalist, found in an old trunk some really dated images—some included in the Italian edition—which gave me strong emotions.

An affectionate thought goes to Martino Casagrande, former Navy Commander, for his professional competence and for the help and support he has given me in difficult times.

Last, but by no means least, I send all my love and thanks to Emilio Latini wherever he may be. There was not a better man in this world who could have lived with me through this life, encouraged me at every turn, gave me the confidence of my convictions, and made every day a wonderful and new exciting experience. I miss our life together more than there will ever be words to express. In one of his last lucid moments, he told me: "Finish writing your book." He made me promise. He knew I would give up otherwise. Per sempre amore mio.

FOREWORD

Aside from our Italian ancestry, Daniela Giordano's life and mine could not be more different. At first, I did not understand why she had asked me to write a foreword for the English edition of her book, *Tre Vite in Una* (Three Lives in One), titled *The Dream Visitor*. But then I realized that our life paths were similar in a way. Our parents or even ourselves could have predicted neither. It occurred to me we both had lived three lives.

We often talk about past lives in the literal sense. Some feel if they have lived more than one life in terms of marriages, professions, and so forth. But there is another way of looking at the stages of our lives.

We can think of our first life as the one we are born in. We have little control over it, at least in the beginning. How it unfolds depends both on nature and nurture. Our nature determines what we are good at, what we can do without having to try too hard. Our nurture determines how we develop our abilities and helps establish a direction in life, what we do for a living.

For many of us, this direction does not change. Merchants usually remain merchants, academics, academics, artists, artists, etc. However, this was not to be the case for Daniela Giordano.

After being crowned "Miss Italy," a career as an actress seemed inevitable. She was good at it and could earn a comfortable living. But Daniela soon realized that there was much more to life. There was a bigger world, one that she had to experience and understand.

Our second life, if we are fortunate to have the choice, is defined by what we want to do. Daniella decided that she would use her success as an actress as the means to do something completely different. This is generally not an easy thing to do. It involves giving up the security of doing what we are good at to do something that we want to do but might not be very good at. It is hard to know. It requires a leap of faith.

With a passion for knowing what exists beyond the veil of physical reality, she became interested in the paranormal, from telekinesis to Kirlian photography and more. So many of us are afraid to try something new. We think we have to copy what someone else has done or is. Our greatest human gift is the ability to find our own path. Although Daniela lacked formal scientific training, her intuition led her to discover new ways of understanding non-physical phenomena, of imagining a broader, richer reality.

If, in our second life, we are successful at what we want to do, that is how it all generally ends. Fame and fortune are for most welcome rewards for a job well done. But again, there is another choice we can make if we are lucky. And that choice defines our third life—what we should do. What we should do is determined by what is needed to fulfill our purpose as human beings in its true sense.

As our senses have become saturated with stimuli of all kinds, amplified by technology, it is becoming increasingly difficult to find our center, that quiet place within all of us, our true selves. Many believe our interest in ancient mysteries is an attempt to return to the source, to a more human spiritual existence, a balance of heart, mind, and soul. Daniela's UFO experiences followed by her pursuit of the key to pyramid power in order to contact the "dream visitor," the consciousness beyond, is an expression of the need to find that balance and our place in the universe. She has decided that this is what she needs to do, what she must do.

Daniela's story is a metaphor of how our lives, if lived well, can play out in the best possible way. Of how we should take what is given, develop it to the greatest extent possible to live up to our obligations to family and friends, and then give back what is needed to ourselves and humanity.

I applaud Daniela in her brave journey through these three lives and beyond.

Mark Carlotto, Ph. D
Aerospace Engineer, Independent Scientist
Author of *Before Atlantis*

PREFACE

Once in a while, a manuscript comes across our desk that makes one stop and pause. *The Dream Visitor* is such a manuscript. With NASA's and the US Federal Government's recent release of reports finally admitting that evidence suggests that Extraterrestrials do indeed exist, this manuscript could not be more timely. (Although for many, this has been a foregone conclusion for some time!)

I became caught up in the physics and engineering of the pyramid because it brought back all my work in earlier years in space systems engineering. This turned into many conversations with Daniela and a friendship developed that will last a lifetime.

This is the story of Daniela's unfinished journey to complete the assignment given to her by an extraterrestrial "Dream Visitor" who came to her one night many years ago. She was instructed to build a pyramid so that she could communicate with them. Personally, I find the concept of a pyramid's primary purpose being for communication, based on science and technology we already understand in part, is not difficult to believe or conceptualize in general.

Daniela is a unique, very sane, very driven individual, whose layperson's approach to the science and technology is one of an innocent, who was open minded and dedicated throughout her life to explore complex science she knew nothing about. She eventually came to understand it well enough to converse with advanced scientists and engineers. It has been a lifelong journey, and as such it is equally important to understand the author as it is to understand the journey itself. So Daniela shares some of her background and personal life to help us understand her journey, why she dedicated a major portion of her life to try to build the pyramid, and to make us want to join her in her quest and carry on her work.

The main problem is how are we supposed to combine and apply these individual technologies into one pre-defined pyramid shaped unit to make it work for the specified purpose. There must be someone who has the big picture insight, knowledge, and the same spirit and drive that the author had, to take the information to the finish line.

In engineering, we often say young engineers find new discoveries " . . . because they don't know it can't be done . . ." The earth needs to find that one young engineer or scientist who doesn't know it can't be done, and so can take this information from Daniela's Dream Visitor, find the solution, and build a pyramid that will allow us to communicate with our extraterrestrial or extradimensional visitors.

That, dear reader, is your task.

Elizabeth Gibson BA, BS (Physics)
MS (Space Technology)—Retired
Acquisitions Editor
Bedazzled Ink Publishing LLC

"Each passing day will become part of History in the future. Therefore, do not advance lightly. The trick is to leave traces that can be followed tomorrow." — Steve Cussler, writer and founder of NUMA—National Underwater and Marine Agency

"The most beautiful experience we can have is the mysterious. It is the fundamental emotion that stands at the cradle of true art and true science. Whoever does not know it and can no longer wonder, no longer marvel, is as good as dead, and his eyes are dimmed."
— Albert Einstein

INTRODUCTION

When I was nineteen years old, I won a beauty contest.

It was 1966 and when the judges announced me "Miss Italy," no one was more surprised than I was. A simple, average girl from Palermo, I hadn't imagined the changes or the opportunities winning that title would bring me. As Miss Italy, I travelled much of the world. As a fresh and pretty face, I found myself cast in about forty movies over the following two decades, most in the 1970s, during the height of Italian film.

In these days of "influencers" and Internet celebrities, some people might believe that my experiences in building a career in Italian film and finding some fame (or even, notoriety) would make a good enough tale for a book. But for me, that's only part of the story—and not even the best part.

My true interests have always been much more unusual—and my acting career, indeed all of the various jobs and experiences I have had in my life—have all been in service to a deeper exploration: an exploration of the unique and unexplained powers of the mind and of humanity's connection to something far beyond what the eyes can see. These are the things that drove me, fueled my curiosity, and led me to reach far beyond what most people expected from a Miss Italy and a some-time actress.

I have seen children move things with their minds.

I have seen the unexplained flying in the night sky.

And most importantly, I have been visited by someone—something—I cannot ignore and given by him/it a message I *must* convey.

This book is the story of what I call my "three lives" and how they converged to lead me on my quest to develop a new technology (or should I say the rediscovery of an old one) that might offer humankind its greatest advance: the ability to communicate directly from one mind to the other.

Believe me or not, I invite you to open your mind. Consider me a messenger—and my story as the blueprint for the research and scientific investigation that must be undertaken to prove or disprove what I recount in the pages that follow.

I begin, therefore, at the beginning, with a restless young actress and a mysterious man in black.

PART ONE:
THE FIRST LIFE
A FANTASTIC ADVENTURE

CHAPTER ONE
RESTLESS

I sat on an old English-style sofa wearing only a nightgown and stared out the window of the large and spacious room. It was a nice window, but one the sun would never shine on because it looked out on the back of a soundstage. Nothing in the room was real; it was a movie set and I was the one of the stars, making an illusion real through the magic of film.

We were on a break, and I sat on the set, playing thoughtfully with the end of the nightgown's belt. On a small table next to the couch lay the remains of what we call in Italy a basket: a nickname for a lunch meal that consists of a dish of pasta with tomato sauce, a little meat and potatoes. I could have taken my basket to my dressing room to eat, but it was far away, and I did not feel like the walk. Instead, I replayed the scene we had just shot in my mind. I knew I could do better, but the director had thought it had gone well enough. I wished there had been time to do it again and challenge my acting skills. But re-doing the scene would have taken time and in film, perhaps more than any other industry, time is money. In the end, the director had decided that good enough was sufficient and was not interested in going deeper to get a better performance.

That seemed to be the story for me with many of the roles I had performed in. I rarely got the chance to stretch myself, to really find out what I was capable of as an actress. Sometimes, I felt bad about it, but usually not for long. Why should I? I was twenty-eight years old, independent, making money, and at least a little famous, thanks to the newspapers and magazines that still wrote about the exploits and achievements of this former Miss Italy. I had been working as an actress for eight years and things seemed to be going well since the offers kept coming and I often had interesting roles. But I say "seemed" because in the Italian movie business, you never knew. Film in Italy, then and now, is not like film in the United States. Actors aren't nurtured, and careers aren't cultivated. In Italy, an actor is only as relevant as their latest film. Today you work, tomorrow? Who knows? Director Lina Wertmuller was right when she told young girls interested in an acting career: "First open a pizzeria and then, when you have a secure income, become an actress." Security is important. Security gives you choice. Security keeps you from desperation and lets you choose roles wisely, building a career based on what will advance you, rather than what will pay your rent.

In this movie, I was playing the female lead, but I knew that this wasn't going to be the role that would change my career. It was just another part, among many like it, where I was a pretty object to adorn the scene. I would perform my role and move on to the next one, without any significant change in my finances or my future. I was happy for the work and I loved acting, but at the same time, I felt trapped by always being offered the same stereotyped roles and the same shallow characters.

I'd tried to escape into theater and had even accepted a role in a musical comedy scheduled to debut at the Sistina Theatre in Rome. I was thrilled, not only because it was a prestigious venue, but because it was the chance to start down a new road. But it didn't work. I quickly discovered that I wasn't cut out for the stage. Always repeating the same lines, every single day for six months. It drove me crazy. And having to stay on the road, touring with the same play, away from everything and everyone I loved for so long? No, I didn't have a gypsy soul. I needed my home. I had fought for it, earned it, and wanted to stay in it as much as possible. Being a stage actress wasn't for me … but what *was*? I felt restless and unsatisfied about my career and I wasn't sure what to do.

Not only was my career unsettled, my relationships were too. I had recently left a boyfriend after seven years together. There was no future for us, I had finally realized. He was a singer who played concerts all over the world and being constantly separated had made our problems worse. Between his tours and my films, it was difficult for us to find the closeness and connection a solid relationship depended on. It was too bad—I liked him—but I had known for a long time that the relationship wasn't working. We did not have the same hopes and dreams, and our professional careers traveled on different tracks. I was at the beginning of my career, (or at least I hoped I was) and he was nearly at the end of his. I was optimistic; he had become jaded and bitter. He liked me very much and we had a good deal of sexual chemistry, but there wasn't that deep sense of soul connection. So, I broke it off.

Now what? I asked myself as I sat on that movie set, staring out of a fake window. A breakthrough film? A new boyfriend? Travel?

Even then, I didn't think my acting career was my *everything*. I liked acting but there was something limiting about it. I had never really sought marriage and family either—even more limiting. Traveling didn't excite me as much as it had before I'd won the Miss Italy competition and gone on a worldwide tour. Now, eight years later, I had seen the countries I wanted to see. I had experienced almost everything I had imagined in my girlhood dreams. No, what I wanted now was a change, a career more in line with my curiosity and true identity. What I wanted was the same feeling of *enthusiasm*, simple and naïve as it had been, with which I had started my professional adventure in 1966, after unexpectedly winning the title of Miss Italy.

Like many of the best things in my life, winning a pageant title wasn't something I ever expected to happen.

It all started when some friends arranged a party on Mondello Beach—a small strip of sand in a suburb of Palermo, Sicily. At the party, I was crowned "Miss Mondello"—really more of a joke than anything. At the time, the standard of beauty was rounder, bosomy girls; I was tall (all of 1.7 meters or about 5'6" English!), thin and rather flat-chested. But the thinner, Twiggy look was starting to gain popularity and my friends recognized it—as well as my spirited sense of fun at the party. Thanks to my uncle being the editor of the *Giornale di Sicilia* (the local newspaper), a piece about "Miss Mondello" ran in the next edition. That little news item caught the attention of the organizers of the Miss Italia pageant, and the next thing I knew, without competing in anything, I was "Miss Palermo" and invited to compete in the Miss Sicily pageant!

At nineteen, under Italian law, I was still a minor. My participation in the Miss Sicily pageant required my family's consent. Given how the whole experience had unfolded at that point, my parents saw it as a game. They agreed that I could participate, not because they thought I had any chance at all of winning it, but because it might be a fun experience. They didn't pay much attention to the fine print of the participation contract—the language that said, if I won Miss Sicily, I was obligated to participate in the Miss Italy contest.

I won ... and then I won Miss Italy. The prize included all kinds of travel, modeling and sponsorship opportunities, money, a mink stole, an American kitchen, and a car. I travelled to the United States to participate in the Italian American-sponsored Columbus Day parade, had my picture taken with handsome young men, met the US President Lyndon Johnson and other dignitaries.

I sat for interviews of all kinds, including one where I was asked by a blonde barracuda of a woman, "What do you think of the Mafia in Sicily?"

And I replied—thrown off guard and only able to think of a gangster film I had seen with Telly Savalas and Sammy Davis Jr., "Mafia in Sicily? They're all gone. They've all rolled here to America!"

I said "rolled" because, at that moment, the word "come" escaped me—English, of course, was not my first language—but the damage was done. It was as if I had thrown a bomb. There was a moment of silence. Then the blonde turned toward the cameramen with her hands up in surrender. A dry voice screamed "Cut!" and the interview was over.

I was amazed. I expected everyone to laugh ... and instead, they bid me a quick "goodbye" and dismissed me.

In many ways, as I look back on my life and career, that experience speaks volumes. People have expectations of me—because of where I lived, what I look like, what I've done—and I rarely deliver what they expect.

As a result, however, of the exposure I gained as Miss Italy, I attracted the attention of the William Morris Agency and was offered my first film role, *I Barbieri di Sicilia*.

Actually, *I Barbieri di Sicilia* was the *second* film offer I received. The first was a film by Carlo Lizzani, a love story between a middle-aged man and a young girl . . . with explicit sex scenes where I would be expected to be nude.

I had travelled to Rome with my father to meet the director at Lizzani's offices. He explained what I'd be doing—as quickly and delicately as possible since my father was sitting right next to me—and asked, "Are you available?"

I looked at my father, but his face was blank. I knew that meant it was up to me to decide.

"Absolutely not," I replied with a smile. "Thank you."

We left. My father never brought up the subject again—and neither did I. It embarrassed me to talk about these things with him!

Fortunately, *I Barbieri* arrived soon after. My first film! I was very happy, but my parents weren't. Or at least, my mother wasn't. My father was happy for me, but my mother's feelings usually ruled in our household, so he was careful not to let his support show when she was around. But as happy as I was to have my first role as an actress, I was soon disappointed. The film wasn't very good: it was very low-budget and aimed at an unsophisticated audience. But it was an opportunity—and that was what mattered the most.

Over the next several years, I worked with some of Italy's most well-known directors and stars—and several American ones, too. I did the western movie *Joe, Look for a Place to Die*, directed by Hugo Fregonese and starring Jeffrey Hunter. I did *The Five Man Army* with Peter Graves and James Daly. I worked with other American actors like John Ireland, Brad Harris, William Berger, Lincoln Tate, and Gordon Mitchell. I played sexy women, abused ones, witches and sorceresses, religious figures and madwomen.

And yes . . . once it had all seemed so exciting! But over time I'd lost my enthusiasm for it. Perhaps it was because I had never gotten the kind of big break that would have really changed my career. Perhaps it was that so many of the directors I had worked with wanted not my talent, but my naked body for their films (and maybe in their beds, too)—something I did not wish to do. Or perhaps I knew that my own heart and brain weren't being used well in the roles I was being offered.

Whatever the reason, by 1975, after eight years in the industry, I knew I needed something new. As I stared out of that fake window into a fake reality, the catalyst for the real adventure of my life came walking through the door.

CHAPTER TWO
INTERVIEW

I was thinking about my career, sitting on the set with my half-eaten basket, remembering my excitement and wondering how I'd come to find myself so jaded after working in the industry for only eight years, when my memories were interrupted.

"Miss?" The stage manager stood near me. "There's a guy here. A photojournalist. He says he wants to interview you on behalf of *Hola*, a Spanish newspaper. Do you want to talk to him? Should I let him in?"

A photojournalist? I was intrigued. Usually, movie sets are closed: no one is allowed to enter unless they are a part of the film crew. That this guy had gotten all the way to the sound stage to have a conversation with the stage manager meant he must have been pretty convincing. I was curious and, at the same time, pleased to have a diversion. I was tired of thinking about the past.

"Yes, let him in," I replied.

The photojournalist was tall, well-built, handsome, and dressed completely black. That was the first thing that struck me: the triumph of black in his appearance. He had wavy and medium-length black hair, fashionably unkempt. Thick black eyebrows rose over large, penetrating black eyes, and on his chin a well-groomed black pirate-style beard with a little fuzz on the cheeks. He wore a black turtleneck pullover, black jeans, black ankle boots. His face and hands were deeply tanned, but with a red undertone that made me think of a Native American. I guessed his age as between thirty and thirty-five—much older than the boys I usually dated.

He offered me his hand and gave me a friendly smile, showing white perfect teeth.

I was twenty-eight years old. I did not know it yet, but from that moment, my life would change course, veering off into new and completely unexpected directions, because after the standard questions (i.e., how did you start your career, what films did you do, which ones you like the most, what directors have you worked with, what was it like working with Nino Manfredi, Dino Risi, and with American actors, etc., all questions I'd answered dozens of times) this man in black noticed my lack of enthusiasm. After a moment of silence, he asked me the question that would change the trajectory of my life and career: "What else interests you? Other than the cinema?"

I didn't answer right away. The question was outside of the box and deserved something more than the usual vacuous "I like painting" or "I like ice skating" both of which I actually like to do. But he wasn't asking me about my hobbies. The question was meant to go deeper and so I dug for the truth deep in my soul.

"I like astronomy," I replied at last, and watched surprise cascade over his face.

"Astronomy?" He repeated, uncertain if he should laugh at me or take me seriously. "And when did you develop this interest?"

I took a deep breath and stared right into the handsome reporter's intelligent black eyes. I saw the skepticism playing across his face and I could tell he was already preparing to dismiss me, drawing conclusions about me based on my looks, on my current career, and the dubious roles I'd played. He probably thought that, since I was an actress, I was too shallow or self-involved to be interested in much more than how I looked on camera, or what was being written about me in the press. The desire to shock him—to let him know there was more to me—blazed up inside me.

"Of course, it's true I don't know much about physics or mathematics," I admitted. "Those weren't my subjects in school. But I've seen the photos taken of the Earth from space, and images of the solar system and stars. I'm fascinated by all of them."

He nodded, signaling for me to go on. It was all the encouragement I needed. A torrent of words poured out of me. All the thoughts that had lived only in my head came tumbling out of my mouth as if they'd been waiting for someone to ask me about them.

"I was in my doctor's waiting room—he's an American doctor—and I saw his copy of *Sky and Telescope* magazine. I've never seen that magazine in any Italian doctors' offices and the cover just called to me, drawing me in. I flipped through it, savoring all the beautiful photographs of space. I hated to leave it in the office, I found it so fascinating. When I got home, I subscribed to *Sky and Telescope* so that I could get my own copy and learn more," I told the reporter.

"But I think maybe my passion for astronomy started even earlier," I continued. "I remember being about eight or nine years old and studying the Gregorian calendar at school. How the calendar is based on the science of the rotations and revolutions of the earth. We even talked about the procession of the equinoxes. It wasn't in-depth or exhaustive by any mean—just an elementary taste of the study of astronomy. Well, I had a lot of trouble with some of the concepts. I couldn't picture Earth, hanging in space, spinning. Taking one full day to turn itself counterclockwise or a whole year to move around the sun. The procession of the equinox was even more confusing." I paused to glance at my listener, who, to my surprise was following every word with wide-eyed interest. "You know what that is, right? The way the earth's orientation changes in relationship to fixed stars?"

"I've heard of it," he replied, and I saw a glimmering light of respect shining in his eyes.

"Well, I hadn't," I confided, laughing. "As a child, all of that movement seemed confusing. I couldn't grasp it. I would still be in the dark today, if it hadn't been for my father. He said, 'Go sit on the sofa in the living room and wait for me.'"

"And did you?" The journalist set down his camera and leaned toward me, those bright black eyes dancing with interest. He hadn't looked nearly so interested when I'd been rattling off the names of famous actors and directors or listing the roles I'd played in films. But then, I had been a bit bored with all that myself. "What is he like, your father?"

"People say he looks like Clark Gable," I exclaimed. "He has the same black hair and black eyes. But other than that, I don't see it. He carries himself with presence—maybe because he was in the military—

and I guess people responded to that. He's a banking officer in Palermo. As a child, when he was disappointed in my grades, he'd get this look on his face—and since I had gotten a zero on the assignment, I knew he was disappointed in me. But when I explained why I hadn't done well, he understood.

"This was when we were living in Milan, before we moved to Palermo. In that house, one side of the room was the dining area and the other side was the living room. From the sofa, I could see him gathering some string in one hand and a pair of scissors in the other. He placed them both on the solid walnut dining room table and then disappeared again. While I waited, he moved around in the kitchen and came back with several oranges and mandarins. He put them on the table with the other things.

"My mother came into the room then, drawn by curiosity and annoyance since he'd disrupted her kitchen. I remember thinking that a fight was brewing if my dad didn't explain himself pretty soon, but my father ignored her and kept working. He cut a few pieces of string in different lengths and tied the strings to the stems of one mandarin and each of the seven oranges, leaving a long piece of string hanging from each. Then he took off his shoes grabbed a chair and climbed up on the dining room table! My mother was horrified as he tied pieces of fruit to the eight arms of the large burnished brass chandelier hanging above the table. Then he tied the mandarin around his own arm and made it turn with his hand. 'See?' he said. 'This orange is the earth. The Mandarin is the moon and this bigger orange is the sun. And he made them all turn. 'This is what they are doing in space.'"

"Oh my!" the reporter laughed. "What did your mother do?"

"I'm sure she didn't like it, " I said. "But to be honest, I wasn't really paying attention to her anymore. I was fascinated by what my father was doing, rotating that fruit dangling from his arm and the chandelier." I glanced back at my questioner. "That was my first lesson in astronomy. I've been fascinated ever since."

The black-clad reporter opened his mouth to ask his next question—and I could see he had many of them by the look on his face—but my time was up. It had been an hour. My lunch break was over. The

Production Manager came to claim me for my next scene and the reporter had to leave. He promised to call to schedule a photo shoot, but at the time, I didn't even remember if he gave me his name.

CHAPTER 3
OLD FRIENDS AND NEW

The phone was ringing, but I was sleeping the sleep of the righteous, as I like to call it—even if, in fact, the sleep of the late-night disco might have been more accurate. I was so deeply asleep that the ringing sounded too far away to be my phone, and even if it *was* my phone, I had no interest in getting up to find out who was calling me on my one day off.

I had a very late night. I finished late on the film and afterward met up with my band, the group of friends that I usually hung around with in the mid-seventies. At the center of the group was my friend Massimo Ricci, the owner of a fairly popular dance club in Rome. Massimo was a couple of years older than I was and we had been friends for a couple of years. He had blonde hair and blue eyes and was a bit chubby. Some people thought he was a bit rowdy, but I prefer to say he a kind of dynamism that drew people in—and that's why he was always surrounded by beautiful girls. His club wasn't the hottest spot in Rome—those were usually either somewhere behind the Via Veneto—or even as popular as The Piper in Via Tagliamento, but his night spot was usually pretty crowded. I liked to go there because Massimo was my friend, and because I usually didn't have a date. As I've said, I was involved with a musician who was often out touring for months at a time. I didn't like to go places alone, even though many girls did. Going to Massimo's club meant that, even without a man, I wouldn't be completely alone. And then of course since he owned the place (or his father did, I don't remember) going to Massimo's usually meant that I didn't have to pay to go in or buy my own drinks once I was inside. I also had the opportunity to meet and hear some of the most important stars of international music at Massimo's club. But most important of all, I got to dance.

I love dancing. I still do. Dancing is one of my favorite things. I feel happy and free when I'm moving to the music, so I was grateful to have a place I could go and indulge myself, even when I was between films and money was low. Massimo and I had become very good friends. I would often drive over to his villa on the Cassia to meet him and our friends. We'd pile into someone's car and go out for evenings of dancing. Other nights, we stayed in, drinking and talking through the night. As I look back on it, I think I loved those evenings even more because often wonderfully intuitive and creative things were said. Utterances like "bread to bread, and wine to wine" made us ponder for a moment. But mostly, there was always so much laughter.

Massimo also tried to look out for me. One night, after quite a few glasses of Chivas Regal, Massimo turned the conversation on me.

"You're doing everything wrong," he told me.

"Me? What am I doing wrong—in your opinion?" I retorted. He was in sensitive territory—challenging the way I chose to live my life—I wanted to make sure he knew it.

"Don't get mad. It's not a criticism, just an observation. I mean, it's nice having you here with us, but we're no help to you if you want to make a career in the movie business. You should be going out with the people in that world if you want a real career—"

"Those old men?" I interrupted. "They only want one thing . . ."

"I know that." Massimo smiled. "But you can handle that intelligently. I know you can."

"I don't want to," I replied. "And it can be dangerous. What if they drug me? Put something in a glass and I don't realize it and drink it? What if they get violent after I say 'no'?" I shook my head. "No, no, no. I don't need any of that. Too much work and too many risks. I prefer my friends *outside* the film world, thank you very much."

I smiled but my tone was clear: the subject was over, and I didn't want to talk about it anymore. Massimo refused to take the hint.

"That makes about as much sense as you continuing to live in that shitty apartment," he said.

I raised an eyebrow at the word "shitty"—I didn't curse back them and objected to the use of the word. Back in Palermo my father would scold me for using the word "crap." Imagine how it felt to hear a much coarser version of the word used regularly in Rome.

"What's wrong with my apartment?" I fired back. "It's beautiful: I've got a large terrace, a fireplace in the living room. It's recently renovated and—"

"Not the apartment itself, the area. You live in Pietralata. That's one of the worst areas of Rome. It's not safe. I know you're from Palermo and you might not know much about the city, but there's a lot of crime in that part of Rome. What do you think people think about you, a single girl, living there?"

This argument had silenced me. It was true I lived in a part of the city that might have been compared to New York's Bronx back at the height of decline years ago. The crime rate was high, and the people were poor. But the apartment itself was nice and I wasn't prejudiced against the people because of their economic circumstances. Perhaps I was a bit of a romantic: I saw myself as a starving artist: a girl from Sicily, not yet twenty-one when I first rented the place, who lived cheaply while pursuing her dreams of becoming an actress. I was living like so many others who had come to Rome to try to make it in the movie business.

And then, like today, finding an affordable place to live in Rome was very difficult. I had spent the first months in the city with my uncle and his family. My uncle worked at the Ministry of Finance. It wasn't my first choice, but after my mother and I had searched and searched, and not been able to find any place secular or religious, that would take a girl who was an actress and who needed to be out late at night, my uncle's home was the only option.

But that didn't last long—less than a year. His daughter, my cousin, was almost my age and he and his wife were uncomfortable that my lifestyle was unsettling the careful expectations they had for her. I did things that "good girls" didn't. I went out alone in the evenings and slept late in the mornings. I did not keep my room neat and tidy. I was not home in time for dinner at the family table. I'll admit, I behaved more like I was living in a hotel than with family, but I was determined to live my life the way I wanted to and refused to concede to their rules.

I did understand, however, that I had put the family into turmoil and, later, I knew that they felt responsible for my safety in a big city like Rome. But the clash between what made them comfortable and my own need for independence made it clear: I had to leave.

But that meant I needed to find my own place which was incredibly difficult. It seemed like if I found a place I liked and could afford, the landlords didn't accept me—a single woman without a steady income—as an acceptable tenant. But when the landlords accepted me, the apartment was often rundown and cramped. I might have solved the probably if I had been willing to revise my budget and look at more expensive places. And I probably could have afforded more—I had been lucky in my film career and often had work—but I worried about doing that. What would happen if I agreed to an expensive lease and then the work dried up? No, that didn't seem smart to me. I wanted a place I was sure I'd be able to stay in, even if my financial luck shifted and roles became harder to find.

In the end, it was my father who helped me find the house in Pietralata that Massimo hated so much. At the time, he was the director of the Frosinone Bank. I asked my father to come to Rome and co-sign my lease. His established name would give credibility to my application, especially since my future landlords lived in a grand mansion in Piazzale Flamino.

Asking for my father's help wasn't something I wanted to do. The general feeling in the family was that I could not survive alone and that I should come back home to Palermo, but when I asked, my father agreed to do this for me. He was peculiar in that way. Many times, when I asked him for financial help, he would refuse . . . and then, out of the blue, when I didn't ask, he would give me money. This help happened from time to time, but not often, and never too much—and usually without my mother's knowledge. She had had me young—at twenty—and was still a young and beautiful woman. If my father was a look alike for Clark Gable, mother was like Olivia de Havilland. We butted heads on almost everything—so much so that my father and I often kept little things from her, just to avoid a fight. When I told her that I wanted to live in Rome, she resisted saying I couldn't afford it. When I reminded her that, thanks to the prize money from the Miss Italy contest, I had a bit of a nest egg, she said it wouldn't be enough. When I told her that the gift of a Fiat 850 (another prize for winning Miss Italy) I could move freely around the country, she told me I would get lost or other bad things would befall me. I insisted that I could live independently and make my way in the world—and she called many family meetings on the subject to attempt to persuade me otherwise. There was a lot of crying and sad faces. But my mother's ultimate weapon was the threat: "If you go out that door, don't come back!" The sentence chilled my heart, but I left anyway. I was almost twenty-one but still a minor, under Italian law. But I knew I couldn't wait until I was legally of age. I jumped in my car and headed for Rome.

All of these memories had flowed back to me as I listened to Massimo criticize my apartment in Pietralata a few months back. He was right, and I knew it. Much as I liked that house, the neighborhood was terrible and not getting any better. Twice somebody had put sugar in the Fiat 850's gas tank. In my two-and-a-half years there, I'd had three burglaries in which cash, gold jewelry, and trophies I'd won were stolen. The first had happened almost immediately when the only furniture I had was the bed and two nightstands and kept my clothes in piles on the floor. I had just finished my first film and collected its last paycheck. That evening, thieves broke in, destroying the door and stole the 250.000 Liras (about $3360 today. My father got 180/200.000 Liras per month working in a bank) I had hidden in one of the bedside tables, tucked into the cup of a bra. I called the police.

Two officers responded to the call, one in uniform and the other in plain clothes and wearing a beige raincoat like he'd seen in *Casablanca*. *Casablanca* cop, after taking my statement and asking my profession, walked around my empty house inspecting my piles of clothes and then asked, "May I take you to dinner?"

Really?

I stared at him icily, thinking of all the awful things I wanted to say. There I was, upset and worried after someone had broken into my home and this insensitive man was inviting me to dinner? Who did he think he was? Who did he think *I* was?

"No, thanks," I replied and led him to the door. I just wanted him and his partner out of my house as quickly as possible. This meeting with the so-called "authorities" had diminished my confidence in the system so badly that I didn't want to talk about it anymore. I just wanted them to go. Of course, none of the stolen items were ever recovered. In hindsight, perhaps he wanted to help me in a difficult moment somehow. Perhaps, he thought I no longer had any money—considering the empty apartment and the theft of my cash. But somehow, I doubt it. And dinner? How was that supposed to help?

Only once did I recover anything that had been stolen from me, and that wasn't because of the police, but because I'd taken the initiative and acted on my own. In one of the thefts, a gold chain that belonged to my great grandmother was taken. It was one of my favorite things and I was heartbroken to discover it gone. For years, I had pleaded with my mother to let me have it—and she had denied me again and again, telling me that I would lose it, or someone would steal it from me. I hated that she had been right—and that was at least part of the reason why I decided to go to extreme measures to try to get it back.

A couple of days after the break-in, I went to a nearby coffee bar. It wasn't one of my usual places—it was a bit seedier and attracted a rougher crowd—but I knew it was the right place for my purposes that day. I approached the lady at the counter as casually as I could.

"Listen," I began. "Somebody stole some family heirlooms of mine that I care very much about. I would love to have them back again."

The lady didn't say anything, she just looked me like "So what?" I didn't let her expression stop me.

"I hope that I can get them back ," I continued. " Of course, I'm willing to pay." I looked around. "A lot of people come through here, if you could ask around, I'd be really grateful."

"No promises," the woman replied laconically. I said goodbye and left, hoping and praying that I'd done the right thing.

A couple of days later as I was leaving my apartment, a little boy about ten years old ran up to me and handed me a piece of paper. On it was the name of an unfamiliar plaza and a time. "For your things," he responded to my question and then ran away. I didn't know him. I had never seen him before, and I never saw him again. I read the little scrap of paper with some trepidation. Meeting a stranger in an unfamiliar place could be very dangerous. But I wanted that necklace—and the rest of my things, too—so I went back into the apartment and quickly looked up the location on my map of the city. I finally found it in an area called Tiburtino III—a neighborhood even further South than the Pietralata and even less reputable. I didn't want to go alone, but I couldn't ask any of my friends to accompany me. They wouldn't do it—and they would have stopped me from going, too.

I made up my mind. I was going, and nothing would happen to me. I was going and I would be fine. I told myself that over and over. Surely whoever I was meeting was more interested in easy money than selling the stolen objects below cost. I was going ... and nothing would happen to me.

I dressed carefully for such an assignation: pants, jacket, head scarf, and dark glasses. I didn't want anyone to recognize me. But I made sure I didn't look too good. I wasn't a rich actress and I didn't want to signal that I could afford to pay a lot of money. So, I dressed in a way that I hoped would make me look like everyone else in that low-rent part of town. The irony, I realize now, is that in attempting to disguise myself I probably attracted even more attention than if I'd simply gone without any extra effort at all. I'm sure I aroused a good deal of curiosity through my naïve efforts.

I parked near the square and got out of my car. It was an ugly day: the sky was like dull, gray lead. The square was a large open space with a dirt floor probably used for ball games surrounded by dilapidated two-story condominium buildings. Something white waved from a balcony: someone's underwear, drying in the breeze. Even though it was afternoon, the square was deserted: no one in sight. As I walked toward the open area in the center, a man of about forty-five to fifty years old, wearing a pair of jeans, a checkered shirt, and a leather jacket appeared from the shadow of one of the buildings. He walked directly toward me and when we were facing each other, he gave me a half smile and said, "400,000.[1]"

---

[1] Probably around $250 in US dollars today and about 200 EU.

"For everything?" I asked. I tried to make my voice sound harsh and tough. I hoped I sounded threatening and worldly.

He looked at the ground and move some of the dirt with the toe of his shoe.

"Not everything. Those trophies and prizes I couldn't get those back," he said. "But all the gold is there."

I thought about it, trying to decide the best thing to do. But I trusted myself and I wanted that necklace. I wouldn't turn back.

"Tomorrow," I said. "Same time, same place. I'll bring the money you bring this stuff. Alright?"

"I'll be here," he replied, and he turned and left without another word, and so did I.

As I drove back to my apartment, I realized I had no idea how much my jewels were actually worth. They were mostly gold chains and little bracelets, but there was also a gold Dunhill lighter that my father had bought me in New York and the delicate filigreed rosary from my first Communion; and of course, my grandmother's precious heirloom necklace. I was a little mad at myself for not knowing for sure whether or not I was being ripped off by paying 400,000 lire for their return, but in the end, I let it go. To recover my things, I would have paid any amount that I could afford. They had sentimental value beyond any amount of money.

The next day I went to the bank, took out the money, and punctually presented myself back in the square. A thousand thoughts and possibilities stirred in my mind—but the strongest of all was the possibility that the man might attack me, take the money, and run away. It would be the ultimate score for him: he'd have both the cash I brought and the stolen jewelry. But everything went as smooth as oil, as the saying goes.

With my heart beating like mad, I handed him the white envelope with the wad of cash inside it. He counted quickly and then pulled a package wrapped in newspaper from his pocket jacket. It was heavier than I expected a few pieces of gold jewelry to be, so I made a quick hole in the paper. My things! I didn't see the wisdom of standing there checking everything—I was afraid something would fall out of the newspaper bundle and end up on the ground and I wasn't sure who else might be watching our transaction. So, I told the man "thank you" and without another word, headed for my car and got the hell out of there.

When I got home, I ripped open the newspaper. Everything was there. I was happy and relieved—and a little proud of myself for how I had handled the situation. It was the sort of thing I would have liked to brag about, but I knew I could never tell anyone, especially not my family.

All of those memories returned to my mind when Massimo challenged me about moving to a better apartment. Along with the knowledge that when my friends came by in the evenings to pick me up in their Bentleys, Mercedes, Ferraris—and one even had a Maserati—I knew the people who lived in the nearby buildings looked out closely at these fancy cars arriving in this poverty-stricken neighborhood. I'd heard some thought I was a high-class prostitute. In one way, I didn't care what they thought: what was important to me was that I was living in Rome, on my own and able to pay my own way. As long as I didn't have to go back to Palermo have to hear my mother say that she knew I'd be back, I didn't care. I could almost hear her saying that she knew I couldn't make it on my own. Going back to Palermo would have sentenced me to her wishes for me: a quick marriage to some oaf of a boy, pregnancy, and a life as dull as her own. I had no desire to be under the thumb of any husband. I had tasted freedom and I wanted to keep it.

But the apartment in Pietralata wasn't the best place for me, I was forced to agree.

"You may be right," I had admitted with a sigh to my friend Massimo Ricci. "Tell you what: if you can find me an apartment in a nice area that I can afford, I'll move."

Massimo smiled. To my surprise, not much later he had found me the apartment where I lived for the next eighteen years. It was small—about the size of the attic of my old place—but in a beautiful residential area in the Cassia, the best new area in North Rome. Massimo himself was in a villa close by. The singer, Enzo Arbore, another good friend, was only a little bit further away. Edwidge Fenech, a fellow actress still at the beginning of her career, lived on the other side of the road. Enzo Cerusico, another actor friend, lived near the coffee bar that I loved to frequent for their good tuna, tomato, and mayonnaise sandwiches and their thick and delicious slices of white pizza with mortadella.

It became the place where I conducted all kinds of experiments into the power of the human mind—and where I was visited by someone/something not from this world . . .

And that's where I was on the morning when my phone rang and rang insistently and repeatedly until at last, I was forced to rouse myself from slumber and answer it.

"Hello," I mumbled. I've been told that my voice is very sexy when I'm half asleep, so I didn't even try to sound like I was awake.

"It's Emilio Latini. I interviewed you last week, remember? On the set of the movie? I wanted to ask you if I could send over a photographer. We need some pictures to run with the interview."

Interview . . . photo . . . the vague memory of my black-clad interlocutor and our discussion of astronomy played in my brain. But I was still too sleepy to care.

"What time is it?" I asked.

"Ten-thirty in the morning. Why?"

"It's far too early for this conversation," I told him. I doubt I was particularly pleasant about it. "Call back later, and I'll talk to you then." I hung up and promptly went right back to sleep.

You might think me rude, but sleep is incredibly important to me. I have always needed more sleep than the average human being—and for some reason, I sleep best at all the wrong hours. I sleep the heaviest in the mornings, when most people are bright-eyed and beginning their days. In fact, I was born at nine in the morning and immediately slept all day. My mother was ecstatic: she thought she had a quiet, peaceful child who would be no trouble. She didn't know that she would never be able to make me sleep at night. Even as a baby, I slept all day and was awake all night. I'm told that I didn't cry very much: rather, I cooed and talked to myself and played with my fingers and toes. To this day, daytime sleep and nighttime activity is my natural biorhythm. Of course, I've had to adjust to different schedules for films and various jobs. But if I have my way, when the sun is out, I'd rather be asleep.

Emilio Latini—that was the reporter's name. He called back in the afternoon and made his request again. "At your apartment," he said, when I agreed to the photoshoot. "See you then."

Emilio was a photojournalist. For years he worked as a freelance photojournalist, then later as the director of a photo agency. He had attended a German University with the intention of studying medicine, but after two years left school for life in Paris and photography. He had traveled the world taking pictures and selling them to various newspapers. He had no particolar specialty: he'd sold Vietnam war photographs to European magazines in 1967 and 1968. *Vogue* and *Harper's Bazaar* had published his fashion photos taken on the beaches of Antilles and Martinique. He'd captured heads of state like Tito (head of the former Yugoslavia) and Prince Rainier of Monaco, then turned his lens on celebrities like Elizabeth Taylor and Richard Burton, Donald Sutherland and Anthony Quinn, Anna Magnani, Orson Welles, Peter Ustinov, and many others. He had travelled to the countries that fascinated him. He lived for six months among the Tibetan monks before moving on to China and Russia. Off to Brazil's Bay of All Saints and then to New Orleans, Louisiana in the United States. He had even been to the Amazon and spent time listening to the teachings of the shamans who lived deep in the thick forests bordering the rivers.

Of course, that left very little room for the typical family life. He was divorced and had a daughter who lived with her mother. He had recently returned to Italy after a legal dispute over his daughter's custody required him to take a more active role in his daughter's life instead of constant globe-trotting, looking for adventures. Reluctantly, he had renounced his long sojourns abroad and taken a job with a Roman news agency that sent photographers out on various assignments throughout Italy. His agency had given him the assignment to interview me. I was now becoming well-known and they knew the interview would make money in magazines across Europe.

He shared none of this with me on the day he called to arrange for my photo shoot. Instead, I learned more about him when I went to visit his office to retrieve the photographs snapped at my home.

Emilio was there, all in black again. I felt as intrigued by him as I had on our first meeting, so when he asked me to dinner, I accepted the invitation. I confess, I was curious about him and dinner gave me the opportunity to study him better. He seemed intelligent and curious. It struck me that he cared very little about money; he was much more interested in living life according to his own terms. He had fried potatoes in some North African village in order to stay there and learn more about the culture. He had taken a job unloading I don't know how many tons of meat at Les Halles (the market hub of food distribution in Paris) in order to keep body and soul together and continue to work on perfecting his photography. Instead of making him less appealing, these adventures and odd jobs made him even more attractive to me. In a strange sort of way, he struck me as particularly cultured—a true renaissance man with a singular sense of himself. He saw things in a way I had never thought about. His company expanded my mind. I liked him and I liked that he liked me, not just because he thought I was pretty, but because he was interested in what I thought about life, about what might lie beyond it, and the connections in between.

Neither of us knew it then, but Emilio was to become my perfect partner for the exploits to come.

CHAPTER FOUR
EXPERIENCES IN A NEW WORLD

A few weeks later, after a restful ten hours of sleep, I awoke to light filtering through the shutters in the way that foretold a beautiful day ahead. Morning had already passed by the time I showered, dressed in a tracksuit, and headed to the kitchen to make my coffee. But the machine was dirty; I would have to wash it first . . . and I really didn't want to. It would take time and I wanted coffee and I wanted it right away. I grabbed my car keys and headed for the nearest coffee house. After four coffees, a cappuccino, and a *croissant*, I returned to my house with a copy of *Il Messaggero*, the local newspaper, to take a look at the news.

The story on the front page changed my life.

It was about Uri Geller, an Israeli boy now living in the United States who professed to have the ability to bend spoons and forks with only the power of his mind. Geller had been invited to appear on Italian television and had exhibited his skills with a public experiment: he had asked the viewing audience to gather stopped watches and clocks. He then used his powers of concentration to attempt to restart them. Hundreds of people had called into the television station to announce the seemingly impossible: minutes after Geller's attempt, their old watches and clocks—some broken for years—had started working again!

The Italian press was having a field day with Geller and the controversial subject. In addition to news reports on Geller and his extraordinary feats, there was a long article exploring the heated debate between parapsychologists and their detractors about the authenticity of teleplastia, telepathy, and ESP—extrasensory perception. There were also articles about Dr. Andrija Puharich, who discovered Geller and his abilities. Dr. Puharich was a well-respected American scientist and the inventor of the technology (still in use today) that enables deaf people to hear using electric brain stimulation. But Dr. Puharich had other interests as well. In 1960s, he and Doctor John Taylor discovered that at eight cycles per second the brain activated extrasensory abilities including remote viewing, telepathy, telekinesis, etc. The two scientists believed that these latent abilities existed in every human being.

Puharich's advancement of these theories made the scientific establishment very uncomfortable. He persisted in exploring the areas of his curiosity, however. He risked his career rather than genuflecting to blind academic policy.

I didn't know all of this when I first read the articles about him in *Il Messaggero*. I was intrigued by what I did read, however. I read the article several times but still did not understand whole sections of it. Parapsychology? Metaphysical? I didn't know the meaning of those words. But instead of being discouraged, I felt excited and eager to learn more. I had always considered myself well educated. I spoke Italian well and thought I had a good vocabulary. But here I was struggling to understand the meaning of words in a common newspaper.

There was no Internet that could easily help me, so I turned to my personal Internet of the time: *Encyclopedia Treccani,* the best resource books in Italy. My father had given me a set (12 volumes) years before as a gift and they had been useful many times. Now, I thumbed through the volumes quickly, looking first for the word "parapsychology." The definition appeared like this:

"synonymous with metaphysics by many however, the term is used to designate the more rigidly scientific orientation of studies of extranormal phenomenon."

What?

That didn't help me. I had to look up the word "metaphysics." The definition I found opened up a whole new world to me. I read with amazement of the search abilities beyond what humanity can observe with our five senses. Metaphysics had a long history, dating back to the ancient times. Indeed, this search for the world beyond the physical had been in common practice until the late eighteenth century, when it was replaced entirely by the scientific method. I read about how metaphysics is usually divided into two different categories, "physical phenomenon" which encompassed things like parakinetics, telekinetics, ectoplasm, contribution, levitation, direct voice, direct writing, and possession; and "mental phenomenon" which included things like telepathy, clairvoyance, cross correspondence, xenoglossia, and precognition. According to my encyclopedia, there were numerous scientific societies in North America that focused on metaphysical examinations, but in Italy there was only one: the Italian Society of Metaphysics, founded in 1936. There were also a few institutes and universities that studied these phenomena abroad. The encyclopedia entry also included the names of many American scientists who worked in this field and one Italian pioneer: Dr E. Servadio.

I read all of this information eagerly and then paused to underline one quote that I reproduced here because of the significance with which it struck me:

"From a strictly scientific point of view, both the possibility of extrasensory perceptions and communications and those related to psycho kinetic effects are now sufficiently demonstrated."[2]

As I read those words, a new excitement dawned inside me. Right there, in the respected *Encyclopedia Treccani*, it was stated that these kinds of events weren't just magical tricks or imagination . They were real, proven and "sufficiently demonstrated." Damn, what news!

I returned to the article I had just read in the newspaper. Was what Geller had done real? Was it a trick to get publicity? And if the encyclopedia seemed to believe that these phenomena had been proven, why was there still such a controversy between parapsychologists and the rest of the scientific community? And why, instead of all of these arguments and counterarguments, hadn't scientists done a controlled study of Geller and his abilities?

I learned the answer later: there was no money for this kind of scientific inquiry—at least not in Italy. In fact, in the mid 1970s, Italy was in the throes of a serious economic downturn. But at the time, I skipped those headlines. I wasn't interested in the politics or the

---

2 Encyclopedia Treccani, Istituto dell'Enciclopedia Italiana(1970).

economics that limited the exploration into paranormal phenomena. Instead, I made a plan to see Geller with my own eyes.

He'd left Italy, and the word was he was touring Europe, but I had no further information. I had just finished shooting another film. I hadn't had very many scenes, but the ones I had were very rewarding because the director had made a real effort to construct a real and believable character for me to inhabit. I had been well-paid for the scenes I'd had, but I was hesitant to spend the money on a trip abroad to meet Uri Geller on his next stop on his European tour. The truth was, my film work was always sporadic, and I never knew for sure when my next job would be. It didn't seem wise to spend the money on a whim . . . but everything I had read had intrigued me to the point that I knew I had to at least try to find a way to go.

I called my father.

Remember, I tried not to ask for his help too often and many times when I did ask, he said "no" to discourage me from relying on him. This time, however, he agreed to a small loan, with the promise that if I was unable to get tickets to one of Mr. Geller's event, I would return the money immediately. I agreed, even though I had no intention of missing Mr. Geller's next show—no matter where I had to travel to catch him. I think my father must have sensed my enthusiasm because he expressed regret that he couldn't join me. He had read about the experiment with the clocks and watches and was touched by the same wave of curiosity that had already swept me away.

Knowing that I had the funds to make the trip, I called the Parapsychology Society of Bologna—the only group in Italy dedicated to the study of metaphysics—and asked for Dr. Cassoli, the only Italian scientist named in the article in the *Messaggero*. I told him who I was and explained that I wanted to learn more about Geller— and to meet him, if possible. I expressed my interest in exploring the phenomena discussed in the article in more depth.

"Are you a scholar or researcher in this area, Ms. Giordano?" he asked.

I told him I was an actress. Usually this got some kind of reaction, but Dr. Cassoli didn't lose his composure or offer any comment on that. Instead he simply said, "I'm sorry. I don't know anything about Geller's tour, but I'm happy to call the people at the television station and see if they have any information. I'll get back to you."

I thanked him, doubting that I would ever hear from him again—or at least not anytime soon. And time was important. I knew that Uri Geller's entire European tour was probably not more than a couple of weeks long. After that he'd be returning to the United States—too far away for me to travel on the little loan my father had given me. But to my surprise, an hour later, Dr. Cassoli called back with the name and phone number of one of the most high-powered and well-known agents of the time, David Zard. A few minutes after that, I had Uri Geller's European tour schedule and after a couple more phone calls and few more minutes, I had made my plans.

Puffy white clouds drifted past me from the window of the Alitalia plane that took me to Geneva, Switzerland to meet Uri Geller. Although Gellar's tour would take him to cities all over Europe, I had chosen Geneva because it was closest to Rome. As I stared out the window, happiness and excitement coursed through me. I was proud of myself. I had not only tracked down Geller and arranged to see him, but I had done it all by convincing total strangers to help me with only my enthusiasm, my voice, and a telephone. It was a victory for me that increased my confidence in a way I hadn't expected. For years, people opened doors to me because they either recognized me for my film work or they found me attractive. I had gotten used to using my face to ease my way. I had even occasionally been recognized on the street or in stores (I didn't go shopping that often, but occasionally, even a film star needs a pan or some soap.) Sometimes the clerks asked me for my autograph. That usually happened when I looked my worst and it had made me realize that fame can be a double-edged sword. While it's nice to be recognized and known, it can be troublesome to not to have the freedom of anonymity when all one wants is to buy bread.

But the experience of tracking down Geller was a completely different one for me. A new kind of confidence was surging within me. I was starting to think of myself beyond my physical appearance and in terms of what I could accomplish with my words and my brain. I expected the trip to Switzerland to reinforce that feeling.

Unfortunately, as soon as my plane hit the ground, things began to go wrong. I reached my hotel and discovered that I had no reservation, in spite of calls to arrange it in the days before. Sorting that out took an alarming amount of time and made me late for Geller's show—so late, in fact, that I reached the lobby of the Palexpo—the massive convention center near the airport—the show was over and the last of the audience was leaving the auditorium.

I was incredibly disappointed, so disappointed I was on the verge of tears. All the confidence and pride I'd felt in myself evaporated in an instant. I hadn't accomplished anything. Instead, I'd spent so much money and time—for what? Nothing.

And then Fate struck.

Uri Geller came striding out of a side door, followed by his old friend Shipi and a couple of other people. I recognized him immediately and stood, mesmerized, trying to build up the nerve to approach him. But even more incredibly, Geller's eyes locked on mine as I stood there debating with myself. To my surprise, he came toward me, smiling.

When I look back on it today, I'm amazed by this synchronicity. Coincidence? I don't think so. I think that meeting Geller was something I was meant to do because it was something that led me further on my path. After everything that I believed had gone wrong in the hours before—missing the chance to see the show as one of thousands of other people in a large audience—Geller now approached me directly with an easy friendliness that was completely unexpected.

"Hello, who are you?" he asked in English.

I told my name, adding, "I'm an Italian actress. I came from Rome to meet you."

He smiled. "We're getting something to eat. Why don't you join us?"

And, of course, I did.

During the meal, as he chatted with me and his friends, I had the chance to observe him. He was about my height and around my age. He had black hair cut short, black eyes, and a prominent nose. A slight dimple lay in the center of his chin. While not movie star handsome, he made up for that with a lot of charm. As he was eating, he accidently bent the fork he was bringing to his mouth and he dropped the anticipated bite of food all over himself. Even at the table he was bending metals. He laughed off his embarrassment as he cleaned up and got another fork.

I seized the moment to witness his skill for myself.

"Can you fold my pendant?" I asked, indicating the gold chain around my neck and the pendant of two intertwined kittens hanging from it. I lifted my hair to take it off, but Geller took it gently between the thumb and forefinger of one hand, waited a moment, and let it go.

The pendant was considerably folded on one corner . . . and I had not felt anything, no pressure, no effort from him, nothing.

An autographed photo from Uri Geller.

The next day, I returned to Rome. The experience with Geller intrigued me and I kept thinking about it. I had always been curious about these kinds of phenomenon especially since others dismissed them so quickly, without any examination at all. It seemed to me that this was as foolish as accepting the phenomenon without any investigation. To me, it seemed obvious that scientific examination of these abilities was necessary. I was frustrated by the usual Italian way of discussion and debate without evidence. I wanted to contribute something to the conversation, but first I had to learn what was real and what was illusion. I needed to read the right publications and research materials and learn what others had done. I needed to discover who was qualified to have an opinion who was not. Fortunately for me, in those years, there were many publications on the subject. Some had been translated into Italian, but most were in English. I started to read. And I read a lot.

I read *Psychic Explorations in the US* by Edgar D. Mitchell and learned for the first time that Geller had been studied at the Stanford Research Institute where some of the most important scientists in the field of paranormal ability had examined his multiple abilities under controlled circumstances. Their experiments seemed to confirm that he had some abilities that science could only partially explain. I also read about the work of Elton Byrd, then a researcher at the White Oaks Laboratory Naval Surface Weapons Center in the United States, who had been baffled by Geller's ability to alter the properties of nitinol. Nitinol is an alloy composed of nickel and titanium that, once deformed, can return to its original form only under intense heat. But after Geller's psychic alteration of a nitinol specimen, the metal had lost its memory and would no longer return to its original form, even when placed in the conditions in which it usual did so.

I read all of these things with great fascination. My belief in Geller's telekinetic ability grew more certain with each book and article—as did my desire to investigate these so-called "paranormal abilities" firsthand.

CHAPTER FIVE
NEW GAMES

In addition to my new field of scientific interest, Emilio and I had developed a strong, if unusual relationship, that extended far beyond our first meeting that day on the film set.

We saw each other as often as we could when work didn't interfere, usually getting together for dinner at our favorite spots in Rome: Pariolina, the famous Ambasciata d'Abruzzo, Sediari, or Poldo. Sometimes, because he knew I loved it, he took me dancing. But after a while, I could tell that he didn't enjoy those evenings, so I stopped asking to go. Instead, after fabulous meals, we would return to my place for good whiskey and even better conversation.

We talked and talked—about all kinds of things that he had learned about in his travels and I knew little about. By now, he understood that my curiosity was insatiable: I asked question after question. I always wanted to know more, even when he'd told me everything he knew. Emilio told me about the Shaolin monks in Tibet who were nicknamed "runner monks" because it was said they could run so fast that they seemed to levitate a few centimeters above the ground. I told him about my experience with Uri Geller and my desire to understand how phenomena like those Geller manifested occurred. Emilio offered his best explanations, but they did not satisfy me. I didn't understand why or what mechanisms could be put in place to explain what I had seen. I wanted to understand—not only for myself, but for others. I wanted some kind of irrefutable proof of the power of the mind to make the impossible, possible.

And then one day, partly because he too was interested in these things, but also, I suspect, because he was tired of my questions, Emilio said, "Let's play a game."

He pulled three small gray containers out of his briefcase. Each had a black cover. All were empty.

"I use these to store the film I've developed," he told me. He placed them in front of me on the little rectangular coffee table. "Have you got something that will fit in there?"

My curiosity came roaring to life. I had no idea where this "game" was going but I was intensely interested and immediately engaged. I searched my living room for something small enough to fit into the little gray cylinders until my eye fell on a steel ball that I kept in an old ashtray. I handed it to him. Emilio dropped it into one of the containers and fitted the black cap over it.

"Sit down and close your eyes," he instructed. He had been wearing a scarf around his neck and he swept it off and tied it around my eyes, blindfolding me. I heard him moving the containers swiftly and deliberately.

"Now you can open your eyes," he said.

I took off the scarf and opened my eyes.

"Now, without touching them, tell me which container the marble is inside."

I was intrigued. I had seen tricks like this at carnivals and local fairs—and even in some movies. And they had always been just that: tricks. Was he making fun of me? I hesitated, demanding to know the answer to that question first. I probably wasn't very nice about it, either, because he said, "Don't get angry. It's a game to help you understand what you want to know."

With these words, I began my psychic training.

I guessed.

I was wrong.

Emilio asked me, "What did you do?"

"I don't know, " I answered. "Just picked one."

"Try again and this time see if you feel anything different," he urged. "Actually *try*. Without touching them, pass your hand over the containers. See if you feel anything."

"Like what?" I asked.

"I don't know," he replied. "Something *different*. The difference between empty and full. Warmth or cold. Tingling. Or something else. Whatever signal your body or brain sends you."

The vagueness of this answer drove me crazy. I wanted something more definite, specific, or concrete. But I tried to clear my mind and tune in to the containers. I tried again. And again. And again. I was amazed when, after many tries, Emilio told me that I was correct more than fifty percent of the time. In fact, as I became more familiar with this game, the more I was able to tune into the containers and the more accurate I was.

I don't consider myself to have any particular gifts in the realm of extra sensory perception or any real paranormal ability, but I was amazed by the accuracy of my efforts—and the improvement that resulted from just a little practice and concentration.

"Imagine if we taught children this in elementary school—or even earlier," Emilio said. "With practice and a greater trust in their intuitive powers, everyone would get a higher than average percentage of correct answers. Imagine the practical application of the combination of logic and intuition."

And then he told me about the Zener cards.

The Zener cards were designed in the 1930s by psychologist Karl Zener. There are twenty-five cards with five different symbols: the wave, the square, the circle, the cross, and the star, each depicted five times in five different colors. In a telepathy session, a sender tries to transmit the description of the card to another person, the receiver. In a clairvoyant session, on the other hand, the visionary names which card will appear before it is pulled. In either case, whether telepathic or clairvoyant, getting more than five cards out of twenty-five correct is considered better than statistically average. The more correct answers, Zener suggested, might indicate some level of extrasensory perception or ESP.

Once again, I was intrigued. But once again, like in my frantic efforts to see Uri Geller, I was blocked. Of course, the cards were not for sale in Italy. And in the late 1970s, there was no Internet to search for a place to order them. So, ever resourceful, I made my own set of

Zener cards with some cardboard, a felt tipped pen, and a few thin sheets of clear plastic and started working on developing my extra sensory perception. The more I worked with these cards, the better I became at sensing which of the five images would appear next. My results supported Emilio's ideas: perhaps some level of extrasensory perception could indeed be taught. Perhaps anyone—*everyone*—was capable of reaching beyond the field of logic and into clairvoyance. And if that was so, mankind was capable of far more than our present understanding acknowledged.

Just as I was reaching these conclusions, two things happened simultaneously that took my exploration of the unexplained into dramatic new directions. The first involved the American anthropologist, Dr. Margaret Mead. The second converged around a tool I discovered in my favorite magazine, *Sky & Telescope*, called a Kirlian camera.

CHAPTER SIX
MARGARET MEAD

During this time, the Italian press didn't often cover the debate about the existence of extrasensory perception (ESP). Obviously, the subject attracted lots of fakers and charlatans. But there were also some serious scientists trying to use scientific means to discover the truth about these abilities. Even with the more serious work, however, I learned quickly that one had to be prepared to read between the lines to understand what was real and what wasn't. There was a lot of conjecture and even more opinion. Unfortunately, especially in Italy, many of those writing and discussing the existence of phenomenon like telekinesis and telepathy hadn't bothered to read any of the books or other material on the subject before expressing their opinions. It made for a great deal of confusion and misinformation.

Still, there was a great deal of interest surrounding the topic and that was probably at least one of the reasons that the national Italian television station RAI aired a documentary that included an interview with Dr. Margaret Mead. As a part of a wide-ranging conversation about her work as cultural anthropologist with the Samoan people, Dr. Meade casually mentioned that she believed that every living being has a vital field surrounding it. Each living thing's field resounds at a frequency unique to it and the frequency will vary according to that entity's state of mind and health. Unlike a pure tone which might emit a steady frequency, she theorized that these vital fields are a combination of a large number of merging frequencies that give rise to a waveform that has unique characteristics that distinguish it from every other living being. She added that one way to see these psychobiological changes was with a Kirlian camera. Dr. Mead then showed her own device in a close up that filled the screen.[3]

I didn't watch much television but the fact that I caught this interview on TV as I had been reading the reports of American researchers studying the energy of paranormal phenomena struck me as no coincidence. I began to wonder if a Kirlian camera would be a suitable tool to quell the ongoing controversy between Italian parapsychologists and their detractors. Indeed, there were only a few Italian parapsychologists at the time; I could count them on the fingers of one hand. Their detractors, of course, were far more numerous than I have fingers and toes since they are practically the entire Italian orthodox scientific community.

I still was thinking about Dr. Mead's interview when my *Sky & Telescope* magazine arrived several days later. I still looked forward to receiving it every month; it had become my favorite publication. But that month, among the various advertisements for telescopes, mirrors, and other tools for searching the skies, there was one for the exact Kirlian camera mentioned in Dr. Mead's documentary. From the photos and technical specifications, I could tell that it was identical to the one US researchers were using in their experiments. The manufacturer was the Edmund Scientific Corp. in New Jersey in the United States.

My first thought was: I need another film job and fast . . . because I have to have that camera.

I wanted to be able to use the same device that the most reputable researchers in paranormal phenomenon of the time were using. I wanted to be able to conduct my own experiments and to compare them to the work being done by American researchers working in the field. I didn't want my efforts to be dismissed because my equipment was poor, or my methods were incorrect or random. I wanted to follow the standard procedures so that I could be sure that whatever results I obtained could add to the conversation about ESP and paranormal activities.

_____

3 Much of this documentary is now on YouTube. See: http:www.youtube.com/watch?v=YF80CN43U1Y

At the time, some "researchers" were conducting experiments with all kinds of homemade equipment. I read years later about some independent researchers who had tried to create their own Kirlian devices using the coil of the Fiat 500 (in place of the Tesla coil) to generate an alternate way to take similar measurements of energy. Those devices failed to earn any serious respect, even among the scientists interested in the matter—and certainly not with the mainstream scientific community. Those homemade devices failed to coordinate their methodology with existing research and ended up undermining the serious study of the phenomena they were designed to support.

I wanted the right device. The same one that Dr. Mead had and one that was appropriately calibrated and accurately used. But I had to be smart about when to purchase it. It would be expensive, I figured, but I knew that with the right film—a strong lead role with some real cachet—I would be able to afford it. Determined, I set about the process of getting a film.

I've never been greedy—I always considered my acting career to be like the whipped cream in a wonderful ice cream sundae. Delicious, yes. But eat too much and you can be sure to get a stomachache. That year I'd been in three or four films, but the roles were minor and not particularly well-paying. In a way, I already had a stomachache: the work was beginning to feel less than challenging and not nearly as delicious.

I had started my career with the excitement and naivete of a twenty-year-old and I had enjoyed it. But the truth was that I had never been the girl who dreamed of being an actress since childhood, or the type who followed everything and anything about the cinema. Acting for me was just fun—but I didn't love Italian films, or live and breathe the work of acting. I loved the independence and the freedom that acting brought me. I loved the chance to travel the world and experience different cultures. I did my jobs well, but I didn't think of them as building a career. I didn't promote myself. I didn't socialize or court directors, producers, or cinematographers. As my friend Massimo had chastised me about, I didn't go the parties, attend the festivals or try to make film friends. I had heard too many unpleasant stories about the things that happened to actresses who put themselves in situations where they were alone with powerful men and I didn't want any part of that. Most of my work came because I spoke English and was able to work in co-productions between Hollywood and Italian filmmakers. I was one of the few young Italian actresses who could perform in English—and most of the others were expensive big-name actresses who worked a lot and only on very big budget films. Co-productions kept me working, but I was never sure just how many or how long I would have to go between jobs.

I had already started to think about what I would do when the offers for roles stopped coming and had taken various part-time jobs, hoping to find something that would sustain me when my life as an actress ended. I had sold Collier Encyclopedias (an English set of books) including my one big sale to a butcher in Centocelle who certainly didn't need them because he barely spoke Italian. I worked as a secretary for an Arab company based in Rome . . . but quit only a few weeks later when I realized that what they really wanted a secretary during business hours and a cleaning lady at night. I worked in an art gallery selling paintings and sculptors. I worked for a vendor in the Fiera di Roma market stalls.

I wrote a few articles for the local newspaper, *Il Messaggero* and the editor of the paper arranged to have me registered on a special list to work as a journalist, even though I did not have a degree. That might have been my next career had he not rejected one of my stories because it didn't agree with the newspaper's editorial board's political stance. Everything I wrote, he insisted, needed to be in accord with the newspaper's views, rather than my own opinions or the facts presented.

I felt like he'd slapped me. I was expected to write according to some political point of view? I might have understood it if he felt that my article wasn't objective. But to reject it because it didn't follow the editorial line of the newspaper? No. I reacted in my characteristic way: I quit immediately.

Instead, I wrote articles for a real estate office's monthly newsletter, and interviewed Rome's housing authorities. Fortunately, the real estate newsletter didn't have the same requirements for the pieces I wrote for them. I could write according to my interests, and except for the occasional interviews with various housing officials, I could write what I liked, as long as it somehow dealt with houses. I challenged myself to do research in a completely new area and searched out information about unusual homes, both in Italy and all around the world. I discovered the Futuro houses, including the "Casa UFO," in Gallicano, near Rome. It was a house shaped like a flying saucer that Mr. Franco Attanasio of the ATAC (AziendaTranvi Autobus Comune) built for his family. The Futuro house still stands, in the middle of the countryside, semi-surrounded by a neighborhood of small conventional cottages. Resting on a single central iron pillar covered with reinforced concrete and supported by twenty steel pillars placed all around the edge of the structure, the circular house is made of wood. Its diameter is about twenty meters and by painting it a luminous silver—like the best of science fiction flying saucers—it looks almost like something from another world that somehow landed in the Italian countryside.

I wrote about the Tesseract house: a house built as a hypercube consisting of eight interlocking cells in design that, according to architect Riccardo Migliari (the author of numerous essays and a lecturer in descriptive geometry at Sapienza University of Rome) lies partially in the fourth dimension. Fantasies? Maybe... or maybe these homes were the evidence of reality being applied in new ways. After all, in 1977, at an international scientific conference in Helsinki, Professor Burkhard Heim of the University of Northern Germany presented mathematical proof of the existence of the fourth, fifth, and sixth dimensions. Professor Heim, a physicist, argued that these dimensions exist from the mathematical point of view, but we do not yet have the experience to know them in our three-dimensional reality. Given my interests, I found the idea of a house that existed partially in one reality and partially in another especially fascinating.

But there were still other ways I could bring my interests into the discussion of real estate. I still remember the reaction of the bulletin's publisher when I brought him the interview I had done with Enzo Nardi, a well-known lawyer in Rome. But instead of exploring the traditional concerns of real estate law, Nardi explained the law surrounding homes which are alleged to be *haunted*. Originally enacted in 1866 and still in effect today, the law focuses on the duty of a seller to inform buyers of the vices or evils associated with the property, including supernatural phenomena. Of course, the vices can be other kinds of problems, but no matter what, the seller is liable for damages if he deliberately concealed the issue at the time of sale.

I loved that job!

Unfortunately, the company went bankrupt and the owner fled to Guatemala with the cash—or so I heard. But finally, an acting job arrived with a role for me as the lead. Soon I was in Puglia and working steadily on a five-week shoot.

I was thrilled to have the opportunity, but I was also in a hurry to finish it and get the film behind me. At that time, there were things that excited me far more than the film. Every evening at the end of the shooting day, I thought about the experiments I would be doing soon with my Kirlian camera. I was determined to investigate the paranormal manifestations I had witnessed and experienced and I hoped I would soon have a role to play in the endless debate among the Italian media about extrasensory phenomenon.

PART TWO

THE SECOND LIFE PARANORMAL INVESTIGATOR

CHAPTER SEVEN
THE KIRLIAN CAMERA

The technology of the Kirlian Camera has a unique history. Years before, Kirlian cameras were used in various branches of science in both Russia and the United States. For example, in 1966, Kirlian cameras were used to discover and locate minerals based on their electroconductivity. In Russia, V.I. Mikhalevskii and G. S. Frantov, were able to discern highly conductive sulfur-based minerals, poor conductor silicate-based minerals, and everything in between, using the Kirlian technology[4]. Similarly, in 1973, in the United States, Thelma Moss and Kendall Johnson, working at the Institute of Neuropsychiatry at UCLA used Kirlian technology for other surprising advancements including:

- Detecting thin fractures in metal—a precursor to the current procedures used to determine stress and fractures in metals;
- Corroboration of work done by English scientists Milner and Smart on the movements of air in atmospheric studies;
- Working with counterfeits and other objects to reveal authenticity and evidence of tampering.

The bottom line of these studies was that the Kirlian camera shows the previous energetic image of an altered object, thus indicating that tampering has taken place. This sort of procedure is useful in identifying all kinds of frauds and counterfeits: artwork, car plates, fingerprints erased by sanding, etc., and, the scientists theorized, could be extended to other disciplines, including

---

4 I read about Kirlian technology in the *Russian Journal of Science* and the citation is in my Bibliography endnotes.

medicine, agriculture, mining, photography, pharmacology, biology, and industrial chemistry.

Other scientists argued that the Kirlian's electro-photography (this is the correct term, but it is easier to say just photography) shows the emission points of the object examined and, in the case of a living being, are for the most part the same as those generated by acupuncture. As such, these scientists argued that Kirlian images should join the recent scientific developments that fell under the general title of systems research.

A system as defined by Ludwig von Bertalanfy is "a complex of components in mutual interaction." R. Buckminster Fuller, the noted architect and futurist, used the term "synergy" to describe the unpredictable behavior of the individual components as they work together to make the system function.

Just as our knowledge of chemical compounds does not allow us to predict the behavior of individual cells, the knowledge of individual cells doesn't predict how they work together in a particular species. Unpredictability explains everything from disease to miraculous healing—and quite possibly the presence of abilities we do not yet understand.

Kirlian photographs of various forms of life show that each species has its own pattern of corona imagery[5]. However, the luminous patterns of each organism cannot be explained by the individual components of the system of the species. Acupuncture is a good example since it suggests a very complex network of bodily reactions, rather than an individual one. The acupuncturist puts a needle for example, in the web between the thumb and forefinger. That should just make a puncture mark or cause pain in that isolated area, but instead, that point may impact systems throughout the body.

I had read the work of Ostrander & Shroeder[6], in which Kirlian photographs of the fingertips of a relaxed man in good health, differed significantly from those of a tense, anxious, and unhealthy one. Kirlian photography records the general state of the person's system—as well

5 Krippner and Davidson, (1972)
6 Ostrander & Shroeder,(1971)

as that system's response to external stimuli. If you think about it, Kirlian photography is one way of seeing the human body as an "open system" in which reactions to various external and internal forces can be captured.

In his book, *Galaxies of Life*, psychologist and paranormal researcher Stanley Krippner writes:

> I think that Kirlian photography gives us images of the light emitted by the ionization of the air, caused by the cold emission of electrons of the various samples under examination. However, the differences in these emissions maybe due to an unusual type of matter such as "bio plasma," a hypothesis suggested by some Soviet scientists. (Inyushin et al., 1968) Physicists have divided the world into four types of material substances: solid, liquid, gas and plasma. The so-called "bio plasma" could be variation of the plasma (which would represent the subatomic particles present in living organisms) or the fifth state of matter. In both cases, the 'bio plasma' can change with every small change in the body's condition. If so, it can influence the cold emission of electrons of the sample under examination, thus modifying the images obtained.

These and other articles, books and reports were my light reading as I worked, saved, and planned for the purchase of my Kirlian camera. Paranormal science has certainly advanced beyond these ideas in many ways today, but as I began my journey into the study of the use of energetic fields to capture the unexplained, this information was at the cutting edge.

As soon as I returned from Puglia with my paychecks from the film, I ordered the Kirlian camera from the company in the United States. Almost a month later, it arrived. This was before the age of digital photography and, according to the instructions, I would need a darkroom—not to operate the camera but to develop the film and print the photographs. That posed a new problem.

A darkroom must be absolutely dark with no light filtering in through shutters or doors that can burn the film or the photo paper. The only light comes from red light or a light bulb painted red. The darkroom also needs a water source for rinsing the sensitive paper used in developing the photograph, a space for finishing tanks, and a safe space for the Kirlian camera itself to sit during the process. If the camera accidentally came into contact with any of the liquids used in developing the film, the camera would short circuit and become useless.

I was living in my small but fashionable apartment in the Cassia then. There wasn't exactly a good space to turn into a darkroom, but I had a friend who was a photographer (Emilio, of course) and I knew that he would help me figure it out. We quickly discovered that, although the bathroom was the easiest place to turn into a darkroom, it wasn't the most practical since I'd have to disassemble everything every time I needed to use the bathroom—from the tanks to the red lightbulb.

The kitchen, on the other hand, was a place I used very little.

Sure, this meant more time in nearby restaurants and cafes ... but that was a sacrifice I was willing to make. I was never much for cooking ... and for my morning coffee, I had a little hot plate that I could put in the living room and leave my kitchen darkroom completely undisturbed.

Photography wasn't an entirely new experience for me thanks to my father. He was passionate about photography and had a beautiful enlarger. When he had the time, he developed and printed the shots he took of our family on vacations and at special events. As a child, I spent hours with him in the darkroom he made in the bathroom at home, counting the seconds of exposure time for his prints.

"Don't run," he used to tell me. "A second is a second. You're not at a race and you don't have win. It doesn't develop faster if you count faster."

Still, the Kirlian camera was different from a regular camera both in use and in photographic process. It didn't have a conventional lens. Instead, on the upper part of the camera there was a box of about 18 x 23 centimeters. A dielectric glass plate with low electrical conductivity rested on top of that. The plate was where you placed the photography paper and above the paper you placed the object you wanted to photograph (finger, hand, flower, coin—whatever). On the front of the camera were two knobs: one for the frequency and one that set the amount of time you wanted to allow for capturing the image. The Kirlian camera then imprinted on the paper or film the difference in electrical potential created between the appliance and the object being examined. The resulting image is a bright corona that varies in shape, brightness, and size depending on the object examined. For an inanimate object like a coin, the crown will be static. For a living object, the fuzziness of the image makes it obvious that the corona was alive. Naturally, on the photo paper, you can't actually see the corona is moving.

Working with psychophysical alterations—emotions, in other words—the electro-potential of the body changes, the corona changes, and you can compare the images that result. From this, I deduced that any psychophysical alteration creates a new frequency in the body. Fear, for example, produces an adrenaline rush in the blood, cardiac acceleration, etc. and these vary the electrical potential of the organism. The voluntary alteration of one's physical state through concentration or deliberate attention also produces electrical variations in the body that can be recorded and compared to Kirlian photographs taken from other states of emotional awareness. At the time, no one had thought to test emotional variations with a Kirlian camera or to compare Kirlian images of psychophysiological changes when certain skills were used. As far as I know, this path of research hasn't been followed since I did it, either.

Using color film, instead of black and white, allows for the observation of many more details. For a while I used regular photography paper, but when I discovered I could purchase the kind of film astronomers used to capture their magnificent photos of the universe, I ordered some right way. This film was very expensive and had to be developed in specialized laboratories, so I only used it on occasions when I thought I might capture something particularly worthwhile.

I took Kirlian photographs of everything and everyone. I did my own hands, then those of my friends. I photographed a dog's paw and I asked my father to place his forehead on the device. Bad idea: he was sick for a couple of days after that as the electromagnetic fields interacted with his natural brain frequencies. I shared these experiences with many friends and colleagues, including an American actor shooting a film at Cinecittà Studios in Rome. He was interested so I invited him to my home and showed him how the Kirlian worked.

"Do you think you could turn it on alone?" I asked. "Take a picture of yourself?"

"I think so," he said. "It looks pretty simple."

"This button," I told him. "Hold it down for seven seconds. And this one is the exposure time on the black and white paper. I'm curious about something, so here's what I want you to do, lock yourself in the kitchen and use *your* ... uh ... Well, put down your ... *apparatus* on the plate and take a photo."

But I had to repeat the instruction a couple of times. Once he understood, he started laughing. And he kept laughing ... until he went in the kitchen and did it. He kept the Kirlian photo of his *hydraulic system* as a memento of his Italian stay.

I also photographed a subject who had taken marijuana to see if there were any differences in the coronas with the introduction of that substance. The variations were remarkable and similar to other images I had taken of subjects who were on various medications.

Many of my friends were photographed with my Kirlian camera, and they told other friends, and that's how I happened to be invited on Raffaella Carrà's television program to take Kirlian pictures and talk about the coronas the images revealed.

In Italy at that time, being on Raffaella's show was a little like being invited to sit down with Oprah. She was (and remains) a very popular television personality. I was excited about the opportunity but the matter of attempting to take Kirlian pictures live—or nearly so—in a television studio setting was daunting. There were many technical issues, but on the whole, the program went well, and I took several interesting photos that I still have to this day.

All of these experiments with the Kirlian were interesting—and I learned a great deal from them—but increasingly I found the photographs that revealed the impact of emotions on the subject's energetic field to be the most fascinating. It seemed to me that I had stumbled into a possible way to test the abilities of people who claimed to have some kind of paranormal skill—and in doing so, validate or refute the existence of such powers. I theorized that, the energetic fields of the psychically gifted should show a variance when they manifested their abilities. The similarities of those corona—or the lack of them—could end a considerable amount of debate.

But if I was going to thrust myself into the realm of scientific investigation, I needed to start using more stringent and coordinated methodology. I borrowed from the scientific method and set up my own experimentation protocol which required three different images:

1. A Kirlian photo of the subject's hand at rest;
2. A Kirlian photo of the same hand while the subject alters his psychophysical state;
3. A Kirlian photo of the same hand after the subject returns to rest.

My idea was that these three images, read together, would offer evidence of a measurable shift in the subject's energetic field while successfully completing some paranormal activity. The only catch was the Kirlian's black and white exposure time was only seven seconds—which meant that the psychophysical ability had to be one that could be expressed quickly. But Uri Geller had bent my necklace in less than that amount of time, so I believed that, if the subject's abilities were real, seven seconds would be enough to manifest it, take the Kirlian image, and see a measurable difference between that manifestation and the images that came before and after.

I put together an entire experiment presentation. I wrote each step of my protocol out on paper, then followed with individual sheets on which I glued the original photos I already had that illustrated the resting, active, and return to resting stages of each experiment. I captioned each photograph then prepared cover sheets on which I had recorded the date of the experiment and the subject's name. The last sheet included any other details which I believed relevant to the experiment or which might have impacted the results.

I was ready to take my theories to the researchers in the fields of paranormal science.

CHAPTER EIGHT
THE CHILDREN

Real or faked, when Uri Geller appeared on Italian Radio Television, he spawned a tidal wave of reports of "bending" in the weeks and months afterward. I called it "the spread" since that's what it seemed like—almost like a virus that had swept through Italy. Many children—especially, it seemed, boys between the ages of nine and fourteen discovered they had abilities similar to Geller's. They could bend spoons, forks, keys, knitting needles, etc.

The media went wild. Geller might be a showman—a skilled magician or trickster—but how likely was it that a child of nine or even fourteen from some small Italian town or village, could achieve the same results? Was the trick that easy or was something else at work here?

I had been conducting my own experiments with the Kirlian camera for a while and following my scientific protocol for making comparisons between images taken of the same subject. I felt I had sufficient documentation to reach out to Dr. Cassoli at the Center of Parapsychology in Bologna again. I wrote to him, presenting him with the documentation I had obtained and told him that I had the feeling that, if I were to take similar images from some of the young people who claimed to have awakened this new skill, I would have found at least a piece of the evidence of paranormal ability that the Italian scientific community was looking for. To my surprise, Dr. Cassoli expressed a great deal of curiosity about the work I had done and invited me to Bologna.

I met him in a quiet restaurant along with his colleague, Professor F. Barbieri and a couple of other men whose names I don't remember. Dr. Cassoli had black hair and eyes, a tanned face and a stylish way of dressing. He sat at the head of the table, on my left, while Professor

F. Barbieri, professor of physics and teacher at the local University sat across from me. He was very different looking man than Cassoli: a more English type, with a thin build, light brown hair, and penetrating and suspiciously clear eyes. He was younger than Cassoli but already balding. He wore a three-piece suit—vest and all—which was unusual in those days. I remember wondering if, somewhere tucked in a pocket, he had a gold watch on a pendant chain.

They spent most of our meeting discussing the various problems they were facing with their research: how the experiments would be done, when they could be done, how much could be accomplished with the limited resources that University could grant, the problem of the University itself, which might not continue to support the topic of paranormal research at all. They turned to a discussion about how to disseminate information about their research conclusions to the public and how to make the media and the wider world appreciate the reality of the phenomena they were exploring. To their way of thinking, advancement of science in this area was synonymous with advancing humanity to higher levels of consciousness.

I listened in silence until at last, Cassoli turned to me and said, "I looked at the photos and read your documentation. I find it remarkable, but I don't know how useful it can be. Or at least, I don't understand how you plan to use it."

I took a breath and launched into my theories with all the enthusiasm I had.

"The Kirlian Camera provides images of the vital energy field that every individual possesses," I told him. "In people, this field is subject to variations due to multiple factors: illness, medication intake, stress, etc. But the camera also allows us to see changes in moods and, therefore, emotions. I think, in fact, I'm almost sure, that if I could take a couple of Kirlian photos of the boys who can bend the forks or similar objects, we would see shifts in their fields that happen at the same time as the bending of the metal. And this would be a proof that something physiological is happening at the same time as the bending and that would be a significant step in proving that the bending comes from something inside them."

As I finished speaking, I slapped the table to emphasize my conviction. Unfortunately, I hit the edge of the spoon that lay next to my plate, and it jumped upward, spinning as it tumbled off the table and landed on the floor with a crash. It was mortifying that I had gotten a little dramatic. That was a bad thing, considering I knew they already thought I was just an actress who had gotten some idea in her head and now thought she was a scientist.

"I'm sorry," I stammered, struggling to lower my voice and sound calm. "But I really believe in this. I think it could work."

"Don't worry about it. It's no big deal," Cassoli comforted me. "In fact, I think you should join the professor when he goes to meet one of these children next week. He has some tests he wants to try. You could accompany him and observe his efforts."

My heart jumped. He wasn't giving me the chance to test my own theories, but it was a step in the direction I wanted to go. I enthusiastically agreed to accompany Professor Barbieri to meet one of the subjects, a boy named Paolo.

The boy lived in a middle-class home in a small town in Northern Italy. He was fourteen years old, had brown hair, and a slightly aquiline nose, set in a face still round with childhood. He was tall for his age, but very thin. He sat on a sofa that had seen better days as his mother left us to our work.

Paolo listened attentively to Professor Barbieri as he took the seat across from him and showed him a device made of transparent plexiglass, more or less the size of children's shoebox. You could see the metal bar inside that divided two clear compartments, one filled with very fine white sand-like material, the other with very fine dark grains. Barbieri wanted the boy to fold the bar—without mixing the light and dark materials. If the materials mixed, according to Barbieri, this meant that the boy had used some parlor trick or magician's technique—and not solely the power of his mind.

"Do you understand?"

Paolo nodded. We waited but nothing happened. So, I started chatting with the boy, keeping one eye on the box. Barbieri joined in and then suddenly I saw it.

"Look, it's bent."

Barbieri's attention snapped back to the box.

"Good," I said encouragingly, patting Paolo on the shoulder.

But Barbieri was not happy. He carefully picked up the box, looked at the powders—which remained separate and unmixed—and eyed the boy suspiciously. I could tell he was thinking that, because he was distracted while the phenomenon occurred, somehow, Paolo had cheated. He considered the experiment null and void and remained unconvinced even when it was repeated on subsequent visits with other boxes, phials with rubber stoppers with metal bars hidden inside, and other objects protected so they could not be manipulated or touched by hand.

I accompanied Professor Barbieri on many of those trips and developed a friendly relationship with Paolo. But as the experiments went on, the boy began to show a certain impatience toward Barbieri, whose suspicions troubled him. Still, Barbieri went to visit Paolo again and again and almost every time he went, I went, too, because Barbieri knew that, when I was present, the boy worked more willingly.

Finally, I found the right moment and invited Paolo to Rome to test him with my Kirlian experiment. His mother was already planning a trip to the city to visit relatives, and that made it the perfect opportunity for me to set up a time to conduct my own experiments. I prepared excitedly for the chance to see what kinds of images our session together would record.

At last, I had him in front of me, sitting in my living room as excited as I was to attempt something new. I took out a bag filled with a dozen pieces of silverware, mostly forks and spoons, that I had bought especially for our experiment at the *Standa* supermarket just the day before. I picked up a fork and placed it on the table in front of the sofa. Then, I took him to my kitchen darkroom, closed the door, and instructed him to place his hand on the Kirlian. I asked him to relax then took a picture of it while he was in a state of rest (i.e., without attempting to do anything special with his body or mind). I put that image into the developing fluid and left it. After asking Paolo to once again place his hand on the device, I asked him to bend the fork I'd left on the living room table within the seven seconds required to capture an image on the Kirlian. If he wasn't able to accomplish this within those seven seconds, I knew there would be nothing on the photo paper and the experiment would be a failure.

We waited and waited. Too long. Finally, he said to me, "It doesn't want to come."

He was so sorry, but try as he might, nothing was happening.

But I had seen him bend so many other objects—and so easily—that I knew he could do it. There was something missing, something about the current setting that was blocking his ability. I searched my mind for ideas . . . and then one came to me.

"Have you ever seen *Playboy* magazine?" I asked.

At first, he was confused (and a little embarrassed!). But after a couple of seconds, he shouted, "I understand."

It may sound suggestive, but what I was trying to do was coax him into the right *emotion* by using a memory of something that had excited him. We tried the experiment again . . . and that's how he folded the first fork I had placed in my living room.

Following my protocol, I took a final control picture of Paolo's hand to use as a comparison to the first resting phase image. When I placed the three images side by side to read the sequence, I was ecstatic. The second picture, the one in which Paolo used his emotional field to bend the fork, the crown of lights around his fingers showed such striking variations from the other two pictures that even a skeptic would have been impressed. Moreover, the experimentation also gave me a bent object to analyze.

I took the bent objects and all of the images I had collected from working with Paolo to friends I had made at the National Research Council (now called the ENEA). They made their own informal analysis and shared with me their results. We concluded that my experiments were important for two reasons: the first, because when an object is bent or deformed with the mind (or mental energy), the object shows a particular kind of molecular alteration that is very different from those observed in objects bent through sleight-of-hand or other tricks. Second, because when a person uses his own mental energy to bend or deform an object, the Kirlian photos show unique changes in his own characteristic psychophysical readings. These changes indicate that something internal is happening within him. The changes in the person's energy also support the argument that the manipulation of the bent objects was not rigged.

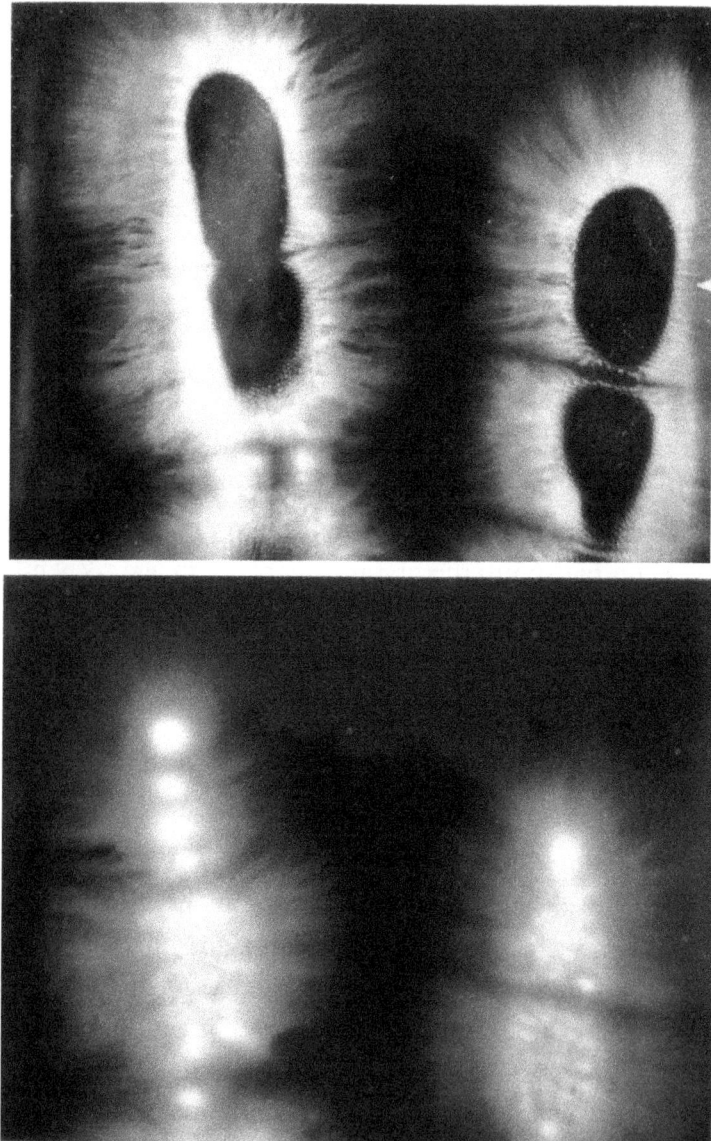

Kirlian photo of two fingers at rest and Kirlian photo of the same fingers while bending the object.

CHAPTER TEN
STUPIDITY

I met with Paolo again the next day. This time he bent a spoon without any difficulty. But our visit was brief because he had to return home with his mother. I thanked him, congratulated him on his bending ability, and he left. I was sorry that he had to go because in addition to the demonstrations of his skills, he'd begun to get comfortable enough with me to reveal more and more about himself. One of his stories struck me as particularly interesting.

Apparently, a few months before, he had gotten into a furious argument with his mother over a motorbike he wanted very much. She refused to buy it for him, telling him she thought that expense should wait until he was a bit older. Upset by the feeling that he was being treated like a child, Paolo ran out of the house, slamming the door behind him. To calm down, he went to the movies and was gone for a couple of hours. When he finally returned home, he found his mother in tears and the house a disaster. Shortly after Paolo had left, all the pipes in the bathroom and kitchen had burst simultaneously, destroying sections of the walls and drenching the house with water. In addition to the mess, the repairs would be very expensive—far, far more expensive than the Vespa Paolo had wanted.

His story made me wonder about the role of extremely strong emotions in the manipulation of objects in our physical world. Could a fourteen-year-old's denied desire for a motorbike have caused the explosion in his mother's home? And if so, what other phenomena that we chalk up as coincidence might be directly related to the feelings of those involved?

After Paolo had gone, I too had to leave for an appointment. I didn't want to be late, so I didn't clean up: I left everything exactly as it was during our session: the spoon on the coffee table in the living room and the Kirlian set up in my darkroom kitchen.

It wasn't until the next afternoon, when I went to the living room to clean and put things away, that I noticed an odd bit of some grainy substance clinging to the glass where the spoon lay. It looked like the residue after a scoop of sugar has been added to strong black coffee—the tacky leftover stuff that dries on the spoon. But we had not used any sugar—or even had coffee—and the spoon was brand new and unused.

I touched the table. Was it dirty before we began? But I didn't think so. The way the spoon had seemed stuck to the table's glass, was more like something wet that that been discarded, than like it had been placed on a table that was already stained.

I couldn't figure it out. But what I was certain of was that there was sticky spot on the glass on my table. I got a damp cloth and a little soap and scrubbed it off. Then I took the spoon and wrapped it in a sheetof white tissue paper to be taken to my friends at CNR for analysis.

A few weeks later, I heard from CNR.

"I cannot tell you anything new," my friend said. "But there are two strange things I noticed this time. The original spoons and forks had a minimal magnetic energy—due to a little bit of iron in their composition. But once bent by Paolo they had become extremely magnetic. In fact, the needle on a compass placed near them spun nonstop. The other thing is that we found a strange substance stuck to the spoon. We couldn't tell what it was because it was too small an amount for a thorough analysis, but it's something I haven't seen before. Do you have any more of it? Or any other objects that were bent in the same way?"

Of course, I immediately remembered the sticky substance I had cleaned off the glass on my coffee table. My ignorance and inexperience mortified me. What was it: a burst of solidified bioplasma, perhaps? Or something else?

But I had played the housewife and cleaned it away. And now I'll never know.

Through a newspaper article, I learned of another child who had manifested the bending ability living on a farm in Central Italy. I had to go. I reached out to the paper, located the journalist who had written the story, and got the address. I knew that Barbieri was in Puglia attempting to verify the abilities of a different child, so I didn't contact him. Instead, emboldened by the results of my own research with Paolo, I set off to conduct my own experiments.

But it would be very long drive and I wanted company. Someone open-minded and interested, but someone who would respect my methodology and objectives. I knew instantly who I would call.

Emilio.

He was the one person I knew who enjoyed talking about these things as much as I did. He was a natural foil to my own thoughts and ideas, and I knew we would enjoy the time together on the drive. As I expected, he enthusiastically agreed to accompany me and a short time later, we had loaded up the car with the Kirlian and the other tools I had invented for my experiments and we set off.

Sergio was about ten years old when I met him. He had one leg, the other having been lost in a tractor accident when he was small. He used an artificial leg and ran to greet us as naturally as any other boy of his age, jumping off the steps of the front porch of his family's home with energy and vitality.

Soon we were all seated around the family's large kitchen table: Emilio, Sergio, the child's mother, father, grandmother, and the teacher who ran his school. I wasn't expecting all of this—it wasn't the way I would have liked to proceed—but I did my best to put a good face on a bad hand. I wondered what reason lay behind the presence of all these adults—and the schoolteacher, no less—and feared that they had some objections to me and what I hoped to do.

After greetings and coffee, we launched into the matter at hand. I quickly understood the problem: They were worried.

"What do we do? He folds everything. My knitting needles, even," his grandmother complained. "I can't even use them anymore. I know he doesn't do it on purpose, but still."

"Folded spoons, forks, ladles..." his mother continued. "But that's not the worst of it. It's the staring off into space. He doesn't even hear us calling him, even though we're yelling in his ear."

"We've taken him to doctors, but they can't find anything wrong with him. They referred us to a psychiatrist. He thinks it's some kind of epileptic fit." The father shook a bottle of pills to show us. "He wants Sergio to take these drugs. Sedatives. To see if they'll help but—"

"But if they don't, he wants to try electroshock therapy," Sergio's mother added with fear in her eyes. "It seems so dangerous and it might not even work—"

"Because it might just be the devil," the grandmother proclaimed, nodding with vigorous certainty. "Maybe he needs an exorcism—"

"I don't think that will be necessary," the schoolteacher interrupted. "He acts normally at school, is quiet and well-behaved. But I do think it's a good idea to rule out any mental illness."

Sergio got up and left somewhere in the middle of this discussion about his affliction. I can't say I blamed him. He had probably heard it all hundreds of times before. Better to be outside in the fresh air than to sit around listening to the same theories and solutions he'd grown sick of hearing.

It was a new situation for me and a very delicate one. I was no expert, but I believed with all my heart that there was nothing wrong with Sergio. He was perfectly well and didn't need the services of either a doctor or a priest. But I understood the feelings of his family—feelings that had been influenced both by ignorance and lack of education about paranormal abilities. I hoped to reassure and inform them, so I threw all the passion and skill I had into my voice as I began my explanation.

I told them about the other boys and girls in Italy and abroad who had the same skills and how those gifts had been perceived not as the curse of the devil, but as a blessing from the Lord. I told them that these children gave us the opportunity to understand these phenomena and to explore the possibility that every human has innate abilities to accomplish similar results. I discussed my own experiments in training my mind toward improving my extrasensory abilities and the theory that, with proper teaching and encouragement, all humans might enjoy the same gifts. I told them about the ongoing research in the United States and abroad on children like Sergio—children who possessed extraordinary abilities. Thanks to those children, many scientists, research centers, and universities were beginning to have some understandings of how these abilities manifested.

I went on like this for a while, building up their trust and, hopefully, allaying some of their suspicions. Then I asked if we could take Kirlian photos of the boy. I left Emilio to explain the process and what the Kirlian images would show, and I went to look for Sergio.

I found him jumping from step to step on the front porch. His speed and agility were amazing—especially for a boy using a prosthetic. He had developed a way of using one leg so he wouldn't have to deal with the brace of the prosthetic, which he disliked.

I asked him to sit down with me for a bit and for a little while we chatted about unimportant things. At last, however, I asked him about what his family called his episodes where he stared off at nothing.

"I'm listening with my mind," he answered cryptically. "But then I forget what I heard."

In short, he experienced the episodes as blackouts during which he was unaware of the passage of time. I searched my memory for some of the other stories I had heard or read about children who behaved in similar ways.

"Has anything strange or inexplicable ever happened to you?"

I wanted his confidence. I wanted to know his secrets. He stared at me for a long time—probably trying to decide if he could trust me—and then told me a story he had not even told his parents.

One night when he was much younger, he was awakened from sleep by a single ray of bright white light outside his open window. He was alone in his room; everyone else in the house was asleep. As he watched, the light beam moved across the fields and the yard and he knew with an absolute certainty that the light was looking for him. He was afraid, but he couldn't move—couldn't run—but only sat terrified in bed as the light travelled across the windowsill, crept across the wood floor and wavered a little on the wall beside the bed before striking him directly in the forehead. Everything went black and he remembered nothing more.

The next morning, he woke up and everything was normal—exactly as it always had been. He told no one what he had experienced overnight, but he never forgot that odd light: a thin white beam that came so steadily and directly toward him.

This was information I hadn't expected. Immediately, I was reminded of Dr. Andrija Puharic's book about Uri Geller, in which he recounted one of the earliest childhood memories of his Israeli friend. Apparently, around the age of four, Uri fell asleep in a garden. It was a spot he retreated to often to escape the questions and concerns of his family. When he woke up, he saw an immense, silent object hanging in the sky. It was shaped like a bowl, and nothing like any of the planes his father had shown him. And, unlike the planes, it was completely silent; it made no noise at all. Dr. Puharic writes that suddenly, "between himself and the basin in the sky, appeared the shadow of an enormous figure similar to that of a man wearing a long cloak, since neither arms nor legs were visible. As he watched that figure, a blinding ray of light popped out of the figure's head and hit Uri so violently that the child fell backward and into a deep sleep."

Sergio's story was so similar to the one I had read in Puharic's book that I knew it was important. But I couldn't figure out what to do with it and that irritated me. Still, with Sergio's family's consent, I made my Kirlian photos. In two sessions, Sergio bent two forks within the seven seconds required to capture the energy of his mental process.

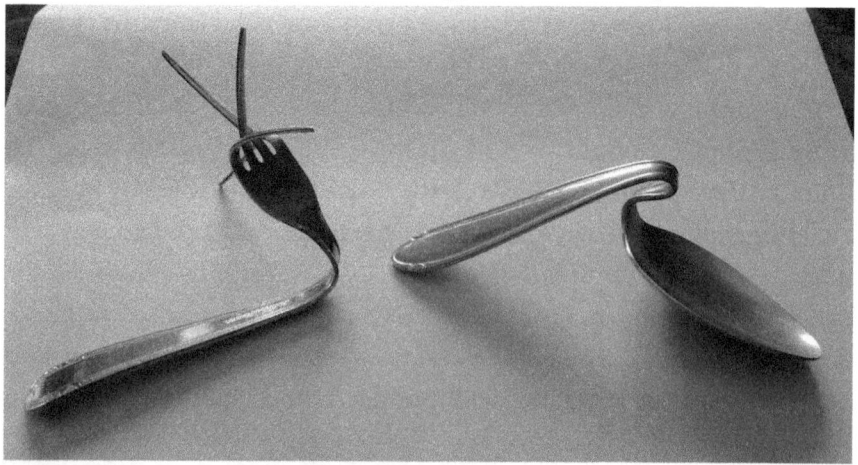

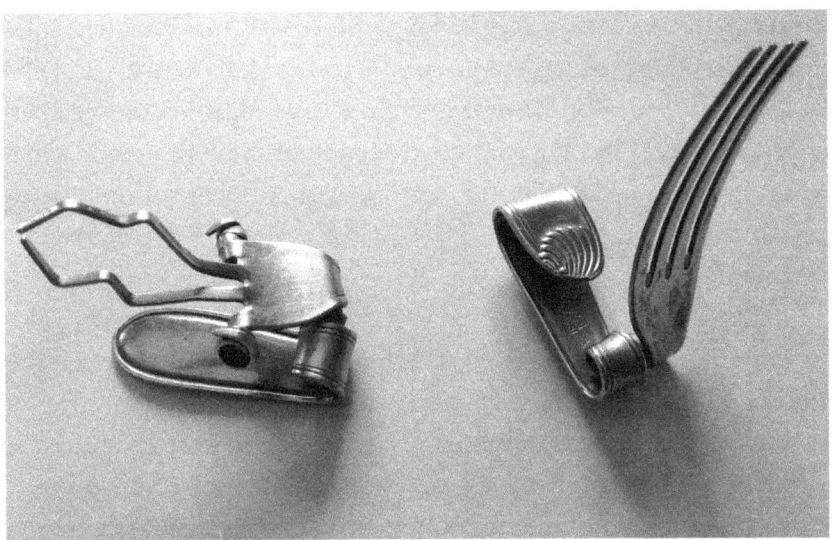
Note: each folded object always follows the style of the subject who created it—like artwork.

I wanted more—more information, more experiments, more understanding. I knew that some US researchers believed that PSI and ESP were a part of the mankind's essential nature, located in an area at the base of the brain called the reptilian brain. This reptilian brain is believed to date back to man's earliest days on Earth. Was it possible that these phenomena were simply a reconnection to an ability lost in man's distant past? Perhaps they were easier to revitalize and manifest in prepubescent children, as yet uncontaminated by the skepticism of our culture?

Dr. John B. Hasted, head of the Department of Physics at Birkbeck College of the University of London, described the more than 10,000 observations made on a dozen British children able to fold remote keys and others who were able to move objects without touching them. Similar observations and experiments have been successfully conducted in six other laboratories worldwide. Several years ago, I read that Sony set up an ESP Laboratory Special Research Department, where extensive research into human PSI capabilities was carried out. Yaichiro Sako directed the lab from its creation in 1990 through its closure in 1998. More recently, American toy manufacturer Uncle Milton Industries launched the Force Trainer that comes with a headset that uses brainwaves to allow players to manipulate a sphere inside a ten-inch training tower, similar to the skills of Yoda and Luke Skywalker in *Star Wars*. In Force Trainer, a wireless headset reads the player's brain activity, in a simplified version of the EEG medical tests, and the circuit translates it into physical action. If you concentrate well enough, the training ball, which looks like a ping-pong ball, rises into the tower.[7]

Imagine: toys that will allow you to test and refine your skills of concentration and perhaps even bring to light some other mental abilities. Mainstream research into telekinetic ability. That corporate entities like Sony have spent years investigating these little-understood powers of the human mind suggests something important. Are we at a turning point in the construction of PSI energy equipment—and its use in everyday work and play?

As we drove back to Rome, I told Emilio about Sergio's experience with the light beam.

"So, he saw a UFO," he said laconically.

"Be serious," I scoffed. "UFOs do not exist."

"Let me get this straight," he continued. "You love astronomy and you study the planets. But you don't believe there's *life* on any of them?"

"Of course, it's possible that there's life," I replied, "but thinking there's possible life to thinking that life is visiting us *here* is a big jump. I'll need a whole lot more proof of that."

The UFO conversation went on until we reached Rome and I closed it at last by decreeing, "I'll believe it when I see it," and that was the end of that.

---

7 (06/January/2009, USA Today).

CHAPTER ELEVEN
THE MEDICINA RADIOTELESCOPE

Out of the blue one day, Barbieri called me. He sounded excited—which was unusual for him—and told me that he had a fantastic idea, one that would finally bring some clarity and eliminate all doubt about the children who claimed they could bend metals with their minds.

"Would you like to come with me to visit Paolo again?" he asked.

"Absolutely," I replied. I'll admit; I was curious about what had Barbieri so excited and I was certainly interested in seeing Paolo again.

"Good," Barbieri said. "We have to make a stop along the way, but I think you'll enjoy it."

I was intrigued.

Several days later, we met to drive from Rome to the Medicina Radio Observatory located about 30km from Bologna. The observatory houses two radio telescopes, including the University of Bologna's Northern Cross, Italy's first radio telescope. There were more than thirty-two parabolic dishes on the campus of the Medicina Observatory, but their shapes were very different from the bowl-shaped discs I had seen in photographs. Instead, the arrays consisted of hundreds of thin U-shaped rails that looked harmonious, light, and delicate. As a light breeze blew over the enormous rectangular structure of many thin threads of metal, a sweet and continuous sound filled the air. It made me wonder if distant galaxies were vibrating in time to their signal.

Barbieri had guessed right: the place fascinated me. Adrenaline coursed through me, along with a sense of exhilaration, as if I had gone dancing at my favorite club in Rome, the Piper.

I was very excited, and I thanked Barbieri for showing me the Observatory.

"Wait," he told me. "There's more."

He led me to the offices, a system of white prefabricated buildings, and asked for the director, who was a friend of his.

"I've managed it, but this has to stay just between us," the director said in a low voice after the pleasantries were complete. He opened a desk drawer and pulled out a thick hexagonal hardware nut—the kind you attach to a bolt or screw—made of a heavy, dull gray metal.

Barbieri reassured him, slipped the nut into his leather bag, and we left.

Back in the car, I peppered him with questions. What was that thing? How did it fit with his experiments? What did that have to do with our trip? Barbieri's answers opened exciting new possibilities—at least for me. I'm not sure Barbieri found them as exciting as I did, even though the experiment had been his idea.

That piece of hexagonal metal was composed of tungsten and titanium, and it was one of many inserted into the rod of the Medicina nuclear reactor to prevent heat and radiation from escaping, he told me. Tungsten and titanium were used to create it because of their properties: they were strong enough not to melt or deform under the intense heat of the reactor. In short, they were impossible to bend or deform, even at extreme temperatures.

When we reached Paolo's house, Barbieri produced the thick hexagonal nut like a magician performing his most famous trick.

"Bend this," he challenged Paolo.

I didn't like the way he said it. He sounded like he was issuing a challenge that he knew Paolo wouldn't be able to rise to. Like, indeed, Paolo's failure to bend this unbendable material would alone be sufficient proof that there was no such thing as any kind of psychokinetic ability. But I kept quiet and waited.

Paolo stared at it, turning it in his hands. I had held it myself and I knew it was heavy, but I could tell by the look on Paolo's face that he was more curious than intimidated.

"I'll try," he said at last. "But only if I can do it in my room."

Barbieri smiled. On any other trip, he would have objected to Paolo taking anything out of our presence to bend it. He would have insisted that he be able to observe, in order to assure himself that Paolo wasn't doing some kind of trick. But this time, he was magnanimous and condescending. Barbieri was so sure that the boy wouldn't be able to bend the hexagonal nut that he didn't much care where he took it. He'd told me in the car that the press for its construction was fifteen meters long, and no instrument could deform it. Certainly nothing the boy might do in his bedroom would make any difference.

"Fine," Barbieri agreed.

Paolo took the ring and went to his room.

While we were waiting, Barbieri explained to me that, with this experiment, he intended to "cut off the bull's head" and put an end, once and for all, to the debate about this phenomenon. He hoped for absolute proof—something that his peers at the University would find impossible to dismiss—that the boy and others like him weren't frauds. In the absence of such proof, he worried that his experiments would be dismissed—and he would be the laughing stock of his colleagues.

I just nodded. He seemed overly cautious to me and at the time, it seemed to me he wanted Paolo to fail. But in hindsight, I understand that he believed in the possibility that the "benders" were fakers, while I had no such caution. He was looking for an answer to the phenomenon, but it had to fit within the laws of known physics. He was deeply interested in these telekinetic gifts, but suspicious of them, too. He wanted an explanation that fit into the known world of science. But for me, at the time, his doubts represented a defense for the status quo.

Paolo returned a short while later. His face was expressionless as he handed Barbieri the nut.

As Barbieri took it from him, all the blood drained from his face. He looked down at the nut in his hand and then at Paolo. Finally, without saying a word, he handed it to me.

The nut was bent, curved into an arch like the top of a lightbulb. Other than that, there wasn't a scratch on it: it looked like it came out of the press like that, rounded not straight.

I jumped up and hugged Paolo, unable to suppress my explosion of joy. Paolo grinned, pleased by my reaction. I explained to him what the bar was and what it was made of. He didn't seem impressed with that as much as he was happy to have received some praise. He had done something "hard," and now he knew it.

Barbieri was very quiet on the trip back to Medicina. I did not bother him. In front of his friend the director's desk, Barbieri opened his leather bag, pulled out the nut, and laid it gently on the leather desk pad. The director stared at it in shock.

"Damn it!" he said in a low voice. "How am I going to explain this?" He remained silent for a while, and we with him. Then, having reached a decision, he said, "This never happened. I will say that we have lost it and that we don't know what happened to it." He locked the nut back in the drawer and bid us goodbye with much less enthusiasm than he had said hello. We left.

Barbieri was disheartened and humiliated. He had had incontrovertible proof in his hands that there was something more than trickery at work with Paolo, but he could never use it without risking his standing in the scientific community.

Barbieri and I did not work together again, even though we sometimes spoke by phone. I appreciated his work, and I was grateful for lessons in physics that he often shared with me. But I did not share his methods—just as he did not share my enthusiasm, or my beliefs. We did not meet again.

CHAPTER TWELVE
GLASS

Time went by.

I continued acting and occasionally was interviewed by reporters from various newspapers and magazines both about my film career and my other interests including my experiences and research into paranormal phenomena. I enjoyed talking about the things that I had learned; about the results I had obtained with the Kirlian and the many people I had met who seemed to have unique abilities.

One day, out of the blue, a young man telephoned me. He'd read about my experiences recording telekinetic phenomena in a newspaper article and wanted to meet with me the following afternoon.

I was a little uncomfortable to meet a complete stranger alone, so I asked Emilio to accompany me. In many ways I was intrepid and fearless, but from time to time my Sicilian roots came out. Having Emilio by my side made me feel safe in ways I appreciated. He had become very important to me.

The young man lived in a single room in downtown Rome, behind Piazza Navona. His place was shabby and untidy, simply furnished with a table, some chairs, a bench, and a sloppily made bed. A few paper posters clung to the walls by bits of cellophane tape. Empty beer bottles and Coca Cola cans littered the table. I was almost sorry to have agreed to meet him when I looked around the dirty little room. The young man himself wasn't much cleaner: maybe twenty-two or twenty-three years old, dirty brownish-blonde curls, worn jeans, and a stained white and brown checkered shirt. He blinked his light hazel eyes as he told me he was a painter. But I saw no evidence of it in the room, whether he meant walls or paintings in the artistic sense.

I just wanted to get down to business as quickly as possible so I could get out of there, so I asked him why he'd called me. The answer to that question was simple: he had read about me and my research. He'd asked a friend who worked in the post office to find my address and then my phone number. It was there that simplicity ended.

Strange things had been happening to him, he told me. The kinds of strange things that he thought might interest me.

He handed me a Zywiec beer. Open. Empty. A completely unremarkable bottle of dark glass . . . except for the bottle's neck, which was folded softly in on itself. It was similar to what I had seen many times with the boys who could bend forks and spoons.

Emilio and I stared at it, speechless. My thoughts raced for an explanation, but the first thought that came to my mind was a question.

"How come the edge of the neck is chipped?"

"It rolled on the ground a bit. Luckily, it didn't break," the young man said.

"Well," I said, "can I borrow it? I'd like to have it analyzed and if you want, I'll give it back to you."

"Keep it," he said with a laugh.

"Do you have any other objects like this?" Emilio asked.

The young man hesitated then headed for a cardboard box on the floor nearby. He pulled all kinds of junk out of the box until, at last, he found an old candle-style light bulb. He handed it to me. At first it appeared normal, but when I looked at it more closely, I could see that the inner filament was broken, and the smooth surface of the glass was marked by bumps like little waves along its exterior.

"I was thinking and holding it in my hand. Those bulges came right between where my fingers touched the glass," the young man said. "I don't know if it can help you. But you're welcome to take it. I don't need it."

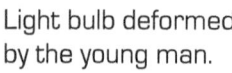

Light bulb deformed by the young man.

I placed my fingers between the bumps and noticed that my fingers, though smaller than his, also rested between the protuberances. I was also fascinated by the filament. Generally, the inside of a lightbulb is a vacuum. So, when it burns out, it usually blackens or breaks the glass. And certainly, any human pressure to extinguish the filament would have more than likely broken the glass, too. The filament was broken, but the bulb was still clear.

I had had plenty of exposure to bending metals, but bending glass was something I had never thought about, heard of, or seen—and because the young man had been so cryptic in his phone call, I was unprepared: we had not brought the Kirlian with us. So, before leaving, we made plans to set up a time for a new experiment, using the Kirlian to test this subject and the objects he bent. The young man seemed happy to submit to these tests.

Bottle of beer bent by the young man.

Unfortunately, it was a while before I was able to reach back out to him to schedule the experiments and when I did, he was gone. He no longer lived in the dirty little one-room apartment, and nobody who lived in the building knew where he had gone or what had happened to him. I never met him again.

My delay wasn't irresponsibility on my part. I had spent a good deal of that time trying to find someone who could analyze the bent bottle and offer explanations about how the folding might have occurred. As I've said, I knew little about glass. For all I knew, the bent bottle could have been a factory error and the young man might have contacted me in an attempt to get some publicity. But the publicity hypothesis did not explain the light bulb. That seemed far more complicated and less likely to have been some kind of factory error.

Finally, I found a laboratory in Rome, a subsidiary of the one of the glassmaking masters in Murano, the famous little town near Venice.

Who better than they to tell me what technique had been used to bend the neck of the glass bottle?

I took the bottle to the lab and placed it gently in the hands of an assistant. Explaining that I was a researcher, I asked if the bottle had already been created in that shape or if it had been subsequently blown into that shape through the heat of glassmaking techniques. The assistant took the bottle and disappeared, leaving me to wait in an office full of beautiful pieces of colored glass. I waited a long time before finally, one of the masters came out, looking perplexed.

"I'm baffled," he said. "I can say only two things with certainty: that the bottle was not originally forged in this way and that it was not blown into this shape afterward." He went on to explain, "When an object is forged, in this case, the bottle, the trace of the bar used to give it its shape remains inside. In this bottle, you see the trace of the bar that was used to forge it. The bending of the neck, therefore, could only have been done by bringing the bottle back to the furnace at a medium temperature. However, you would see the traces of the torch that was used in that process—the one used to bend the neck. But there is no trace. It makes no sense. I have no idea how this was done. I'm sorry."

With this information, I was ready to reach out to the young man and try some of my experiments. But as I've said, he was gone. The opportunity was lost. Instead, I expanded my reading, looking for similar experiments and phenomena that might offer an explanation.

William A. Tiller, Professor Emeritus of Materials Science and Engineering at Stanford University, wrote that the visible emission on a Kirlian photo passes through any kind of material (paper, metal, fabric). This means that if, for example, a person puts his hand on the Kirlian Chamber wearing a glove, the resulting photograph will show the characteristic emission of the hand as if the glove did not exist. The only material that can disturb the results of a Kirlian photograph is wood. As I considered Professor Tiller's experiments, I thought that the emissions that I was investigating (ESP, PK, etc.) had to have particular radiation and, consequently, frequency. I wondered if they could be blocked or changed to material that blocked light, or if they would pass through, unaffected by the addition of any intervening materials. I tried with the only material I had on hand that could block light: the black plastic bag in which the black and white photosensitive paper I used was wrapped.

It turned out to be a good idea. The photographs of the hands obtained by inserting the black plastic between the hand and the dielectric plate, came out completely white (i.e., not exposed), except for some scattered black dots. (I'm talking about black and white photos.) Of course, the color photos were totally dark, except for some scattered blue dots. The radiation, or whatever it was, did not pass through a material that blocked light. So, I tried to take the same pictures using that process I invented: the first Kirlian photo doing nothing (at rest), the second photo voluntarily altering the emotional state, and the third photo as final control. My idea was right: all the second pictures showed the typical crown around the fingers—despite the black plastic that prevented the passage of light. The control photos were either all white or all dark.

What did all this mean?

My conclusion was that the theory of bio plasma might be accurate. Under certain conditions, human beings emit a particular type of radiation that passes through any material and can, with the right equipment, be read. And if this is true, it destroys the arguments of those people (orthodox scientists and others) who think the Kirlian effect seen on the photo paper is just the effect of the combination of electrical discharge and humidity.

This shouldn't really seem far-fetched. Thanks to electroencephalography, we also know that our brain produces alpha waves (8 to 13 cycles per second), beta (15 to30 cycles per second), Theta (4 to 7 cycles per second), and Delta (.05 to 3 cycles per second). The question is: at what frequency does the ability to bend forks, spoons, glass, etc. correspond?

Peter Bender, the psychologist, posed this question, in his preface to the book *Where Do My Powers Come From?* by Matthew Manning, a British psychic almost as well-known as Uri Geller in the mid-1970s. In fact, in the summer of 1974, Dr. George Owen, director of the

New Horizons Research Foundation in Toronto, Canada, organized a special seminar to study Manning's extraordinary abilities. Among the scientists in attendance was Professor Brian Josephson, a member of the Royal Society, and winner of Nobel Prize in Physics in 1973. Dr. Joel L. Whitton conducted the experiments, connecting Manning to an electroencephalographic device and an electromyograph. A normal course of Manning's brainwaves was taken in relaxation conditions and another one in concentration conditions (key bending). Whitton found an unprecedented electroencephalographic pattern while Manning "psychically" folded keys and other similar objects, but the electromyograph did not detect any muscle activity. Instead, rapid eye movements (R.E.M.) detected by the readings suggested that Manning was in the fourth degree of a deep sleep—but it was clearly evident to all that scientists that the young psychic was wide awake. The electroencephalographic pattern Whitten recorded looked like a ramp and was actually called the "ramp effect." The "ramp function" contained up to forty-nine percent Beta waves and lasted up to twenty seconds, distinguishing it from the remaining Theta waves, i.e., deep sleep.

As a result of these experiments, Whitton published a booklet entitled *Ramp Functions in EEG Energy Pathways During Actual or Attempted Paranormal Phenomena*. Dr. Owen, on the other hand, published his own report, *Preliminary Report on The Physical Phenomena of Matthew Manning*. Sadly, I have never found either scientists' complete report, but the summaries of their experiments suggest that a great deal of exploration in this field had been done at the time I was making my own work in these areas.

The more I experimented and read, the more I became convinced that there must be a specific frequency or emission that occurs when certain faculties are manifested. It was around this time that I had the idea that perhaps connecting Kirlian to an electroencephalograph might offer a different visual representation of the electroencephalographic patterns that Whitten and others documented. Perhaps electrophotography could offer another way to demonstrate the existence of certain "skills" to a skeptical, orthodox scientific community?

But I didn't have access to that kind of equipment or the money to buy them. An electroencephalograph isn't something that the average actress (or any private citizen) can easily acquire. Instead, I looked for something more accessible and that was how I began to expand my "experimentation protocol" and update it with various tools. The first of these was a heliogiroscope, also known as Crooke's integral radiometer.

Heliogiroscope or Crooke's integral radiometer.

Usually used as a teaching tool, the heliogiroscope was designed by W. Crookes in 1875. It consists of fourpieces of mica each blackened on one side and then mounted on the arms of a whirling reel set inside the vacuum of a glass sphere. When exposed to light waves—for example, direct sunlight—the blackened mica absorbs the waves and heat, releasing gases that gives them greater kinetic energy than the energy around the non-blackened (white) laminas. The pressure imbalance between the blackened and unblackened lamina makes the reel turn with a speed proportional to the intensity of light source. Or at least that's what my *Encyclopedia Treccani* said. In addition, according to a law of physics that I can't now recall, the rotating is always clockwise.

I began adding Crooke's radiometer to my experiments with the boys who could bend metals. I placed the radiometer on a table, away from any light source. When the reel stopped moving and the mica slats were completely still (any little movement will make them sway) I asked the boys to make them move.

Not all of the boys were able to do this but those who did so did it not only without touching the radiometer (of course) but also turned the reel in the opposite direction: *counterclockwise.*

I do not know much about radiation and properties of light (it would be better to say that I know nothing about it), but in my opinion, these unusual results suggest something important about the effort to establish the "mental" frequency that creates telekinetic and paranormal activity. It is, in a manner of speaking a kind of "light" or electric energy, but different from that typically measured by scientific inquiry.

But as interesting as these phenomena were, they weren't exactly what I was looking for. I did not want tools that would only work with the Olympic champion runners of psychic ability. I also wanted tools that would indicate the abilities of those who could only run or jog psychically. In other words, I wanted a way to measure the abilities of someone who might be able to produce a frequency, but not necessarily in the strength that might bend a key or bubble glass or make Crooke's radiometer turn backward.

But how?

I added a neon tube to my experiment protocol—yes, an average neon tube like the kind that hangs above a typical bathroom mirror. I placed it on a chair in a dark room, disconnected from any power source and asked the boys to turn it on. Usually they could and the neon tube would emit a weak, intermittent brightness. I concluded that the neon gas molecules inside the glass tube were excited by certain mental "frequencies." But as I continued to experiment with the neon tube, I realized I had found what I was looking for: an easy tool for weaker energies. In fact, almost anyone can create the same phenomenon—even so-called normal adult people. Many times, I successfully used the neon tube with friends and acquaintances who saw the same result when they recalled strong emotions. There was one significant difference, however: the adults needed to hold the tube to achieve a weak brightness. The children lit it without touching it.

Evidently, the ability to project one's energy outwardly, without touching the object, is part of the PK phenomena. But even for the children, this can be difficult. Recalling emotion on command is, frankly, stressful. I think that's why so many psychics fail in laboratory experiments. The experimentation process strips the individual's sense of peace and that makes it harder to get the desired results.

My search of the psychic research carried out by the many qualified US researchers between 1970 and 1980 didn't reveal any experiments similar to mine but I still believed it was possible to define our mental frequencies with simple experiments if we could develop the right equipment. Was there a frequency at which we can excite neon molecules? Was there a different frequency for mentally moving other noble gases such as argon, xenon, etc.? What mental frequency turns the lamellae of the Crooke's radiometer? Once we discovered those "frequencies," could we find ways to support and amplify it? Since the "natural" frequency is like a small burst of energy that doesn't seem to last long, amplification would be the key to working and experimenting with it.

At least, these were my theories in the 1970s and 1980s when to most people, my ideas and experiments seemed nefarious and dangerous. Today, they may be tame or obsolete, or both. However, through the study, research, and results that I obtained from working with various children, I concluded that certain paranormal phenomena are generated as follows: *The thought creates an emotion, the emotion creates energy, the energy creates the frequency, and the frequency influences and/or interacts with the matter (our reality).*

Today this sounds very New Age spiritualism. It even sounds a bit like quantum physics. But in the 1970s, if I said this to other people, they looked at me like I was crazy. I had no academic qualifications to help legitimize my opinions—if you believe that a degree means something. In my experience, however, a degree isn't everything. It doesn't always mean that one has an open mind, creativity in pursuing research, and flexibility in developing hypotheses and conclusions.

Dr. Giulia Sellers, in her 2018 book *I Have Seen It Tomorrow* describes her own experience with extrasensory perception as a *sensation* that precedes thought. She outlines the sequence of mechanisms that trigger these beautiful skills as follows:

At the beginning of human evolution, thought was a sensation. The sensation should not be confused with emotion. Emotion arises from feeling. The feeling is actually the mother of emotions. Moreover, emotion is the mother of thought. Feelings, emotions, and thoughts form this sequence. Feelings are of vibrational origin. Emotions, like thoughts, are of electromagnetic origin. The only difference is that everyone has a different speed of vibration and oscillation. Emotions are more magnetic, while thoughts are more electric. When feelings are transformed into emotions, mechanical vibrations are converted into electromagnetic oscillations. Feelings are based on vibration. Emotions and thoughts are based on oscillation. They are electromagnetic waves.

Dr. Sellers words are the present statement of what my research suggested forty years ago.

CHAPTER THIRTEEN
LUCID DREAMS – 1976

Emilio stood on my doorstep with a plant in his hand.

"I usually get bouquets of flowers," I said, laughing and letting him in. "This is the first time I've ever been given a plant."

"Flowers don't last long," he retorted. "I hope this plant, a Maranta Leuconeura—a prayer plant—will last longer. I've seen your balcony. Anything left out there is dead. This one stays inside."

"It can die inside, too. Who's going to water it when I have to leave for weeks at time?"

"Give it to the lady downstairs. She'll do it with pleasure. She has so many healthy plants already," he suggested.

I took it reluctantly. The truth was work was just an excuse for rejecting this gift. I had never been interested in plants. But for this plant, his solution seemed appropriate. And I liked the name. And I liked the man who had brought it even more.

It seemed to me that my dear friend was reaching for something more in our relationship. Was he courting me? In one way, I hoped not. So often men changed in relationships: I'd seen it happen. Once they were sure of the woman they claimed to adore, she became a piece of property in which they quickly lost interest. Our friendship was so rich and interesting and challenging. I had no desire to surrender something I valued so much for the role of a wife.

He came inside and we talked as we always did. We talked about so many subjects that I don't remember how or when I started revealing to him some of the dreams I had had. Dreams that struck me as particularly unusual.

"They are beautiful," I told him, "and different from normal dreams. They are sharper and more real. I am aware that I am dreaming, and sometimes in the dream, I am able to steer the dream into the direction

I want it to go. It's amazing how clear everything is. Clearer than real life," I concluded emphatically. My vision has always been a little weak and being able to see so clearly was a unique experience. "I know that dreams are the unconscious speaking to the rational mind, but I don't understand what these dreams mean. They are always of places—places I've never been and do not recognize except that they are beautiful. I'm not sure what that means."

"Have you ever tried to find them?" Emilio asked. "These places?"

"They're just dreams."

"I know, but maybe the places are real?"

"But how can I dream of a real place I've never seen?" I replied. The conversation had drifted into a very strange direction, even for us.

"Give it a try, the next time you have one of these dreams, ask yourself in the dream where you are and see what happens," Emilio suggested.

The "dream talk" ended there, and we moved on to other subjects.

But a few nights later, I had one of those dreams.

In it, I was high above the trees and below me lay a highway leading to a small and picturesque village. Sunshine lit the scene: it was a bright and beautiful day. The village had a small square, lined with charming homes with their balconies full of flowers. The nearby shop windows exhibited plates, vases, bottles, and even decorated bricks. There were so many of these shops. At the end of an uphill road was a small fountain decorated in wrought iron and fed by water gushing from a pipe in the wall. Everything about the place gave me a sense of peace. Where was it? And, as if by magic, the information flowed into my mind: Flaminia. I got emotional, the dream stopped, and I woke up.

I told Emilio.

"So, let's go," he said.

"Are you crazy?" I said. "All I got was Flaminia. The Flaminia Road goes from here to Rimini. That's more than 300 kilometers. And who knows where to turn to find the village. I don't even know the village's name."

"Today is Saturday. I do not have to work and it's a nice day. It's early enough to start out on a trip. Pack some sandwiches and couple of bottles of water and let's go. If you see something familiar, okay. If not, we had a nice drive on a beautiful day."

I didn't have to think about it long before agreeing. No one had ever asked me to take a spur of the moment trip like that before and I loved the idea.

We climbed into his car and set out on our journey. I was happy to have the chance see more of the countryside. The truth was I didn't know much about Rome or its surrounding areas, and what I knew was always linked to travels related to films. I had never driven on the ancient consular Flaminia Way. I found it to be both a beautiful and sometimes mysterious road, lined with trees with beautiful dark leaves and often skirting rock formations with strange veins—especially as we passed near the *Faggeta*, an ancient and majestic forest. These landscapes were very different from what I had grown up with in Sicily and I found them wondrous.

We passed turns indicating the exits for various towns, but we kept going straight, following the Flaminia Road. I chatted with Emilio as he drove further and further along it until I started noticing things that seemed familiar: the way the road curved, a certain tree, the gash of a small clearing . . . and I felt I'd seen them before. But I distrusted it: there had already been so many trees and bends, what made these different? I did not know but I was determined to surrender to the intuition.

"Slow down and take the next turn," I said to Emilio.

He obeyed. We turned onto a narrow street that looked derelict and abandoned. We followed it for a few miles before I told him to go back. I had lost the feeling I had had when I saw the curve, the tree, and the clearing.

We returned to the Flaminia and headed back toward the curve and the tree.

"I know this is stupid," I said to Emilio as they came into view, "but instead of turning right, try left."

I was surprised by my feelings, but I was also starting to have fun.

We went back and forth like that for most of the morning, turning off on the side roads that intersected the Flaminia near that tree and curve. Finally, about three o'clock in the afternoon, I said, "I need two things: a bathroom and to eat. Let's find a rest stop and a place to eat our sandwiches."

"I hear and I obey." Emilio smiled, saluting me like a soldier.

We returned to the Flaminia, and about two hundred meters from that curve with the tree, there was a sign indicating Deruta. We headed in that direction and entered in a tiny village with a wide and open square. Emilio parked the car near a tent that shaded the entrance to a coffee bar. I got out of the car, looked around, and was shocked.

It was the little square I had seen in my dream. There were the low houses with the geraniums on the balconies. I could not believe it. I was very excited. But I was still hungry, and I still had to go to the bathroom. So, we went inside and used the facilities, then sat down at a table, carrying our sandwiches of tuna and tomato, and we ordered coffee.

When we were finished eating, Emilio said, "So now we have to see if we can find the little road that leads to the fountain."

I stared at him in surprise.

"Do you really think it exists?" I asked uncertainly. "I mean, I'm surprised that we found this much. Don't you think it's possible some of it was just a dream?"

I left out the part I was thinking, about not relishing the idea of sweating through a walk in the hot sunshine so soon after eating.

"You're really something," he replied, laughing. "You're rigorous about your experiments on other people, but you do not want to check out something that directly concerns you."

"What's that got to do with it?" I retorted. "This isn't science. It's a game. Incredible, yes. But it could all be just a very strange coincidence."

"Perhaps. But don't you want to see how far a strange coincidence can go? I'm not sure yet, but I think you might be having lucid dreams."

"Lucid dreams?" I asked.

"Do you want the complicated explanation or the simplest one?"

He knew me well. Maybe too well, I thought, wondering again about this special friendship. A little mystery in a woman never hurts ... but at the same time, I liked how well Emilio could anticipate my questions, patience, and interest.

"Simple."

"Lucid dreams are the ability to be awake and aware while we are dreaming. They say you can develop the ability to bring the experiences gained in the dream into your waking life. It's supposed to increase creativity and the ability to solve problems."

"Do you have them?" I asked.

"I don't believe so. Or to better say I never remember what I dream. Maybe I don't dream at all."

"Everyone dreams."

"Maybe, but I don't sleep much so maybe there's no time to fiddle with dreams."

"If you had one, you would remember it. They are unforgettable. They are too vivid. Anyway, you've convinced me. Let's walk around and see if we can find the shops with the ceramics and the bricks, and the fountain."

"Deruta is famous all over the world for its ceramics, you know."

"So, you knew all along that this was the place in my dream and that Deruta was the village we were looking for." I felt suddenly irritated, as though Emilio had been having a joke at my expense.

"No!" he insisted. "It was only when I saw the road sign that I realized maybe Deruta was your village. And if you hadn't said you were hungry, we'd still be driving around the countryside."

I accepted his explanation and led the way. We strolled along until at last we stood in front of a street that looked exactly like the one in my dream: a gently ascending lane with ceramics shops on both sides. And then, at the end of the road, I saw the fountain with its mural decoration in black wrought iron that looked like a coat of arms.

The day had been fun and amazing, and I couldn't resist buying a small ceramic flower vase as a souvenir.

That year I had worked in three films, including a couple as the lead, and I had had very little extra time for my experiments. In a way, I was glad to have a break from the Kirlian: too many people had started showing up at my apartment in the Cassia, wanting a Kirlian photo to see if they had "energy." It irritated me, not only because of the waste of photo paper, but because they treated the subject as a party game. Other times, I had professed psychics visit seeking Kirlian photos to use to market themselves in their pseudoscientific practices. I had begun rejecting requests for Kirlian photos altogether since so many of them were just a waste of my time.

Occasionally I still had lucid dreams, however. I channeled my interest in psychic phenomena out of the energy of the Kirlian photos and into the exploration of those dreams. Emilio and I made many weekend trips all over Italy. More often than not we couldn't find the exact locations I dreamt about at all and other times we found partial matches where only some of the elements of the dream were present, but others were missing. Indeed, we only found another exact location once more.

I had dreamt that I was flying high above a valley partially surrounded by mountains. On one of the mountains about halfway up, a small village was tucked into the trees. From its height, I could see the sea, but it was far away. In the valley, amidst the tall grass, there was a very small airstrip with big black tires lying abandoned on the tarmac—perhaps airplane tires. Close enough to the runway, there was a small gray rectangle that had been some kind of modular structure. That was all. I looked around for some point of reference or landmark, but apart from the distant village, I did not see anything that identified this place. I asked myself "Where am I?" But no enlightenment came.

At the first opportunity, I told Emilio the dream and, that, to my disappointment, I had no clues about how to locate the small airport.

Emilio thought for a few moments and then asked, "Have you tried a map?"

"What good is a map if I don't know what town to look for?"

"Try," he insisted.

It seemed like a waste of time, but to make him happy, I looked through my desk drawer for a good map. I had several because I liked geography, and I always purchased them when I was shooting films abroad, so I'd know where I was and what else was nearby. I found one I thought would work and spread it out on the coffee table.

Emilio was already smiling in the most irritating of ways.

"Let's start big," he said."Were you abroad?"

I thought for a moment. "No."

"Okay. Italy. North, center or south?"

I mentally returned to the dream, focusing on the light, the sky, and the grass and the sea. "Not north," I said.

"Fold it so you can only see the center and the south of the country and look at it carefully. Remember our experiment with the steel ball in the film containers? How you tried to feel which one held the ball? Try to do that with the map. Try to feel something."

I remained silent, but it crossed my mind that anyone listening to this conversation would think we were crazy. He was right: I had had some success with the game with the ball. And I did believe some people could manifest great mental abilities. I just didn't believe that I was one of them. Still, as skeptical as I was, it cost nothing to try ... and it might be fun.

I stared at the paper for a long time and then suddenly, I folded it again, eliminating central Italy. My eyes kept coming back to the Calabria region, and then, all at once I locked in on one area in particular, a small town Lamezia Terme. But the map didn't indicate that it had an airport.

"It seems crazy to me," I said, "but I think it's here."

"Ready to go?" Emilio asked in the same tone he might have used when we had just finished our meal at a restaurant.

"Are you kidding?" I replied, "Do you know how far that is?"

"About 600 kilometers, I think. Maybe a bit shorter on the highway," he replied after a few moments of concentration. "You're right: it's not a day trip. Let's take a bag and stay the night in a motel."

I stared at him for a moment to see if there were other goals behind this proposal. But he stared back at me, waiting.

"I'll pack," I replied and before too long, we were in the car.

I had woken up early and was not really in a great mood even though Emilio had stuffed me with coffee, cappuccinos, and croissants. I was regretting the long drive to Calabria and the hours that we'd already spent searching around for something that probably wasn't even there. In the cold light of morning, I regretted that I'd been persuaded to seek out something I'd only seen in a dream. It didn't help that we'd spent an uncomfortable night in a crappy motel. I was spoiled by now: I was used to the best hotels and the cramped old roadside place we'd found depressed me.

Usually wandering around with Emilio was fun. We usually had great conversations and he knew how to steer them to the subjects that interested me. But not today. Emilio was quiet and I wondered if he, too, had decided that this excursion was sheer lunacy. That was what I was thinking when Emilio said, "We're running out of gas."

I looked at the dashboard gauge. He was right: we were running very low on petrol. I stared around the mountainous countryside and saw ... nothing. There certainly wasn't any place to get gas in this place forgotten by God and the world.

"You should have said that before," I snapped.

"I didn't know it before," he snapped back.

We were both on edge, facing the possibility of running out of gas on these deserted winding roads. I kept looking ahead, searching for a gas station, but saw nothing. The tension between us grew, the gas gauge sank lower and there was still nothing in sight. Right when I was sure that we'd run out and have to leave the car and walk to find fuel, we saw a station ahead on our right.

We both sighed with relief as Emilio pulled in and filled the tank. But the experience was enough for me to doubt the wisdom of continuing our trip without a little more information. As Emilio returned to the car, I was getting out of it.

"Where are you going?"

"To ask the attendant for answers," I told him and headed toward the garage.

"Please, could you tell me if there's a small airport around here?" I asked the man.

"There is our new Lamezia airport," he replied as proudly as if he had built it himself. "About forty miles from here."

"No, I'm looking for a smaller one. Very small and very near here," I clarified.

"I do not know..." he said thoughtfully. "Ah... wait, there is a very small old airstrip a couple of miles further on, if that's what you are looking for. But it hasn't been used for many years."

He gave me directions, and we were off in search again.

After a while, we turned onto an unpaved road and continued for about a mile before the road ended suddenly in a thicket of tall weeds. When we got out of the car, we saw a trail cutting through them... partially surrounded by huge, old black tires. We followed the trail until it ended and when it did, I was standing on the broken, cracked asphalt of the airstrip. The gray rectangular structure was nearby, its single door locked with a padlock.

I looked up and saw the little village perched on the mountain—just as I had dreamed it.

"This is the place," I said excitedly to Emilio, pointing to the village.

"Do you want to go up there?"

"No, this is enough for me. I didn't visit the village in the dream. I only saw it from here. This is it."

We climbed back into the car and began the long journey back. Although we traveled the same number of kilometers back as we had travelled to get there, it seemed so much shorter to me. I was happy but filled with more questions. The awareness that my own mind was open enough to receive images beyond my conscious reality had impressed me deeply. Could it be that my experiments with the children had awakened some latent ability in me? Was there such a thing as a "contagion" of frequencies? Did the brain adapt to the frequencies that surrounded it?

More questions to explore. More research to be done. More reading and more experiments awaited me.

CHAPTER FOURTEEN
THE NATURAL WORLD

Between the constant hullabaloo and noise of any Italian city and the incessant chatter of our own minds, the one sound nobody listens for is silence.

By "listening for silence" I don't mean the relative quiet and peace of night. I mean the active silence of forgetting oneself and quieting the mind in order to hear one's silent, deep internal dialogue. This internal dialogue is different from the dialogue of speech. It's a dialogue that has a thousand languages. It is the dialogue that connects us to Nature.

All living things—man, animals, plants, and even insects—express their emotions and concerns. Humans are often able to interpret the behavioral signals of animals. Indeed, the more clearly an animal communicates its needs in human ways, the more intelligent we consider it. But in an unfortunate and colossal twist of fate, the different species do not understand each other's languages beyond these cues. Nature could be compared to the biblical Tower of Babel, with every living thing speaking its own language simultaneously with every other living thing—without any places of harmony or agreement. In many ways, it would be fair to say that humans are deaf to any language that doesn't involve verbal expression—and that therein lies our problem.

Consider the Macaca Fuscata species of Japanese monkeys. For more than thirty years, scientists have been studying the monkey colonies on the island of Koshima, east of the coast of Kyusgu. Since 1952, researchers have placed food for the monkeys on the island and studied their behavior when new food sources were introduced. The researchers wanted to see how the monkeys responded to unexpected variations in their everyday experiences. How did the monkeys respond to new and different foods? How long did it take them to recognize something was edible? How did they determine that something was food?

For example, the researchers placed sweet potatoes covered with sand and slush in the monkeys' feeding area. They hypothesized that the colony monkeys would not know how to clean off the sweet potatoes and that, as a result, the food would be left uneaten. To their surprise, one day in 1958, a young eighteen-month-old female named Imo solved the problem. She took the potato to the river and washed it before eating it.

Normally, it is the mother monkey who teaches her children what they should eat and how they should use food. Imo subverted the order of things by teaching the potato trick to her mother. She also taught it to all the young monkeys in the group who, in turn, taught it to their mothers. The whole colony took the sweet potatoes to the sea, washed them, and ate them. Imo had not only discovered that the saltwater cleaned the food but also that it gave the potatoes an interesting new flavor.

What does this have to do with silent communication? With the listening that goes beyond actual sound? In monkey colonies of other islands off the coast of Japan, including the ones living on the monkey preserve on Takasakiyama, a large island almost 300 kilometers away, monkeys started doing the same thing. Coincidence or information? Telepathy or a language that we humans don't yet have the ability to understand?

Children, who are not yet polluted by the dictates of our culture, very often manage to penetrate a more authentic, more natural dimension. Because they don't know the limits of possibilities, they are open to talking to *all* things, not just those that speak in words. It is only by socialization that they begin to believe that it is useless to talk with the cat or the tree. By adulthood, we have learned these lessons so well that we no longer even think about the opportunities lost to us in the process.

Science calls unexplained or anomalous animal behavior "instinct." Instinct is the knowledge that guides so much of what animals do.

We do not discuss animal instinct, but very often, instinct transcends the boundaries of logical behavior and becomes something more. For example, all of us have heard stories of animals traveling remarkable distances to get home. Short distances are easier to explain since biologists agree that the animal follows visual and olfactory signals to orient itself. But it's harder to explain the phenomenon when the animal is able to return home from a place it has never been before, a great distance away.

A long time ago, a West Virginia police officer's twelve-year-old son was rushed into surgery. About a week later, while a snowstorm raged outside, the boy heard a flutter of wings at the window of his hospital room. He called the nurse and told her to open the window because his pigeon was trying to get inside. To satisfy the little patient, the nurse opened the window, and a pigeon fluttered in. The boy asked the nurse to check the band on the pigeon's leg for the number 167 and sure enough, it was there. The stunned nurse had to accept the reality: the pigeon had flown through a snowstorm and found its master, even without knowing where he was. The boy's parents confirmed that for a few days after the boy had been taken to the hospital, the little creature had been nervously fluttering around the house, looking for him. The pigeon had not followed any kind of olfactory or visual cues and had still managed to travel about 100 kilometers and somehow locate the right window, in the right building, in a city it had never seen, at night and during a snowstorm.

There have been numerous attempts to give scientific validation to what appear to be psychic communications between animals and people. Electromagnetic, gravitational, acoustic, and chemical explanations have been evoked, but the results of these efforts have led only to weak conclusions that, so far, haven't offered any satisfactory explanation. For example, Joseph Banks Rhine and his Duke University researchers have tested hundreds of cases of what they call "PSI tracing" (or ESP—Extra Sensory Perception) in animals, trying to get a precise understanding of how it might work. But the results simply reinforce that some kind of communication is taking place but offer no explanations about how or what that communication is.

In a park in the town of Fribourg, Switzerland, a monument stands to a duck, that on November 27, 1944, began to squawk so violently that the townspeople, fearful and alarmed, ran for the air raid shelters. Half an hour later, a tremendous bombardment occurred. The duck was killed, but the inhabitants were saved. It is well known that animals are very sensitive to the approach of any natural phenomenon—long before an earthquake occurs, for example, they show signs of anxiety and fear. Biology usually explains this with the sensitivity of animals' senses—the ability to hear at higher or lower decibels than humans, among other traits. Since an earthquake is still a natural phenomenon, it is likely that animals might have an ability to sense slight vibrations humans cannot. But the advance notification of a coming bomb combines something else with the sense of vibration, since the duck's cries indicate not only the ability to sense the vibration of the coming plane, but also the understanding that the vibration represented the arrival of a dangerous enemy. Without telling all the stories of dogs or cats returning home, sometimes after years, from places hundreds of kilometers away, through mountains and all kinds of territories and obstacles, we can all understand that these phenomena occur. But research has not been able to clarify how or why PSI tracing, or telepathic recall exists in animals so strongly.

Several countries around the world (but, unfortunately, not in Italy), conduct experimental research in fully equipped and specialized laboratories to try to understand how biological phenomena like this occurs. For example, at the University of Utrecht, Sybo Schonten has trained mice to press a lever when the light was lit in their cage, using this baseline experiment as a gateway to possibly distinguish between telepathy and clairvoyance in these animals. The reward for the correct action was (and is) always food or water. Similarly, Dr. Helmut Schmidt of Duke University has also conducted numerous experiments in this field to ascertain if animals have psychokinesis (the ability to act mentally to direct matter). In Dr. Schmidt's experiments, a cat was placed in an unheated shed with an electric heater connected to a computer. The heater would turn on at random intervals for brief periods of time. The experiment attempted to determine if the cat, due to the need for heat, could psychokinetically prolong the heating period. The results were surprising. When the temperature dropped beyond the cat's comfort zone, the heater ignited more often than expected, suggesting that, under the impulse of a very strong stimulus, in this case the cold, the cat had acted psychokinetically on the ignition mechanism and kept it going more frequently than random programming would have done.

Hunger, cold, thirst, loss of one's master—these basic survival concepts have been expressed by animals and humans through ESP. Apparently, insects also receive and transmit information through extrasensory perception, but because their behavioral systems are harder for us to understand, the mechanisms by which they communicate become more obscure.

Italian anthropologist Lidio Cipriani has devoted many years to the study of insect communication, focusing particularly on butterflies. Zoo semiotics—the study of how animals use signs to communicate their knowledge—posits that female butterflies emit a chemical "love call" through their glands. The smell is carried by the wind and received by the males through their antennae. This transmission apparently happens even when the males are upwind of the females. The male butterflies follow the scent and find the female butterflies ready for mating. While this scientific explanation is widely accepted, Cipriani noted inconsistencies that suggested that there may be other explanations for the butterflies' behavior. For example, the scientific explanation relies on the presence of the wind to carry the female butterflies' scents to the male. But in experiments carried out in completely calm air—the absence of wind—in which it would take hours for the female's odorous secretions to travel thirty meters to reach the males—the butterfly males arrived within a few minutes. Furthermore, in many studies male butterflies travelled distances ranging from three to ten kilometers—far beyond the distance that the tiny glandular secretions could have reached in any concentration carried by wind—depending on the species. Under these conditions, a male would have about one in five thousand probability of encountering the smell for each meter of flight and would have to fly for several hours before encountering the same species of butterfly.

In short, explained by the olfactory transmission alone, the male's search for the female butterfly should last several hours. But it doesn't. It happens within minutes. This suggests that the theory of chemical communication is insufficient to explain how male butterflies know that female butterflies are ready to mate. A telepathic call, however, could explain the phenomenon.

Reading about these kinds of possibly telepathic communications in the animal world reminded me of a very special experience I had as a child.

I was probably about seven or eight years old. My family and I were living in Milan in the early 1950s, in a house that sat in front of the Naviglio, a dark green river that aroused in me everything except the desire to get wet. Beyond the road, there was a pier and a dock where piles of dirt and gravel formed a sort of ugly beach.

I was often at the window or on the balcony, watching children playing on the pier. I wanted to join them, but my mother would not allow it. Instead I watched them and the barges full of gravel steam by night and day. At night, their lights bobbed up and down on the water; the boats themselves were too dark to see. It always seemed magical to me to see those lights on the waves, as if they were a signal of something strange and beautiful about to happen.

One winter evening, I looked out and saw something dark hovering about twenty centimeters from my windowsill. I opened the window and leaned out to see better, then screamed and immediately closed the window tight. My father, who had just returned from work, came running.

"What is it?" he asked.

"There's an animal outside the window. Kill it, Daddy!"

"What? Let me see," he said and moved toward the window.

"Don't! Don't open it!" I screamed. But he had already done it.

He remained silent for a few seconds, staring out into the night. "But it's a butterfly," he said at last. "Why should I kill her?"

"A butterfly? That ugly thing?" I said incredulously.

"Yes, a big one. Actually, it's called a moth."

To my horror, he reached out a hand and gently caressed the creature's wing with one of his fingers. The moth shivered a little but did not move. "See," my father said. "She's hurt her wing and can't fly."

"How did she hurt it?" I asked, coming a bit closer to peer at the moth hesitantly.

"I don't know. Maybe she ran into the tram wires. Anyway, we have to help her."

"How?" I asked.

"Well, to begin with, let's keep this window closed so we don't scare her. Let's make sure your mother doesn't shake out her dust rags from this window. After that, I'll have to think about what else might help."

The next day, before I went to school, I checked the window. The moth was still there. At lunchtime, my father came home with a bunch of flowers. At first, I thought they were for Mom, but no. He went to the window, opened it slowly and gently placed the sprigs of grass and the wildflowers in front of and around the moth—which did not move.

"Is she still alive?" I asked in a whisper.

"Yes," my father replied in the same tone of voice. "I hope she eats something, and the smell of the grasses and flowers should help her to heal."

Every day I went to the window, hoping for the moth to get better, cheering her on from the other side of the glass. After four or five days, the moth disappeared. I was happy. She had done it. She had gotten better and flown away.

This little childhood experience taught me to cultivate the sense of positive expectation. I still practice it to this day, but I confess, with mixed results. Through his explanation that the creature that so terrified me on first sight, my father also taught me that not everything that is aesthetically unpleasant is also dangerous. Over the years, too, other questions about this event have arisen. What was a moth doing in Milan in winter? How did she come to be at our window in the evening on a road without trees? What was she doing so close to the canal? Why did she choose ours from so many windows on which she could have stopped? Did she know in some way that we would help her?

Old wives' tales tell us that moths symbolize messages about one's destiny or fate, and that a beautiful one suggests a good message and an ugly one the opposite. I don't believe that the moth delivered any special symbolic or esoteric meaning about my future during those cold winter days—and if it did, I probably did not believe it.

Like animals, plants suffer. They are afraid. They sleep. They may even think, remember, and understand us. The reality of plants and their ability to feel is based on a working hypothesis of the world of natural science called the Backster Effect.

Cleve Backster was the most renowned American expert on the subject of plants and their feelings. A former CIA interrogator, Backster began experimenting with plants in 1968 and eventually his research became so well-known and controversial that over 7000 scientists asked for copies of his reports.

Backster's experiments began, almost by chance, in February 1966, while he was working with his polygraph in his New York laboratory. After several hours of working with the polygraph, he needed a distraction, so he watered his plant. Watering made him wonder if the polygraph could measure the level of water salinity by the response of the leaves. In humans, a polygraph measures changes in breathing, blood pressure, and heartbeats, as well as the electrical potential of the skin. Backster theorized that the leaves would show different reactions based on changes in stimuli, specifically the addition of different qualities of water. Backster placed an instrument electrode on each side of a philodendron leaf and attached them to the polygraph paper strip. About a minute later, an unusual result appeared on the polygraph paper, which Backster described as being similar to the reaction of a human subject in the grip of a short-lived emotion. Intrigued, Backster tried again, immersing a leaf in a cup of hot coffee. Nothing happened. Backster decided to make a more direct attempt by burning the leaf with a match. But before he actually touched flame to the leaf, the polygraph chart showed an immediate and dramatic jump upward. Since there was no other stimulus to the plant and Backster himself was not actually touching it or the instruments, he hypothesized that the response could not have been influenced by anything other than his *decision* to harm the plant. The plant sensed his intention and responded. Backster also cooked live shrimp in the presence of the plants—dipping them in boiling water –and discovered that the plants, through the polygraph, reacted violently to the crustaceans' death.

All of these observations confirmed his hypothesis that an unknown method of communication binds all living beings together. Many years later in the movie *Avatar* (2010) James Cameron explored a similar theme for a popular audience, but during Backster's time, this theory was extremely controversial—and rejected almost entirely by the orthodox scientific community. Backster could not explain or document this interconnected communication. In fact, he acknowledged that it was indeed very mysterious. "It seems that the signals do not belong to the known range of the electrodynamic spectrum," he wrote. "However, in some part of the process, the signal is converted into a measurable electrical current with the polygraph." Plants seem to have the ability to analyze signals and selectively identify them.

Backster also discovered that plants were particularly in tune with those who paid attention to them. Good thoughts and cheerful mood seem to be a determining factor. But anxiety, depression, or, worse still, *hate* can damage their growth, especially if those emotions were directed towards the plants. Perhaps this positive emotional field explains, at least in part, why some people seem to have a so-called green thumb—even in the absence of practice or knowledge about plants. Something in their energy field communicates directly with the plants to stimulate the growth of plants and eventually to revitalize them.

There is a world that surrounds all living beings, and which goes beyond our five senses. There is a primordial form of communication that we catch glimpses of but unfortunately cannot yet detect with our instruments. Sadly, Western men seem unwilling to accept anything that instruments cannot prove—even when it is something that is a part of our very nature. Scientists become blocked by the debate over how to understand and codify the tide of information inherent in our very tissues. This field of energy is the "Bio plasma" we discussed earlier. It has always been understood by seers and philosophers since the dawn of written history. But for the scientist, for the cold positivist, observing these hieroglyphics of light, whose colors vary from milky blue to pale lilac, orange, and red, requires the realization that much of what we have understood is wrong, and that to move forward into a new scientific understanding means rewriting the theories of the past.

For example, radiation surrounds us in every moment of our existence. Cosmic rays, light rays, rays transmitted by radio and television stations, shortwave radiation, heat, light, to name a few. Science tells us that all matter emits radiation; even every living being. And when humans, plants, and animals stop emitting radiation, life has ceased. The first to realize that these emanations were our "vital energy" were the Russians, with the discovery of the Kirlian camera and the photographic process that enables us to capture the aura that surrounds living beings. But Kirlian imagery is considered to be eccentric and extremist by many Western scientists and is not accepted as proof of the existence of our energy field. Still, however, research continues into more solid ways to prove and measure this field.

The big scientific talents aren't only found in America or in Russia. They are also here in Italy, even if the Italian scientific community doesn't always recognize their work. In 1979, biologist Alberto Crocetti, of Macerata, in the Marche region, discovered a system to decode the signals emitted by plants, concluding that plants communicate with each other at a frequency of around 800 megahertz, more or less. After capturing these frequencies, the then young biologist transformed them into diagrams which he then, in turn, translated into language. Because each plant had its own specific frequency, it appears that each species has its own language. But it also appears that plants can modulate themselves to communicate between different species. Dr. Crocetti also planned experiments which would have used the energy of a single seedling to power a 5-watt bulb. The only labor involved would be the commitment to water the seedling to keep it alive. Expanding on Dr. Crocetti's theory would mean that a single small forest or park would contain enough energy to light an average provincial town. But of course, as mankind continues to destroy forests and damage environments all over the world, it seems unlikely that there will be enough nature left to sustain us. Perhaps we'll have to look to the stars?

L. George Lawrence, an American researcher, has done some research that suggest that plants can help us even with the search for intelligent life beyond our Earth. He discovered that living plant tissue was able to perceive signals in ways that were much more sensitive than electronic sensors. He was convinced that biological radiations transmitted by living things were better received by a biological medium than an electronic one. He built what he later called "a biodynamic field station for receiving signals from space." In fact, he connected plant tissue to both his apparatus and a telescope and found that plants received well-defined signals from space. Lawrence wrote that biological communications could ultimately supplant our radio telescopes—and have far reaching impact on the search for extraterrestrial life. Still, however, his research and findings remain virtually unknown.

Building on Backster's work, for example, researchers discovered that it was possible to distinguish a leaf of a healthy plant from a sick one, even before the appearance of outward symptoms. Before manifesting itself in the physical body, disease is evident in the energy field of the plant. William A. Tiller, a professor at Stanford University observed that a wilted leaf placed under Kirlian imagery does not have a bright halo. Instead, as the leaf dies, its brightness diminishes until it ceases completely. It can be deduced that the spontaneous emission of living tissues constitutes a direct measure of the vital processes that take place within them.

Dr. Douglas Dean, a professor of programming and statistics and also one of the world's leading experts on the use of plethysmographs (an instrument for measuring changes in volume within an organ or whole body), was able to establish just from the electrophotographic imagery of seeds, which would grow into strong and luxuriant plants and which would be sick and stunted. Because the bioluminescence of a weak seed is lower than that of a healthy seed, it can be used as a complement to the current seed selection process, making it easier to more clearly establish possible pathological anomalies and increase production.

In 1980 I discovered by chance that Dr. Dean was giving a lecture on his experiments with the Kirlian camera at a conference just outside Rome. I dragged Emilio to it, because I had no intention of missing the opportunity to hear Dr. Dean speak. Mostly he spoke (in English) of the experiments that I had already read about in various industry publications, documenting his assertions with slides and video images. But the presentation that was worth the price of admission were the Kirlian images in motion of a woman giving birth.

I had never seen the crown that fingers make as they move in my Kirlian electrophotography. In addition to the basic image, there were also small luminous globules that swirled erratically just around the shape of the mother's fingers like a fascinating universe of light. But the biggest thrill came at the moment of birth. One of these luminous globules moved away from the shape of the thumb, remaining initially connected to the finger by a long luminous filament, until then, at the moment of birth, it finally detached and disappear. It was beautiful, emotional, and thrilling.

CHAPTER FIFTEEN
TURKEY

A new film came to me—my twenty-eighth—and with it, another item on my bucket list was fulfilled. I got to travel to the city of Istanbul, the capital of Turkey, to make an adventure film complete with sultans, heroes, and princesses. The script was not bad, and I was the female lead. Of course, it wasn't as strong as *Angelique* (1964) starring Michelle Mercier and Robert Hossein. I'd seen all of the episodes of the popular TV series that told the story of a feisty teenaged heroine who becomes entangled in a political assassination plot and has encounters with a sorcerer. But this movie was similar in theme and I was eager to travel to Turkey, another place I had longed to visit.

And, of course, a film meant that I had more money to invest in my research. I remembered the Canadian experiment I had read about using the electroencephalograph to measure the brain waves of Matthew Manning as he folded objects. It revived my intention to obtain one and attempt to connect it to Kirlian. But I had no idea where to buy one or how much would it cost. Would I be able to understand how it worked? And would I be able to get the results that I expected?

I was debating with myself about how to resolve these problems when Professor Giorgio Monaco, head physician of the Surgical Pathology II of the Policlinico Umberto I in Rome contacted me. Occasionally, when the condition and health status of a patient did not allow the use of general anesthesia, the professor had used acupuncture to create the same effects locally, allowing him to proceed with the actual operation. It was generally a small intervention, used in relatively minor surgeries, but the hospital management did not look favorably on this practice as it was not recognized by official medicine. As a result, Professor Monaco had recently founded a center of Ayurvedic and Tibetan medicine, where he could apply both his passion for oriental medicine and training as a surgeon. The idea that energy surrounded every living being—a new theory for many of us at the time—was for him a fact already acknowledged and confirmed.

He had reached out to me with a specific request. He was eager to bring the medical community more concrete scientific information on the movement of energy as he applied the methods he had discovered on his travels to Asia. He wondered if I would consider taking Kirlian photographs of a hand under the effect of acupuncture.

I was in seventh heaven! To hear from a respected Italian surgeon asking me to do some experiments in my field of interest—and who offered to pay for the cost of the plates and the developer and not just on standard black and white paper, but the beautiful and expensive film (size cm. 17.5 x 12.5) astronomers used? It seemed like a beautiful miracle. I enthusiastically agreed.

A date for the experiment was set and, once again, I asked Emilio to accompany me. We traveled to the hospital and walked the halls for a while, lost, looking for Profesor Monaco's office. After quite a bit of circling the corridors, at last we arrived at the right location, confirmed by his name plate outside the door. We carried the Kirlian in its case along with all of our other equipment and my heart was pounding nervously in my chest as we stepped inside. I felt the pressure of Professor Monaco's expectations and hoped so much that everything would work out all right.

Monaco welcomed us and immediately escorted us to a room without any windows, to ensure we had the absolute darkness we needed, and offered us a place to set up the Kirlian. Then he called in a couple of his assistants and we started our work. I took Kirlian pictures of both of his assistants' hands. One at a time, they sat on the only chair in the room for the initial at rest image. Then Monaco used a classic long and very thin acupuncture needle on each of them, beginning with a point of stimulation on the shin. He vibrated the needle for a while, then removed it. I immediately took pictures of each of the assistants on the Kirlian plate after the acupuncture stimulation.

We went on like this for a while: taking an initial photo, followed by Monaco inserting needles at different acupuncture points, according to the energy plans he knew, followed by more pictures. From time to time, the two assistants complained of some slight pain from the needles, but other than that, the experiments continued without interruption.

When we were finished, Emilio and I said goodbye to Professor Monaco and told him that as soon as we developed the slides, we would contact him again. But the sheer number of pictures we had taken presented us with a new problem: convincing the only technician in Rome who had agreed to develop our slides to work on such a large number of images. It was a difficult job for him because of the oversized plates he'd have to deal with, compared to the usual slides. Not only were the plates oversized but they had to be printed and organized in the specific order that we had outlined (e.g., right hand, point S38, right shin). If he made any mistakes and accidentally slipped a slide into the wrong box, the whole experimentation would have been lost its validity.

Fortunately, everything went well. The technician correctly inserted the plates into the right boxes, and the slides showed considerable variations between the at rest photos and the images taken after the administration of the acupuncture procedures. The energy field and the crown of the fingers had been re-formed substantially, confirming a shift of energy as a result of the acupuncture—at least on an experimental basis.

Professor Monaco was very happy with the results we obtained (and so were we). He paid us and I was proud of that payment, much more than most of the paychecks I earned doing films. I never heard whether the images ultimately assisted him in his efforts to convince his hospital to recognize acupuncture as an alternative to anesthesia. We did not hear from him, and we did not meet him again.

Following the experiments with Professor Monaco, I felt increasingly restless for more exploration and experimentation. I was still thinking about an electroencephalograph when I saw an advertisement for a new piece of equipment in the next issues of *Sky & Telescope*. The ad was for the biofeedback electroencephalaudio ("EEA" for ease of reference) device. Basically, instead of recording brain activity on paper as a normal electroencephalograph or EEG does, this device recorded the activity in an acoustic signal. It was used, I might say today, as a kind of personal trainer, to enable one to reach various stages of relaxation. The device enabled the user to select a favorite rhythm and attempt to synch the brain to that sequence. When the user dropped out of that rhythm or sequence, an audio signal announced that the user had lost relaxation or concentration. I was intrigued. This device solved a major concern for me—that I did not know how to read the frequencies of an electroencephalograph. With the audio signal, I wouldn't have to worry about that problem any longer.

I wrote a short and concise letter in English to the American company that produced it for information and took it to the post office to make sure I had the right postage. Then I waited. In the meantime, I had received more requests from various associations in and around Rome to give lectures on my experiments. I was excited about it, but being a performer, I worried about how to best present the material. I knew that any audience, even those were deeply interested in my work, would get bored after ten minutes if I just stood in front of a microphone and talked. I needed to find a way to make sure that my presentation was dynamic and interesting.

I shared my concerns with Emilio, who, as always, had some ideas to help me.

"Don't worry," he told me. "I can take photographs of the Kirlian images and the folded objects you want to talk about and make slides. With my slide projector, all you need is something white—any white wall in the room will work—and you'll have a visual presentation that they can see for themselves."

I liked his plan a lot—so much so that it gave me another idea.

The next day, I went to the American Embassy on the famous Via Veneto and asked to speak with someone from the United States Information Service (USIS). With my Visitor card pinned to my blouse, I followed an assistant down a long corridor interspersed with massive mahogany doors until I reached the elegant office of a charming middle-aged man with blue eyes, tanned skin. and a crown of hair around the back of his head. He rose to greet me and pointed to a chair across from his desk.

I won't lie. I was excited and nervous. As usual, I hadn't prepared what I would say in advance—I usually just evaluate the person in front of me and figure out how best to proceed. I took in the man and made a decision.

I explained to him that I had seen the documentary with Dr. Margaret Mead in which she mentioned the use of the Kirlian camera. I went on to explain that I had an upcoming speaking engagement in which I would be presenting my research using my own Kirlian camera and it would be helpful to have a copy of Dr. Mead's documentary.

My interlocutor asked several questions about who I was, the nature of my research, where I could be reached and so on before saying, "I'm sorry. I cannot give you a copy of the movie. We can only lend it out for cultural reasons."

My heart dropped.

"And the conference I'm attending? It's not considered a cultural reason?" And before he could respond, I launched into the full explanation of the research I had done as a result of the purchase of a Kirlian identical to the one I had seen in the documentary, the amount of interest my results had received and so on.

After a while, he lifted his hands, stopping me.

"All right, all right," he said, grabbing the phone on his desk. "I do not know much about this subject, but given your enthusiasm, we can let you have the use of the film."

We shared a few phrases about Rome's beautiful weather before a man entered with the film case in his hand. I signed a couple of sheets of paper, indicating my responsibility for the material delivered and the date I was required to return it. I signed, thanked him warmly, and went away happy . . . but there was still one problem.

I didn't know the exact date of the conference. Now I was afraid I'd have to return the film before I had a chance to use it. Once again, Emilio offered a practical, if not entirely legal, solution.

"Make a copy of it."

"It's forbidden. They do not want people to make copies," I replied, thinking of the paperwork I had signed when I was permitted to borrow the movie.

"I understand that," he replied, "But do you think it will be the first and last conference that you will be asked to do? What will you do the next time? Go there to ask for permission again? What if they won't let you have it that often? Things could get very complicated."

I knew he was probably right, but even if I could overcome my fears about being caught, making a copy wouldn't be easy. This was the late 1970s—and at that time there were no video recorders. The reel I held was the exclusive property of USIS and the film's producers. Copying it would require professional equipment. But I was an actress, after all. I knew people in the worlds of film and TV who had that professional equipment. I reached out to a friend who worked at Italian RAI TV and asked for a favor. He agreed and that's how I obtained a copy of the video that I used in the many conferences that I was asked to do.

A few weeks later, on a particularly hot day I was heading into my apartment, sweaty and ready for a shower. I had parked my beloved FIAT128 Blue Coupé in the garage and all I could think about was getting under the cool water . . . until I saw that there was a letter in my mailbox from the Edmond Company—the makers of the EEA device—in the United States. They could not process my order because the machine could only be sold to medical professionals or technicians in the field. Could I provide references as to my credentials to qualify for purchase?

I hadn't expected that reply and it came as quite a blow. Of course, I had no references that would satisfy them. Now what?

I spent several sleepless nights thinking about how to solve this problem. It never crossed my mind to give up: I wanted that device at all costs.

"Try Dr. Cassoli," Emilio suggested to me one day. "He's a scientist but he's also available and open-minded. He helped you once; he might be willing to do it again."

I phoned Dr. Cassoli, but I will confess that I felt more than a little fear as I dialed. This seemed like a very big favor to ask, and I wasn't at all sure that he would agree. Still, I explained the problem to him and asked if he could give me a letter of reference to be sent to the company. Dr. Cassoli was very kind, listened to my predicament attentively and then asked for a couple of days to think it over before giving me an answer.

A few days later, he called to instruct me to visit Professor Servadio, the acting director of the Center for Parapsychology in Rome, who would have a letter for me specifying that I was a researcher on their staff. He had arranged for me to pick up the letter in person rather than waiting the time it would take for it to be mailed to me from Bologna.

I was so grateful and relieved I could barely stutter my thanks. I promised to let him know the results of these new experiments and hung up, excited to meet Professor Servadio.

Servadio was something of a luminary among Italian scientists interested in the field of parapsychology. Indeed, my trusty *Encyclopedia Treccani*, noted him as the only Italian among the most important researchers in parapsychology. The fact that he was willing to write a letter to help *me*—someone with no formal education or experience in the field—filled me with excitement and emotion. I visited his office, obtained the letter, and on a separate piece of paper, I translated it into English. I sent the whole package to Edmond Scientific, along with a copy of the order already sent. Once again, there was nothing to do but wait for several weeks until at last, I received instructions on how to pay for the device. I paid and I waited again.

Almost a month later, I found a notice in the mail from the Fiumicino Airport Customs Office alerting me of the delivery of a parcel from the United States. I was sure it was my EEA at last. Excited, I telephoned Emilio, who hurried over as quickly as possible, and we headed for the customs office with the notice in hand.

A uniformed officer stood behind a counter with a large box—already opened. He asked me for my documents, and after looking at them for a while, he pointed to the box and asked, "What is it?"

"It's an electroencephalaudio," I replied, smiling.

"What?" He didn't smile back.

Oh no. I hadn't considered there might be some import laws that would interfere with my taking possession of the device. My mind raced ahead, trying to think of a way to circumvent any problems.

"It's a device that sends an audio signal for relaxation . . ." I began, but the officer stopped me.

"So, we can say it's a record player." It sounded more like statement than a question.

I was about to launch into a detailed explanation of precisely what the machine did when Emilio interrupted me.

"Yes, we could say that."

The officers sealed the box with a strip of tape and slid it across the counter to me.

I was stunned and a little upset that this sophisticated piece of machinery had been marked down as a common record player. I said as much to Emilio as we loaded it into the car.

"That might have been a mistake," he said. "All that guy wanted was to get rid of it. If he'd understood exactly what the thing was, he might not have delivered it to you. He offered you an elegant exit by calling it a record player, don't you see? That closed the matter and everyone's happy." He raised an eyebrow at me. "You *are* happy, aren't you?"

"Of course, I am," I replied. "Thank goodness you were there." I probably would have said too much if he hadn't been, I knew. My enthusiasm would have won out over good sense and, without Emilio's grasp of the situation, things might have ended very differently. His presence that afternoon at the customs office ensured that, a few hours later, I was holding the EEA device's instruction sheet in one hand and a cup of coffee in the other. My Italian-English dictionary was nearby as I settled into a comfortable position on my sofa and began to wade through the technical details of the machine.

It took a while. I had to keep thumbing through my dictionary to find and translate the words. But I soon read a few lines, highlighted in bold text, that left me stunned. For example, the machine was recommended for use in rooms *shielded entirely from other electrical emissions*. Furthermore, connecting it to other equipment was discouraged. Together, these instructions meant that I could never connect the device to the Kirlian. My intended experimental hypotheses were destroyed.

I was crushed. The EEA device seemed now to be a useless expense—at least for the original purpose of attempting to measure brain activity while simultaneously recording the shifts of energy captured by the Kirlian. However, I thought, perhaps I could still use it for experiments like the ones undertaken by Cleve Backster?

I placed the EEA on the living room table, unwound the electrodes, and connected them to the apparatus. Then I brought my "trunk of happiness" plant (botanical name is Dracaena) from the corner of the room near the window and placed it next to the machine. It was the oldest plant in my home, one of the few that had survived my frequent absences and chronic inattention. I gently placed the electrodes on the leaves, adhering them with a bit of tape. I did not select a special frequency on the machine—I didn't know which one to select. So, I simply put the potentiometer in the general position and waited. I waited a long time. Nothing happened. I kept waiting, but nothing happened for so long that I gave up and decided to go out to buy cigarettes. I was already at the door with my keys in my hand when I heard a strange sound.

I headed back to the living room but as soon as I got there the sound stopped. I looked around, but I didn't see anything that could have made the sound. Nothing was disturbed. Nothing was any different. What was it? What had I heard? I could not come up with an explanation. Was it the sound of the EEA itself, signaling that it was working? I didn't know what it sounded like—I hadn't heard it make any noises before. But why had it stopped? Had the plant "spoken" for a moment? And if so, why?

Anyway, I still needed cigarettes. Once again, I headed for my door, ready to leave. And once again, as I turned the knob to go, I heard the sound. I paused for a moment, then decided to go ahead on my errand. I'd only be away for five minutes—ten at the most. Let the plant continue to "talk" if that was what it was doing, I thought, and left.

When I got home a little later, I heard the sound as soon as I stepped into the house. But when I entered the living room again, it stopped.

For a good fifteen minutes, I went in and out of the living room like a fool. Each time I left the room, I heard the sound. When I returned, it stopped. It was strangely exciting, and I was swept away by the pleasure of having a "result" even if I wasn't entirely sure what it meant. The room was certainly not screened from all electrical emissions as the instruction book had recommended, but the television was turned off, and there no other sounds or electrical devices at work in the room at that time. It did not seem that there was any other easily explained electrical interference causing the sound.

At long last, I began to understand what was happening: the plant was reacting to the presence or absence of a person, in this case *me*. It was a confirmation of Backster's experiments in my own home.

Around seven p.m., Emilio rang the doorbell. He'd stopped by after work with food, since he knew how excited I got about these kinds of things and he was sure I'd forgotten about eating. Of course, he was right: I had forgotten about it. But even then, food was the last thing on my mind. I wanted to talk to him about the experiment with the plant. As I talked, he loaded the empty refrigerator with the things he'd bought.

When he was done, I wanted to try the experiment in a new way. I had him go in and out of the living room several times, hoping to get a different sound out of the plant as a reaction to a different person. But the plant did not react. But when I went out, and the sound returned. I tried again with Emilio, but when he went out nothing happened. After hundreds of trials, we realized there was only one conclusion to make: the plant "recognized" me but not Emilio. I had had that plant for years and it reacted only to my presence. Emilio, after all, was a new arrival; the plant did not consider him to be important.

"I hope you don't feel the same as the plant," Emilio said to me. His tone was something between serious and facetious.

I smiled mysteriously but didn't answer. I wasn't sure what to say but of course, by then I knew that Emilio was far from unimportant in my life.

CHAPTER SIXTEEN
A NEW CHALLENGE

In the summer of 1976 Emilio's news agency sent him to southern Italy to interview a controversial doctor who claimed to have found a cure for cancer. He'd developed a serum derived from a sheep's gland and his proponents and detractors were hotly debating his methods and results. Emilio was driving back to Rome after the interview with the doctor. It was very late—around two a.m.—and he was traveling on an unlit road near Agropoli, a very small town in the Campania region. There were only three cars traveling on the road that night.

Emilio was the second car in this mini caravan, in his old two door Opel Kadet. As usual, he kept his Canon camera on the front seat with its 50mm lens attached. The camera was loaded with a 36-exposure roll of black and white film. The first car was about twenty yards ahead of him, about to take a curve around the hillside when suddenly a huge glowing light illuminated the night. Emilio slowed down, thinking they were the headlights of a large truck. But it was brighter than the headlights of a truck. From behind the rocky ridge of the hillside ahead of him, suspended in the sky, hung a ball of light five or six times larger than the Moon.

Driving with his knees. Emilio reached for his camera and quickly snapped all thirty-six frames, trying to capture what he was seeing. Meanwhile, ahead of him, the first car slid off the side of the road, smashing into the guardrail. As soon as the accident happened, the bright ball of light completely disappeared. Emilio slammed on brakes and pulled over to help the driver. The car behind him, the third car, sped past them and kept going, disappearing behind the ridge.

"Did you see that?" Emilio asked the driver in the first car, after he made sure he was unhurt.

"I didn't see anything," the guy answered, shaking. "I'm okay. I think I just fell asleep." And with that, he got back in the car, started it, and headed on with his journey home.

Emilio stood there on the side of the road for another twenty minutes or so. He reloaded his camera, making ready for something else to happen . . . but nothing did. At last, he got back in his car and drove on.

We met the next day and he told me with his usual nonchalance about the strange event that happened to him. Then with a casualness that belied our shared interest, he gave me the roll of film to develop. He knew I would be intrigued by both his story and the opportunity to see what was recorded on that roll of film. But I played it cool, too.

"Sure," I said. "I guess since it's Kodak black and white we could do it at home ourselves."

But the truth was I was so curious to see what was on that roll of film there was no way I was willing to wait a week or ten days for a professional lab to do it.

"I'll help," Emilio offered and off we went.

In his experiences as a journalist, Emilio had heard stories about UFOs, but I hadn't. As we transformed the bathroom of my apartment into a dark room by hanging a black curtain and balancing a small basin for the acids on the sink, Emilio told me all he knew about this phenomenon. It was not much, but it was enough to give rise to my skepticism.

But as soon I saw the negative, I was astonished and baffled. I had believed that perhaps Emilio was tired: fatigue can certainly cause hallucinations. But fatigue is unlikely to project itself onto photographic film. And this film showed anomalies and contradictions that made no sense. Although Emilio had snapped all thirty-six exposures, only the three central frames—seventeen, eighteen, and nineteen—recorded images. They showed clearly a ball of light: it appeared in the top left corner of frame 17, almost perfectly in the middle of frame 18, and in the top right corner in the frame 19. It was a perfect photographic sequence—a copybook. But what made us crazy were the remaining frames. Some were so overexposed they were completely black and others so underexposed that they were transparent. Even stranger were the reference numbers. On every roll of Kodak film, the word "Kodak" and the roll's reference numbers usually appear along the bottom. They do not have photographic emulsion and can't be altered by the acids used in developing. But on this roll, the reference numbers were also overexposed and blacked out. How could that have happened? Radiation, perhaps? Something else?

Also, there was another oddity: the ball of light showed a solid body with an additional strange shape inside it. This was something Emilio had not noticed with his naked eye, but the photographs revealed it clearly. And the photographs clearly showed that the light was actively moving in places, pouring out of the center like water shooting out of a fountain. Usually rays of light shine more directly and don't have that fuzzy, watery effect. Years after, a friend who worked in a physics laboratory told me that luminous emission plasma behaves in this way. It's called the "Cherenkov effect" in honor of the Soviet physicist Pavel Alekseyevich Cherenkov, who won the 1958 Nobel Prize for his study of this phenomenon. A Cherenkov refers to the visible electromagnetic radiation of particles that are moving faster than the speed of light. Something about whatever was shining over Emilio that night might have had a Cherenkov effect.

I was very excited to have learned about something I had never heard of before—and even luckier to have photographic proof. I must have talked about the images to half the world—and even more, if you count the many friends and acquaintances who visited my apartment to see the photographs with their own eyes.

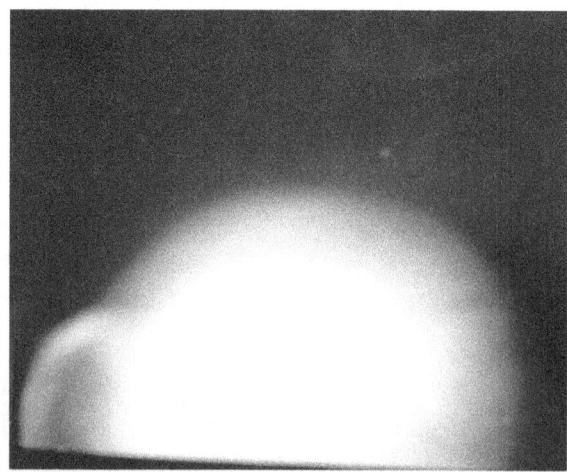

Emilio's photograph of the sphere of light. Note: the fountain of light on the left.

Second frame increasing exposure times to highlight the inside of the sphere. Note a tail on the right. Possibly an antenna.

About two weeks later, I went out to the theater with a group of old friends. That hardly ever happened anymore: it seemed like I didn't have as much fun with the old crowd as I used to. I was often bored in their company and preferred to spend my evenings with Emilio who, by comparison, always had something interesting to say. I always seemed to enjoy myself when we were together. But I agreed to go out that evening because it had been such a long time since I had seen them.

I returned home to find broken glass under the dining room window and my apartment torn up. Thieves had broken in and everything was topsy-turvy: my books were scattered on the floor, the drawers turned inside out, and my dresses pulled out of the wardrobe. I didn't touch anything, I just called the police, even though my prior experiences with them left me doubtful that they would do anything. I guess social conditioning dies hard.

"What was stolen?" the officer asked when he arrived at my apartment about half an hour later.

I was a little embarrassed to admit that I didn't know. I hadn't checked yet.

And indeed, on first inspection, nothing was missing. Jewels and fur coats were on the floor, but not taken. Everything was in disarray, but nothing seemed to be gone. The police officer did his report for a housebreaking/attempted burglary and left.

I wanted to call Emilio a thousand times, but I knew he had to do a *special* (an on-call photo service) that night of an American actor passing through Rome. He was working and I would have to wait.

Little by little, I returned all my things to their appropriate places. It was almost morning by the time I finished, and I was exhausted. I went to bed. I had been asleep only a couple of hours when I suddenly awoke with a single precise thought—unusual for me with only a little sleep. I got up immediately and went to the writing desk in the dining room. I opened the left drawer and felt around for the plastic bag where I had put the film negative of the object that Emilio had photographed on that dark road. The plastic bag was there . . . but it was empty.

The negative was the only thing missing—that and the Zippo lighter I had placed on top of it as a paperweight. The lighter itself was special too because it was engraved with the name of the aircraft carrier Forrestal. The USS Forrestal had been anchored in the port of Palermo many years before and the lighter was given to me as gift when I visited the ship. A group of my friends and I had gotten the chance to visit the ship and in talking with one of the sailors, it came out that I had recently won Miss Italy. The news that a beauty queen was aboard spread throughout the ship and the next thing I knew I was invited to the bridge for small *cincin* (cheers). I remembered it clearly: the thrill of being aboard the vessel was like stepping into the World War II movies I'd seen. Years later, I learned that after leaving Palermo, the Forrestal had proceeded to the Gulf of Tonkin. A serious electrical fire aboard had killed more than 130 men and injured almost twice that many. Every time I saw the lighter, I remembered all of those poor boys.

Anyway, that lighter and Emilio's negative were the only things stolen in the break-in. My stories about the "mysterious flying object" came to an abrupt end. I still had the prints, but of course, they proved nothing without the negative to show they had not been altered.

Emilio scolded me for telling so many people about the images. On this subject, he said, I had to learn to be much more discreet. During that time, some American intelligence services were actively interested in the subject of unidentified flying objects both at home and abroad. Interested enough, Emilio believed, to have relieved me of those images. Naturally, I dismissed that possibility. I knew nothing about these things, and it seemed to me that he was being dramatic about a couple of lights on a half-burned roll of film. Oh, blessed innocence.

The arrival of another movie role distracted me from thinking about the lost negative and UFOs for quite some time. It was an important movie, set during the Spanish Inquisition, about a country girl accused of witchcraft and the Inquisitor who falls in love with her. Both ended up being burned at the stake. I had been chosen for the role of the country girl—the lead. (*Inquisicion*, 1977). I was excited to have a new film—and excited to have money coming in once again—and it would be about a year before the subject of UFOs returned to my mind again.

CHAPTER SEVENTEEN
A CLOSE ENCOUNTER

It was almost dark on a Friday night in July 1977 when UFOs re-entered my thoughts.

Emilio drove us along the old consular Aurelia Road. By then, I had stopped thinking of him as a "friend" and adopted the word "boyfriend" to describe our relationship, though I liked to tell myself that our romantic relationship was just a "trial period" to see if it worked. I loved our friendship and didn't want to lose it because we were dating.

It was a beautiful summer evening after a pleasant day on the beach at Pescia Romana, in the Civitavecchia province. Of course, in summer the beaches are always very crowded, but that day we had found a beautiful beach secluded by trees and surrounded by barbed wire. There was a little sign on the fence that said, "MilitaryZone, Do Not Enter" but there were no guards or dogs protecting the property. Indeed, someone had already cut a hole in the barbed wire making the trespass so easy we could not resist—especially since we could see the seashore just a few yards away. The calm, clear, blue water beckoned to us. We crept through the opening in the fence and took a spot on the white sand of the deserted beach.

We swam and sunbathed, feeling privileged for that magnificent solitude. The water was perfect—so clear and clean you could see straight to the bottom. I liked it so much better than the beaches of Ostia and Fregene, though in Fregene there was a restaurant, little more than a shack really, near the latter where they cooked wonderful anchovies *au gratin*.

Even without anchovies *au gratin*, it was wonderful day. Perfect in every way. I was happy. I had not thought about work at all. I had breathed the fresh air and embraced the salty waves of the sea. We climbed in Emilio's old Opel Kadet and left with more than a little regret that the day was over, but it was time to go home to my apartment to shower off the sand and salt before dinner. It was not long after dusk, the sky was still clear as we started back toward Rome.

But then, after such a peaceful day, a glittering ribbon of multicolored taillights quickly let us know that our streak of happiness was about to come to an end. Traffic. A line of cars wound ahead of us, bumper to bumper and barely moving at all—and we were still many, many miles from Rome.

"It's a lot of traffic." Emilio sounded as irritated at the prospect of delaying a hot shower and rinsing off the sand as I was. "It's going to take at least two hours to get home."

The thought of spending the next two or three hours in the car, creeping along in traffic moving at the speed of walking was insufferable. I reached into the glove compartment for a map and spread it along the dashboard, taking on the role of navigator in the hopes of finding an alternative route.

I loved maps. I could read them well, unlike Emilio, who often had difficulty orienting himself. I identified our location and used my finger to trace the Aurelia Road, the old roman way that wound through rolling hills and tiny villages. After a few moments of study, I found what I was looking for.

"There is a road ahead on the left that connects the Aurelia with the Cassia," I said. "Road" was probably not the right word. On the map the route appeared not as a solid line but as a series of dashes, which we both knew translated to "it's tough, try at your own risk." To Emilio I said, "It's a very narrow, winding road that cuts through the Tolfa Mountains. Look for the turn. Be careful, though. I don't think its marked."

"Are you sure?" Emilio asked and I knew he was asking if I really wanted to take a chance on some tiny mountain road. He knew there was a good possibility that we'd find this little detour to be under construction, unpaved or, even worse, blocked by a landslide or some other natural disaster.

"Yes, take it," I said confidently, pointing out the turn. "Here."

Emilio turned and I crossed my fingers that I was right.

The road turned out to be perfect: it was paved, smooth and apparently, not well-travelled. We did not meet a soul as we travelled quickly along under a canopy of trees. We were delighted with the discovery of this shortcut and it felt wonderful to be moving quickly toward home. The sky was beginning to darken with the first stars, but the sun had not yet completely set. The miles flew past us. It was like an extension of our perfect day at the beach and the irritation the traffic had brought us evaporated. Emilio and I chatted happily as the little car carried us closer toward our hot showers. And then suddenly, a light flashed in the bit of sky peeping through the thick trees.

I bent slightly to be able to see better through Emilio's open window. It was a dot of light, moving but not in the regular way of a vehicle or a plane. It rose and dropped then rose again, zigzagging through the air erratically as it came closer and closer, growing bigger and brighter as it advanced.

"Slow down," I told Emilio, pointing. "Look at that."

Emilio slowed the car down so that we were barely moving and turned to look.

"That's strange," he said. "I've never seen anything move like that. And it's so bright and white. What is it?"

The light came closer and closer. It grew brighter and brighter.

Emilio stopped the car. We climbed out to better see the light as it moved up and down, coming closer and closer, growing brighter and brighter. We looked around for other people, hoping to see if there was anyone else seeing what we were seeing. But no. We were totally alone on this winding and deserted road.

In a flash, the bright object was less than thirty meters in front of us and about twenty meters off the ground. It slowly crossed the road in front of us, while we stood there bewildered and amazed.

It was a classic flying saucer.

It was just like the ones I'd seen in science fiction magazines or in comic books: an upside-down dish of a craft that hovered in front of us while we stared at it in disbelief. The saucer was about twelve meters wide and a metallic dark gray. Its bright milky light came not from the dome at the top, but through three or four vertical black bands rotating beneath the dome. It seemed to be studying us just as we studied it because it hung there above the road in front of us for several seconds. A deep and heavy silence lay between us; the craft was soundless, and Emilio and I were struck dumb with amazement. Not even a bird call penetrated the silence, until at last, driven by a wild impulse I still don't completely understand, I ran to the car and flashed the headlines and pounded on the horn in attempt to signal—to communicate—with whatever or whoever was inside.

I was very excited. I do not know what I expected to happen, but nothing did. The incredible aircraft, after having remained just above our heads for so long without any sort of noise—not even a hiss or a buzz—suddenly jumped away from us and disappeared behind the ridge.

"You scared it," Emilio said. "Get in, quick."

We drove, hurrying to catch another glimpse of it as we followed the road along the next hairpin turn. But it was gone.

Emilio and I had seen a UFO. We never had any doubts that what we saw was a craft from another world. There was nothing about it that was recognizably earth-bound, nothing that suggested that it was a military aircraft or anything else that might have come from our world. Unlike Emilio's pictures from his experience a year before, this time I spoke to almost no one about what I had seen. I'd learned my lesson. Over the years, I have tried to learn more about UFOs and visitors from other planets. But like many others who have gone down that path, I've found that most of this information leads nowhere. Those who claim to have seen spaceships are quickly deemed to be mentally unstable and are discounted as mistaking simple weather balloons for flying saucers.

But I know what I saw . . . and what I saw cannot be dismissed or easily explained.

CHAPTER EIGHTEEN
CONSIDERATIONS ABOUT ART

Today, after much research and investigation, as well as a roller coaster of enthusiasm and frustration, I have concluded that the biggest problem is not what is "up there" but what is "down here." I am convinced we have almost all the information we need already in our hands. The difficulty is in understanding how to phrase that information appropriately and how to deliver it to people—especially to those people who do not want to know. But I am an optimist. I think in a century or so, we should be able to change our mentality. In a hundred years, what now seems to be taboo will be accepted and I hope, commonplace. Perhaps, we shall one day consider the very things that are now laughed at and deemed ridiculous to be the pioneering ideas of the next Age.

I have studied art and have painted since I was a child. Since that day on the winding road home from the beach, I look at the art of painting differently—and find new things in analyzing the works of other painters. Painting communicates in an entirely different way than, for example, speech. Speech at its foundation is a series of sounds organized in a certain order to form words. Behind the words are thoughts and emotions. You can express a thought relatively coherently with words. But words are often inadequate to express emotions.

To communicate emotion often requires other means. Dance, for example can communicate more powerfully than words, even if that movement happens just at the local club on a Saturday night. If you've ever been dancing, you've seen people unloading their repressed emotions on the dance floor. Those dance moves could be graceful or awkward, they could be beautiful or ugly, but they always express the dancer's feelings in ways that are beyond words. Art is the same way. Art's imagery communicates beyond language. An ugly picture painted by a garret artist speaks of his or her circumstances in every stroke of the brush, every choice of color, every shape. The artist's ideas and self-concept present themselves on the canvas, revealing thoughts and emotion he or she couldn't have expressed in a thousand years of conversation.

When we look back at works painted hundreds or even thousands of years ago, our modern perspective enables us to analyze the ideas and beliefs expressed in them with a clarity and immediacy that the surviving written word cannot. For example, there are many worthy works that include images of extraterrestrial aircraft. These works—all dating back hundreds of years—tell us that UFO sightings can't be explained by the modern explanations of too many science fiction movies or by secret military technology.

Take *The Madonna and Saint Giovannino* attributed to Sebastiano Mainardi or to the Jacopo del Sellaio school—just one of many works that raise the issue of UFO sightings long before the present day. Displayed at the Palazzo Vecchio, in Florence, Italy like many paintings of its time, it depicts the Virgin Mary. But in the top right corner of this sacred image, near the head of the Madonna, one finds a curious detail: a lead-gray object with a dome or turret on top. Bright yellow-gold rays of light emanate from its hull. The oval object appears to be flying above some kind of barely visible spherical structure. On the opposite side of the painting is the sun, with three small fires (symbolizing the Holy Trinity, Father Son, and Holy Spirit) immediately below. These details show that the artist knew the difference between a mystic-symbolic representation and a real event. As if to confirm the artist's will to communicate something of special emotional intensity, a small human figure stands below, observing the object in the sky with his hand shielding his eyes—a sign of attention—while a nearby dog barks at the mysterious object.

It is important to remember that in our historical past, much like now, artists were subject to ostracism if their work deviated from the certain social and religious expectations. Talking about certain phenomena could lead to the loss of work or worse: the loss of freedom or even loss of life for heresy. Thus, it might be far safer to "hide" a message through skillful brushstrokes.

"La Madonna e San Giovannino" exhibited at Palazzo Vecchio, in Florence, Italy.

Detail on top right

I find the painting a fascinating communication that reaches beyond the political and religious prohibitions of its time. Whatever is going on "up there" did not begin in the twentieth century and it is up to us "down here" to acknowledge it, include it in our discussion of our shared history and ultimately, to attempt to understand it. Our current scientific knowledge allows us to understand better the importance what else might be "up there" better than any other time in history.

In 1999, an article I had written on this topic entitled "UFOs and the History of the Arts" won the first prize in the Donald E. Keyhoe Award competition promoted by the Fund for UFO Research (FUFOR) located in Washington, DC. The article was published by Greenhaven Press and has appeared in several other magazines and journals. I think the article was a bit of an eye-opener for many people who had not realized how many hundreds of years mankind has been spotting unusual things in the sky.

Since that strange and unbelievable day that I stood by the side of the road and saw a flying saucer, I have continued to attract unusual and exciting opportunities—and to conduct experiments looking for more proof.

CHAPTER TWENTY
SERENDIPITY

"An attitude for making desirable discoveries by accident; good fortune or luck."

That's the dictionary's definition for "serendipity." Coined by the English writer Horace Walpole—son of Great Britain's first prime minister—in 1754, it derived from the accidental wisdom encountered by the characters in a fairytale called "The Three Heroes of Serendip." In the story, the Sultan of Serendip (an ancient Arabic name of the island of Ceylon), sets off on an adventure in search of gold. After crossing mountains and valleys, he didn't find any gold at all. Instead, he discovered some excellent quality tea, which turned out to be far more valuable than gold and made him a fortune.

I didn't make a fortune, but serendipity led me to some great new realizations and opportunities, too.

I had known director Luigi Cozzi for many years—thanks to Libra Editrice and Ugo Malaguti, both friends from my acting work. Cozzi and I shared a passion for books and often recommended titles to each other. When I learned he wanted me for a small part in his science fiction film *Star Crash*, I was thrilled. The other actors were big stars: model Carolyn Munro, the British actress known for being a Bond girl, Christopher Plummer, the unforgettable Atahualpa in *The Royal Hunt of the Sun*, David Hasselhoff, famous for his action movies, Nadia Cassini (a relation of designer Oleg Cassini), and many others. I think Cozzi called me because he liked me and because we had bonded in our book discussions more than because he really needed me for the role. He could have hired anyone for the small part he had in mind, and it surely would have cost him less. However: a week in Calabria, near Vibo Valentia, close enough to visit the sea in late September, in a film with a respectable cast, with a director who was also a friend, *and* being well-paid for a part that didn't require any nudity—well, I couldn't wish for more. Unfortunately, many parts—including mine—ended up being cut from the final film because it was too long. But that was okay. It was a wonderful week made even better by the chance to get to know Carolyn Munro and Judd, her husband—and I got paid anyway. It was a worthwhile experience.

Between scenes and during "basket breaks," Carolyn, Judd, and I would talk. I'm not one for gossip and I didn't really know that many people in the entertainment industry well enough to talk about them anyway, so I told Caroline and Judd about my experiments with Kirlian. To my surprise, they were very interested and listened carefully to my stories. They shared that they knew someone who was also interested in the subject and expressed an intention to put us in connection with each other.

A few months later, thanks to their introduction, I received an invitation from an English foundation asking me to speak at conferences in London and Paris about my experiments with the children who could bend metal. Astonished but very excited, I accepted and a few weeks later, Emilio, the Kirlian camera, and I headed to London.

The Orb Foundation was located in Belgrave Square, a prestigious section of an elegant district in central London. When we reached the address we had been given, we found a three-story building that looked more like the home of a noble lord than a conference center. For a moment, I was concerned, but when we were showed to our room, I was speechless. Emilio and I had done a few conferences and events by then and we had gotten used to the "poverty" of many of the Italian associations interested in paranormal phenomenon. Most had very little money and no sponsorships and conducted their events in small rooms where the participants sat on folding chairs. If they covered our lodging at all, it was in the cheapest place available.

But clearly the Orb Foundation was different. Our accommodations were of the caliber of a luxury hotel or an ornate movie set. Ours was a large room furnished entirely in white: two single beds, both with thick white comforters and headboards in white damask satin; white lacquered bedside tables, a huge white four-seasons wardrobe with mirrored doors that made the room seem even larger. In the corner, next to an elegant window, a large white leather armchair rested on a huge white carpet, tufted and shaggy, like the skin of a polar bear.

But the bathroom was a different kind of surprise. When I went in to take a shower, I discovered that there was no bidet, the tub was very old, and the water pressure was so poor that it dribbled out of the nozzle in two weak streams. Worse, every time you used it, the hot water heater clanked and clattered like something out of an old horror movie. Any illusion of privacy in the bathroom was shattered by the hot water system, which announced to everyone in the house that you were in the bathroom.

I soon learned something else unexpected. I would be presenting the results of my experiments—in English (a difficult thing for me and an experience I would not like to repeat)—not to the *public* as I expected to do, but to a swarm of paranormal *scientists* from all over the world.

I was paralyzed with fear. If I'd been told that scientists were my audience, I might not have accepted. After all, I had no formal education in these matters—I was an actress. And worse, in English? Even if I felt confident in my presentation, I was sure I didn't have the vocabulary to communicate to these scholars. For a moment, I seriously considered packing up the Kirlian and going home.

But of course, I didn't. I prepared a good presentation and I hoped my English would be sufficient to deliver it well, even though I didn't know the scientific terms of another language. It must have been enough however, because in spite of the communication and translation issues, some American scientists were fascinated by my experiments. Douglas Dean and John Mihalasky of the Newark College of Engineering, co-authors of *Executive ESP,* Dr. Andrija Puharich, the scientist who had discovered Uri Geller during his trip to Israel, and Christopher Bird, botanist, and the author of *The Secret Life of Plants* were among the scientists who approached me after my talk to ask questions and encourage my efforts. It was thrilling for me to be in the company of researchers whose work I admired—and to have their interest in me and my experiments.

Following the conference, there was a meeting with the attendees and then a buffet in the foundation's dining hall. I remember clearly biting into a "pastry" that was flavored with garlic. A "sweet" . . . with garlic? Who came up with that idea? It was one of the more unfortunate things I've ever tasted—so unpleasant that I can't think of the conference without mentioning it. It tasted terrible.

After spitting out that abomination, I mingled with the scientists, talking to this one and that one. One of the conference attendees followed my every move. He was a wiry guy, graying and middle-aged, with eyes made smaller by his glasses. He hovered on the edge of all my conversations and every time he could fit it in, he asked me the same question: "What kind of florescent tube did you use in your experiments and where did you buy it?" I guess he thought I didn't understand English well, because he'd change the sentence almost every time, using slightly different words. But it was still the same question. I answered it exactly the same way every time: it was just a regular white florescent tube—like the kind typically found above a bathroom mirror, bought at a local hardware store. This went on and on until, finally, irritated by his persistence, I spoke to the Orb Foundation's director, a small woman with black hair and intelligent-looking eyes.

"Who is that idiot who keeps following me like shadow?" I asked in a joking tone that (I hope) concealed how annoyed I was. "He keeps asking me the same question, over and over."

She didn't match my good-humor or levity. "He's an official with MI-6, the British Intelligence Service," she replied soberly.

My shock was so complete that I folded my lips and didn't say another word.

As the day went on, there were cocktails in a small living room of the grand old home. Four or five of the scientists I had met asked me to take Kirlian photos of them. As a researcher, I knew that a single photo wouldn't illustrate anything important—the value is in the comparisons between photos taken under different stimuli—but, given the setting, I didn't feel comfortable saying "no." So instead of sipping cocktails, Emilio and I ended up back in the bathroom setting up all the equipment. Knowing that electricity in England runs on a different current, we had thought ahead and bought a transformer in Rome. We were ready.

We electro-photographed all of them and repaired to our improvised darkroom to develop the black and white photos. I was eager to show these prestigious scientists my work and to explain their images to them. But when the pictures were developed, my hopes sank. Instead of full, bright images of their fingertips, the photos revealed only partial impressions; some were little more than a few streaks of black.

"What the hell happened?" I asked Emilio, but he was as perplexed as I was.

"Maybe Kirlian doesn't work as well with this kind of electrical current," he suggested.

It seemed plausible, but something told me to try a photo using my own hand, then Emilio's. Our pictures came out perfectly and we agreed that the problem wasn't the Kirlian. It was working perfectly.

"Now what do we do?" I asked myself more than Emilio. "From these results, I would say they're all really sick. But that can't be right: they all look perfectly well."

"Well, if they weren't well-known researchers and scientists—if they were just your average person—what would you say about these results?" Emilio asked me.

My mind raced through the hundreds of Kirlian images I had seen, looking for similarities.

"Well," I said at last. "I'd say they're closest to the images I took from a man who told me he'd been smoking marijuana. But I can't go out there and tell these scientists they're all high."

"No, you can't say that exactly," Emilio said, smiling. "But maybe you can find a way to put it diplomatically?"

He was teasing me. He knew fully well that diplomacy wasn't a skill in my toolbox. We rinsed the pictures and took them, wet and as they were, into the living room where the others were waiting for us. I sat on the edge of a small armchair and showed them the results.

"So, what do they mean?" one of them asked.

"Well . . ." I began carefully. "How should I say this? These images have a special appearance. I'm sorry, maybe it's something different in this case—I don't know—but these look like the images of those who've recently smoked marijuana or substances like it."

I was mortified and uncomfortable saying that to them. But there was nothing else to do but tell them the truth.

For a moment, they looked at each other in silence. Then to my surprise, they all started laughing. Now I was worried. Were they laughing at me? Had they concluded that I was a charlatan and that in the future, I should stick to films and leave these kinds of investigations alone? I was sure they were about to tell me to "go to hell" and take my "alleged" experiments with me.

Finally, still laughing, one of them took pity on my alarmed expression and explained that, the night before, they had all been at a party together ... and smoked marijuana.

We stayed in London for a week longer than we anticipated for an unexpected reason. There was no smoking allowed in the Orb Foundation's house where we were guests. At the end of our long days, however, when we returned to our room, Emilio and I would open a window and smoke anyway, using the plastic cap off our deodorant as an ashtray. It was a nice way to relax at the end of the day but leaving the window open let in the cool English air. The combination of long days and cold nights gave me a terrible cold and a very high fever. Poor Emilio! He ended up having to walk around a strange city at three a.m. looking for an open pharmacy to find medicine for me. But he did find it and I was grateful. It took a while to recover enough to travel home.

Back in Italy, I soon discovered that the good word about my presentations at the conference had travelled. I began to receive more serious invitations to speak in my own backyard. The first, and the most prestigious happened thanks to Dr. Cassoli and Professor Servadio and occurred at the Bologna Press Club. Speaking engagements became routine: I presented my results with the Kirlian at events all over Italy.

Today, almost half a century later, the same experiments that were of such great interest all over Italy and most of the developed nations, are practically obsolete. Some governments, the United States in particular, have done similar experiments and research into these phenomena but have only partially understood them. They have become part of protocols used by certain military and intelligence units, with mixed results. Perhaps you saw the 2009 film *Men Who Stare at Goats*, directed by Grant Heslov, with George Clooney, Jeff Bridges, and Kevin Spacey? Based on Jon Ronson's book of the same name, it tells the story of a reporter who discovered a secret US military department researching the use of paranormal faculties as a tool to achieve victory during the Iraq war. A satire against the American military establishment, the film questions how, without understanding much about them, this department tried to teach soldiers to use psychic powers against the enemy. The film did not do very well in America, but it was a colossal flop in Italy. I went with Emilio to see it—by then we had been married for many years—and there only six other people in the theatre. Our companions thought we were crazy, I'm sure, because, having followed the development of PSI skills in humans over the years, we laughed at the soldiers' attempts to replace or add to their conventional military training with subtle energy work. We were the only ones laughing, though, because most people don't know anything about these matters. Or rather, they only know what the media reports: skepticism, sensationalism, and cultural confusion. This kind of limited coverage and understanding is why psychic phenomena (PSI, telepathy, psychokinesis, PK, psychopathy, OBE, out-of-body experiences, clairvoyance, dowsing, and many others) remain "fringe" experiences that don't enjoy scientific adoption or replication. The individuals who have lived them know and understand, but it's difficult to get others to accept or believe in them without any real proof.

In fact, in Italy, there isn't even a specific agency or individual to whom one can report these experiences or abilities. It isn't like going to a doctor and saying that one has pain. At most, a psychic ability might be revealed to a friend in the strictest confidence—and even then, one might be afraid of being perceived as crazy. Better to remain silent about these experiences rather than being seen as mad—or worse, being treated like a lab rat and being subjected to all kinds of tests which can be draining and, perhaps, even dangerous.

In the end, personal and direct experiences are the ones that convince us anyway. Personal experiences with psychic phenomena are what makes us want to more fully understand the potential implications—philosophical, technological, military, and social—that these abilities, now considered *avant-garde* science, involve.

PSI and UFOs get the same reactions from conventional science—but interestingly, even the academic researchers in these two areas do not want the disciplines to become intertwined. The feeling is that the association of one with the other somehow lessens the validity of both. But in reality, their struggles for acceptance by the mainstream scientific community could be bolstered by the union of the resources of these two fields.

CHAPTER TWENTY-ONE
UNUSUAL DOORS

Once, I was invited to "guest host" a magic show in a city near Rome. I had heard of him, water cooler gossip pegged him as a character who sometimes produced strange phenomena that seemed to be beyond the typical prestidigitation of the average magician. I have sometimes been asked to host shows like these, but it's a job I hate, even when paid to do it. You are obliged to stand and smile and improvise witty jokes that usually aren't that witty under the pressure of the moment. I usually think of much better ones hours later, at home, when it doesn't matter anymore. However, I was curious enough about this particular magician to agree to participate. As usual, I couldn't turn down the opportunity to meet a person who may have had some exceptional talent or to mingle with the crowds of interested spectators.

In meeting this man and watching his show, I was surprised to find that in all likelihood, he had some skill. There was definitely some psychic ability present, though not at all as powerful as the children I had worked with. But since he had claimed "magician" as his profession, he was useless to me as a subject for any kind of experimentation. He had downgraded his skills so that they would always be seen as little more than parlor tricks. But the thing that struck me most about him was a story he told me in confidence.

He was performing in a small city in central Italy. One night, he woke up suddenly in the middle of the night. He was wide awake, so rather than lie sleeplessly in bed, he decided to leave the hotel and take a walk, hoping to burn off some of his restlessness and get back to sleep. He set off aimlessly, reflecting on the work he would do in the day ahead and found himself walking along a suburban, tree-lined avenue. To his left was a chain link fence that enclosed a large, and apparently, vacant lot. The occasional streetlight provided enough light for him to see his way forward, but it was still pretty dark. Suddenly he saw a gap in the fence's wire mesh and, like a little boy, was overcome by the strong impulse to slip through it and onto the lot. Even though he was aware that he was on private land, in a place far from home, at night and that once he left the street, there wouldn't be enough light to see anything, he followed his impulse and ducked into the opening. He moved through a patch of trees and almost immediately found himself in a small clearing. He stopped and looked around, feeling "like a fool," he said, and then suddenly, the air in front of him seemed to become denser, as if it were turning into fog, while at the same time becoming more and more luminous. A few seconds later, a door made of white light materialized in the clearing. The center of the door blazed the brightest, emitting a very intense and very bright light.

The magician considered in a fraction of a second. Should he step toward it and cross the threshold into the unknown . . . Or should he stay and make his show the next day? He darted off back to the hotel and told no one what he had seen.

If that had happened to me, no one and nothing would have prevented me from crossing that threshold—or at least that would have been my answer forty years ago when I was told about this experience. Maybe now, I would be more cautious—but I'm not sure. Curiosity usually wins.

But the point is this: how many of us have experienced firsthand strange phenomena—but have never told anyone? Or have only told one or two people whom we trusted to keep that secret? How many of these stories are never investigated beyond that single conversation? Of course, upon investigation, the experience may have a rational explanation. But when there is no rational explanation, these experiences suggest realities beyond our current understanding. Indeed, there may be different levels of reality altogether, completely beyond our comprehension. Are we open to that theory? Can we speak of it as a real possibility, beyond science fiction movies? Although today we acknowledge and study quantum physics, I do not believe that most scientists are ready to revise their beliefs about the nature of reality in the ways that experiences like my magician friend's suggest we could. We close our minds to the possibilities and dismiss those who experience them as fakers or crazies.

You might wonder what has happened to the children I studied in the seventies. So do I. I lost touch with all of them as they grew older. Did their powers fade, eclipsed by the requirements of a "normal" life? Did they suppress them as they grew older to "fit in"? Or perhaps they were undone by their own mistrust of their abilities. Mistrust of experiences we cannot readily classify, and fear of the unknown are very much alive. In the grand scheme of time, it has not been very long since the witch-hunting of the "holy" Inquisition in which people who exhibited strange powers were burned alive. And certainly, in my own experience, people who have these abilities and gifts have faced a maelstrom of doubt and skepticism—as have the scientists who have attempted to explore them. Since the seventies and eighties, scholarly examination of psychic phenomena seems to have disappeared from the popular culture, replaced instead by horror movies and television psychics. Is this because the real research is now the purview of corporations, the military, and intelligence communities?

One thing that has always struck me is how science divides itself into sectors: astronomers study space; botanists, plants; physicists, physics; and so on. But these divisions often interfere with an interdisciplinary approach that encourages the sharing of information that could accelerate and enrich the ongoing evolutionary and technological process. By discounting the study of the paranormal and dismissing it as pseudo-science how many opportunities to raise our understanding of how the human mind, the world, the Universe—and beyond—have we missed?

This opinion of mine may seem controversial, but in reality, it just illustrates one of the many gaps that threaten our ability to truly advance.

Consider Remote Viewing. It's been around for a while—and it's one of the techniques that was attempted by the US military in that movie I was talking about, *Men Who Stare at Goats*. I hear it's now taught in various private and semi-private US institutions, but it's something you rarely read much about.

Remote viewing, also called psycho-energetic perception, is a form of clairvoyance. It is the acquisition of information about people, places, and events through the mind. People who can access this ability can clearly see objects and people at a distance (the next room, for example, or in another country) or through obstacles (walls, for examples) or at different points in time (i.e., the past or the future).

Remote viewing has an interesting history. In 1971, Ingo Swann, an American artist who had achieved some fame, met Cleve Backster, who by then had also become well-known for his experiments with plants. In addition to his artistic talent, Swann claimed psychic abilities and participated in research experiments conducted by the Stanford Research Institute (SRI), the American Society for Psychical Research (ASPR), and ultimately, the CIA—who wanted to know if these "practices" would affect national security and if they could be used militarily.

Under the direction of Dr. Hal Puthoff and physicist Russell Targ, the SRI launched a series of experiments on Swann—and became the founders of parapsychology as we know it. Together they conducted hundreds of experiments, from underwater tests to space trials, involving civilian and military personnel. They presented hundreds of lectures for the public and wrote several books on their results. Their work with Swann focused on his ability to "see" objects that were located out his range of vision—like his ability to affect the readings of a magnetometer and other unique experiments—completely through the power of his mind.

At the time, however, Swann's abilities and the results of Dr. Puthoff and Dr. Targ's experiments were dismissed outright.

Reading about the experiments done with Swann some years later gave Emilio and me an idea about to raise awareness about this and other work being done in the so-called "ESP world." In 1980, we organized an exhibition of paintings we called "PsychoArt" at the Quirinale Hotel in Rome. We hoped to expose the public to some ideas about psychic powers in a different way, and in the process circumvent some of the traditional rejection and skepticism these concepts faced. We hoped people would understand that, in the artist's life, in any field in which he/she works, there is a magic, inviolable element of inspiration—and what is inspiration, if not an alternative condition of one's mind or a wider, unexplained perception of one's own faculties? Rather than confronting the existence of ESP directly, we tackled it from a milder perspective hoping to encourage people to realize that what we call "psychic phenomena" is simply an expansion of powers we already recognize and accept.

We contacted a couple of famous painters and invited them to show their works and lend their names to this exploration. They consented and the show was on. As Emilio climbed a ladder to hang the various paintings around the hotel's lobby, I contacted Ingo Swann. He had been staying in Milan and I hoped to invite him as well as the noted artists Jack Frankfurter and Karel Thole. I received a very kind letter from Swann, declining the invitation due to commitments in Milan that made it impossible for him to get to Rome, but the others accepted and mailed their original works, too.

The six-day show was quite successful. I don't know if any minds were changed, but it was certainly a well-received effort to raise awareness of the connections between the unconscious mind and inspiration. To my surprise, years later, Ingo Swann sent me a copy of his book *Penetration: The Question of Extraterrestrial and Human Telepathy*. He, too, had naturally arrived at the same place I did in associating ESP and UFOs.

CHAPTER TWENTY-TWO
PRESS SERVICES

Of course, I had not forgotten the object that Emilio and I had seen on our trip back from the sea. The more I thought about it, the more I felt compelled to seek out others who had a similar experience. I began to look for stories in the newspapers about strange sightings or occurrences, but it was rare that I found anything. I read books, reports, and reviews but I soon realized that the Italian press didn't cover this phenomenon very often. In those years, most people didn't take the subject seriously and as a result, the news articles I found were often in esoteric, spiritual, or religious publications. In the mainstream press, articles about an alleged UFO sighting were entrusted not to a writer with any real interest or background in the subject, but to any journalist available. A sportswriter, a gossip columnist, a crime reporter—any of them might be assigned to a story about a UFO sighting. Of course, these reporters sensationalized the sightings, which also simultaneously diminished or discredited the experience.

The result for me was a gap between the information I wanted and the information available to me. Then, one day, I discovered a press service published by a small American publisher who was an aficionado of UFO sightings. His name was Lucius Farish, and he lived in Arkansas. Every month, he printed a twenty-page newsletter in which he compiled all of the press clippings that mentioned a UFO sighting from the entire English-speaking world.

Reading articles and accounts of UFO sightings from China, Russia, or America each month opened up another new world for me, perhaps a more slippery and, sometimes, more dangerous one than any of my previous interests. Information is, after all, fundamental. As I read clipping after clipping, I began to understand that what I had seen was part of a global phenomenon. But the information alone is nothing unless it is accompanied by the four Is:

- imagination
- interaction
- identification
- integration

I knew that I had a role to play in sharing the information Farish had begun collecting—and making sure that others could interact with it, identify similarities to their own experiences, integrate the reality of what they'd seen and imagine new ways to process the truth about extraterrestrial visitors.

I started a collaboration with Farish to translate selected clippings he had compiled and reprint them in Italian. My thinking was that if Italians could read about the number sightings reported worldwide *every month* the information would fill that "gap" in information that had troubled me for so long.

I had the time. I was working less: film roles were becoming less frequent. Often, I was offered roles I declined because, in my opinion, they belittled the profession. But that left me constantly worried about money and what my next moves would be to pay my bills and stay financially afloat. I wondered if publishing a version of Farish's newsletter could help me, so in 1983, Emilio and I started one of the most difficult jobs of our lives.

I would have liked to start big, but Emilio advised against it, so we started with a photocopy of a twenty-page mockup of a selection of news articles about UFO sightings, all translated into Italian, all typed, designed, and printed by just the two of us. I typed the translation on Emilio's old Underwood typewriter, then cut out the typed words, and glued them onto another sheet of paper. Attribution was given to the original newspaper that published the story, the name of the subscriber who had sent it to Farish, and, of course, to Farish and the UFONews Clipping Service. It was time-consuming work—and the workload got even heavier when press clippings began to arrive from our Italian readers too, and then more from readers abroad, in French, German, and Spanish. So reluctantly, Emilio translated from German and French and I from English and Spanish into Italian. And then, after laying out all of these new reports too, we made photocopies and sent our clipping service to UFO followers across the Continent.

This work lasted for fourteen years. We always hoped the number of subscribers would grow to the point we could afford a proper typesetter and printer, but it never happened. We never got enough readers to justify the cost of investing in a more professional look—and our own cost of living was rising dramatically because of a national economic crisis that was rippling through all aspects of our lives. Even the movie industry had suffered a heavy blow—and at last, the moment I had been dreading came. There weren't likely to be any more movie jobs.

But for all that hard work and anxiety about our survival, the readers and fans of the publication brought us moments of intense satisfaction. Sergio Bonelli Editore, the founder of a prestigious publishing company that focused on Italian comic strips became a devoted subscriber and sent us a congratulatory letter for our work. He even said that we had inspired some of his stories. General Salvatore Marcelletti, a former military pilot and later a commercial airline pilot, told us about his terrifying encounter with a UFO while he was on a training flight with his squadron. He and many other pilots read our UFO-Express and they didn't care that we published from our kitchen table, with scissors and glue. They appreciated that the contents included and supported their experiences as Italians and recounted stories from around the world in a credible way. Whether you were looking to validate a personal experience or just interested out of curiosity, our little publication filled the gap in coverage of these phenomena and the readers were grateful.

Obviously, given the work—and the amount of reading I was doing—I learned a great deal about sightings happening outside of Italy. The more I read, the more I realized that we would know so much more about UFOs, aliens, and extraterrestrial contact—almost everything, really—if we could only compile all the pieces and connect them. Reading the stories from all of the individual sightings made me certain that almost everything we needed to know was already in our possession. But what was lacking was the connection—the opportunity to put all those pieces together into a coherent whole. But if those connections were being made at all, they were the exclusive property of some scientific "entourage" who were either not interested in linking their data with others from different sectors or to disclosing them to the public.

The Internet has made it easier for us to communicate and investigate some aspects of the sightings of UFOs and while I believe this has improved the access to information for many people, the situation hasn't improved as much as I would like. I think it's time to acknowledge not only are we not alone, but that we are often visited— as the number of sightings suggests.

One morning, my doorbell rang, and I found myself face to face with a gentleman in his fifties. He clicked his heels on the doormat and said, "I am Colonel Attilio Consolante, stationed at the Sigonella Airport, in Catania. If it's convenient, could I speak with you?"

I was dumbfounded. Why had this man shown up at my home without calling in advance or at least seeing if we were available? What did he want? A thousand thoughts thronged in my mind about this strange visitor, but he was there in front of me and irritation was overpowered by my curiosity. I waved him into the living room.

With a glance, Emilio cautioned me to be prudent. But "prudence" wasn't my strong suit and his look was largely ignored.

Consolante came directly to the point: he wanted to receive a copy of our UFO-Express. Now I was really amazed. What did a man of his position want with our press service?

So, I asked him, "Why? What do you do at Sigonella?" I know. It *was* a bit abrupt. "Diplomacy" isn't my strong suit, either.

"We catalogue sightings of unidentified flying objects in Italy," he replied.

"And then what?" I pressed him.

"Well, we send them to the United States."

"That's it?" I asked.

"Yes." His answer was brief and certain, as though it should have been obvious. But I felt disappointed that he wasn't launching his own investigations or trying to learn more.

He subscribed to our service and left.

"Of course, he wants to subscribe," Emilio said when he was gone. "We're already cataloguing Italian and foreign news on the subject—something no one has ever done—and that saves him a lot of work. But his visit confirms it: all the governments are tracking UFOs. For all the denials, they know it's real and they're taking this topic seriously."

Later, I discovered that following a wave of sightings of UFOs in 1978, the then Italian Prime Minister Giulio Andreotti gave the Air Force the authority to collect, verify, and monitor reports concerning UFOs in Italy. The Air Force held the power to launch technical investigations into UFO sightings to determine if there were any correlation between their appearance and human events and/or natural phenomena. In addition, they could compel other agencies and entities to support their investigations. Private citizens were encouraged to report sightings to their local Carabinieri (like your police force) and the Carabinieri were supposed to forward the details to the Air Force.

The idea of putting the Carabinieri in charge of receiving UFO reports left me perplexed. All the jokes about the ineptitude of the Carabinieri came to my mind. Did they now suddenly have a squad of officers dedicated to hunting UFOs? It was ridiculous. Or least it was in the early 1980s when this policy was first announced. I think in the last ten years or so, there's been a change in the specializations of local police. Maybe they really do have a UFO squad now. Stranger things have happened . . . and some of them have happened to me.

CHAPTER TWENTY-THREE
THE PYRAMID—THE BEGINNING

One night in the summer of 1978, as I slept in my bedroom, dreaming as I often did, I had a very strange experience. The dream—whatever it was about, I don't remember that part—was interrupted by a sudden black screen as though the film in an old-fashion projector had broken. It wasn't that I woke up; I didn't. Instead, the dream story ended and a "being" appeared. He might have been a male—we'll say he was—but he was strange looking to me with his big round head set on a body that did not seem to be either particularly slim or fat but wasn't particularly muscular either. I had the impression that he had never been in a gym in his life and his body wasn't the most striking thing about him. Instead, what drew my attention was his head. It was milky-white, and I could see thin blue and pink capillary vessels through it. It reminded me of the delicate head of a newborn baby, born a little premature.

The nose was just outlined, the mouth was only a short, horizontal cut on a little chin. He had no hair at all—not on his face or chin or on his head. The neck was thin but not very long. But the eyes were really big and the clearest blue, placed above very high cheekbones. He gazed at me sweetly, simultaneously like someone who had lived a thousand years and had experienced and understood everything—while remaining perpetually young at heart.

His chest, arms, and hands were white-grey, maybe only a half-tone darker than his head, as if he wore a very thin, tight suit. I don't remember having seen nails or ears. In his hands, he held a pyramid of about 27.5 cm (about a foot, perhaps in English measures) high that looked to be made of some kind of opaque plexiglass. I couldn't see inside it. The pyramid rested on the open palm of his right hand and he gripped the apex of it with his left. He faced me like in the drawing below.

He let me watch him for a moment before beginning to talk. When he talked, the pyramid emitted an intense and yet somehow soft white light that pulsated in the same rhythm as his speech.

"You must build a pyramid like this one," he said.

"Why?" I asked. I wasn't afraid of him in the least, odd as he was. And as a general rule, I don't like strangers telling me what I should or shouldn't do.

"To talk to each other better," he answered.

The reply made complete sense to me . . . but the device did not. Considering my limited technical and engineering abilities, I knew I had no idea how I could construct what he asked.

"I can't," I said. "I don't have the skills. I don't have the technical knowledge."

"Don't worry, it is not difficult," he answered with a reassuring smile. "Listen, this is what you do. Take a phial and fill it half with mercury and half with salt and put them in a vacuum—"

"What kind of salt?" I interrupted. In my kitchen I had two kinds of salt: fine-grained salt for seasoning dishes and a coarse-grained "kitchen salt" for use in boiling water for pasta.

"Kitchen salt will be good," the being answered. "Then connect the phial to a spiral and the spiral to a pyramid's frame, then . . ."

"It is too difficult!" I interrupted again, troubled because I had lost the thread of his instructions. But this time my interruption was ignored. He continued as if he had not heard me.

" . . . place quartz inside the spiral over the phial . . ."

"But I don't know how," I repeated.

"Place an aluminum disk on each face of the pyramid. One of them must have a hole in its center . . ."

The more he talked, the more worried I became. He gave me no time to think and kept going, providing me with so much information that there was no time to assimilate it or understand it. I had almost forgotten the first things he'd said.

"Stop," I shouted. "Please, stop!"

"Build a pyramid as the frame. Use copper for the spiral and connect them . . ."

Now I was really angry. This man/being/thing appears in *my* dream and starts giving me orders and ignoring my interruptions and questions? No, no, *no*.

"Stop!" I shouted again. "I don't understand!"

But it was like he was a recording of a person and not the actual person. I was talking but he wasn't responding to me like he heard me.

" . . . when you connect them, remember that all must have a ratio: the one between the pyramid and the spiral must be the same; the quartz and the frequency must be harmonic. Even the inner volume of the phial's contents in the vacuum must be in balance . . ."

I don't remember what else he said. He continued to talk and talk . . . but I stopped listening. Instead, all my efforts concentrated on breaking the contact. If I was dreaming, I didn't want to be in this dream anymore. But it wasn't that easy. His will was incredibly strong, and he wanted me to hear him. I felt like I was at war with a power far mightier than I was. It took all the strength I had to finally break free.

I woke up breathless and with my heart beating wildly. I was surprised to find myself still in my bedroom, and even more surprised that it was still night. I could hear the distant traffic noises of the highway, but other than that, Rome was silent. I turned on the bedside light and looked around: everything about my bedroom looked exactly as it usually did. There was no light coming through the slats of the blinds and the clock on the nightstand announced an early morning hour not exactly conducive to investigation. I knew I had a busy day ahead of me, so I shook the "dream" from my mind, turned off the light, and fell asleep again within a few seconds.

Later, however, I remembered everything about the night before and I was filled with questions. I hadn't asked the being its name—not that it would have mattered, except that it might have been easier to tell this absolutely true, crazy, and not very credible story if I had been able to give my visitor an unusual name. But since I didn't ask—and since I prefer to stick to the facts—I will simply call him Dream Visitor.

Dream Visitor had given me very specific instructions, all of which I remembered vividly as well as the appearance of the pyramid he'd held in his hands. I had not seen the inside of it, so I had to rely on what he'd told me about that, but I had seen how it pulsed white light—bright when he talked but dimmer when I talked or shouted. But what did it mean? Was it just a wild dream?

I tried to remove the memory from my mind and got on with all of my usual morning routine—shower, teeth, coffee. But as soon as I had taken the first sips of my favorite drink, I found myself thinking about it again.

He could have been a creation of my unconscious mind and in my dream-like state I had given voice to some piece of technological information I had read or seen somewhere. Possible? Maybe. But if it were my unconscious mind, I would have made him beautiful: tall, blond, and muscular. Not some pale, fragile, big-eyed thing. If I was trying to tell myself something, it would have been more logical to choose a messenger I would listen to.

Oh well, I told myself. This dream, strange as it was, would fade like all dreams do. Within a few hours I would forget most of it. I got on with the rest of my day and was soon busy with other things. But the dream stayed with me. It was like my mind was split between the present reality and those technical directions—directions Dream Visitor set forth so clearly and logically that I could remember them even though in my daily life, mercury, spirals, copper, quartz, and the like were hardly typical items. In fact, they were almost completely foreign.

The morning after the dream, I had to meet a director I'd worked with before. I got in my 128 Fiat coupe and dealt with the traffic to get into town. For some time in Rome, it was forbidden to enter the city by car. So, I parked outside the old walls of Porta Pinciana and called a taxi to reach the director's office at the end of Via Veneto.

It was a good role and I was a good fit to play it. I left the director's office with the job booked and since the film would be shot entirely in Madrid, Spain and the surrounding areas, plans to travel for a little over a month—the time it took to make a low-budget film in those years. The Dream Visitor and his pyramid would have to wait.

It was weeks later when I thought of him again, on a beautiful Sunday afternoon when I wasn't scheduled to be on the set. I had slept well, but I didn't want to be at the hotel all day. I left, looking for a place not too far away where I could sit and think in peace. I smelled water, and my feet led me to the right place. I soon found myself at the edge of the Cibeles Fountain, one of the most beautiful in Madrid, in the large circular square from which it takes its name.

I had left my colleagues in the hotel lobby chatting about the glories of movies past and future, and the scenes that would be filmed the next day. I needed to get away from all that. The sounds of the water spurting upward and pouring into the fountain's basin were the perfect accompaniment to my thoughts. The Greek goddess Cybele watched me from the top of her chariot pulled by lions: beautiful, regal, and softly elegant. I craved the security and peace she symbolized. As I sat there admiring the talent of Francisco Gutiérrez, her sculptor, I felt free from worldly cares, far from everything and everyone. But only for a little while. Now that I was away from the film and its duties and requirements, my thoughts quickly returned to the "bomb" that had gone off in my life following the visitation by the strange little man.

Was he a dream? And if so, what did it mean? And if wasn't a dream, what was it? Was it connected to the experience that Emilio and I had with the UFO as we returned from the sea the year before?

I had no answers, only more and more questions. It was odd that I still remembered it so vividly and that I could recite almost all of the instructions I had been given about the construction of the pyramid. I have a good memory, but it was unusual for me to remember technical specifications so well. I had no training in that area and there was no reason that those details should have stuck with me.

I returned home from Spain with my finances stabilized from their constant oscillation and my mind still whirling on pyramid construction. I found myself assembling all kinds of materials into that shape. I wondered how to connect a glass phial with a copper spiral, and then the word "windings" gushed up inside me, and then the word "magnets" and then again "mirrors." Between my various commitments, words popped into my mind like answers. I realized that I had absorbed much more information than I consciously remembered. Just thinking about constructing the device Dream Visitor had told me to build seemed to open the doors of my mind. Solutions and new information that I hadn't remembered being told appeared simply by focusing my thoughts.

Edginess grew inside me. The impulse to attempt to build the thing became stronger and stronger every day, but my logical mind resisted it. I had no intention of doing something I didn't understand, that I didn't know how to do and that I had no rational basis for even attempting. It seemed crazy.

But was that true? How could I say it was crazy—that all Dream Visitor had told me was complete nonsense—if I hadn't tried it? If I had insufficient knowledge to say that what I had experienced was just a dream, it was equally true that I had insufficient knowledge to conclude that it wasn't real. In short, I hadn't investigated either way.

And the impulse to *do* something—to try to build this device—was very strong. I had to at least follow my own curiosity and see where it led, so I decided to proceed—but as rationally as possible. I told myself that I would investigate a bit and if it turned out there was something logical in what Dream Visitor had told me, I would continue and try to build the pyramid-device.

Having made this decision, I immediately felt relieved—but also intrigued. Here was a new project—something completely different for me to focus on. I began my search for information and quickly discovered that I didn't know anyone to ask the specific questions I had about what this device could be or how to build it—not even Emilio. So, I did what I always did in those days: I got out my encyclopedia and began to look up all the words related to the elements of the pyramid. For the Internet generation, I'll add this: a funny thing about using an encyclopedia was that explanations often referred you to other topics with the words ": *see*®" and the little arrow was always followed by another new word to look up. I followed those little arrows through volume after volume of my *Encyclopedia Treccani*, opening up all kinds of new possibilities and prospects.

Most of the time, the definition of the word I had searched for did not clarify anything for me about how to build this pyramid. Nevertheless, in the process of searching, I felt my mind humming and buzzing as ideas bubbled in my brain. I knew I was on the right track, even if I didn't know why.

I discovered that mercury reacts with non-metals such as halogens. Then I learned that halides are relatives of halogens. Then I learned that that sodium chloride (NaCl)—or table salt, as we know it—belongs in the family of halides. Therefore, combining kitchen-salt and mercury would have produced a volatile mercuric chloride—and perhaps formed some kind of power source. Maybe that actually made sense, I thought and read on. At the word "piezoelectricity," I learned that some crystalline substances, including quartz and various kinds of salts, can show a superficial electric charge, and that through applying alternating electric fields to these substances it is possible to produce continuous oscillations—frequency waves. Therefore, quartz combined with salt and electricity maybe had some validity in terms of constructing a communication device.

But what finally convinced me that I should attempt the pyramid's construction was the word "coherer." The encyclopedia explained a "coherer" was a piece of apparatus once used in telegraph machines of the early twentieth century. It was the first radio signal detector. It's no longer in use today, having been replaced by more sophisticated technologies, but it consisted of a glass phial containing two rustproof electrodes and metal filings (usually nickel, silver dust, and a little bit of mercury) and kept in a vacuum. When a radio signal was received by the electrodes, the metal particles would "cohere"—bind together—and in doing so ring a bell in tone identified as a "dot" or "dash" in the old telegraph Morse code.

This information was important to me. Someone had already put mercury in a glass vacuum—and achieved a communication device. I had never read anything about the workings of the telegraph before, but this—and the other reading I had done—began to convince me that my Dream Visitor wasn't talking complete nonsense. Maybe there was some truth to the device he proposed … and maybe it would be as easy to construct as he said.

A new experiment had begun.

CHAPTER TWENTY-FOUR
PRELIMINARY EXPERIMENTS

I bought a test tube—about the size used for blood tests—half a kilogram of mercury (I didn't know it was so expensive), and some kitchen-salt.

My encyclopedia hadn't told me what to expect when mercury interacted with non-metals, so I initiated my own cautious first test. I put a small pan on the kitchen gas, I threw in a bit of mercury and a bit of kitchen-salt, and I mixed this with a wooden spoon. Nothing caught fire—there were no sparks or lights—but the mercury melted into a thick fluid. I didn't see how it could power anything. Unluckily, or probably it is better to say *luckily*, at that moment, Emilio arrived. When he saw what I was doing, he shut off the stove and pulled me out of the kitchen, upset and concerned.

How was I supposed to know that heated mercury produced a poisonous vapor? It wasn't in the encyclopedia.

After the near disaster with the mercury, I decided to shift my attention from what was inside the pyramid to building the outside.

Constructing the first prototype

The strange guy with those big blue eyes had told me how to build the pyramid. I decided to follow his instructions exactly as I remembered them, even though I was very puzzled about how it would work.

I removed some copper wire from an old string of Christmas tree lights and wound it thickly around my test tube of mercury and salt, leaving both the top and the bottom of the tube wire-free. On these open ends, I attached a little magnet, as he had instructed. Then I framed the whole thing in a pyramid the planes of which I held together with more copper wire about 3mm thick. But immediately I ran into a question. He had said nothing about the pyramid's base. Was it supposed to be open or closed? If it were closed how would I add to the interior's contents and connect additional wiring? I couldn't see a way to keep the structure together well without a base, so I included a base, but cut into it a small gap (about 1.5 cm) that would enable me to thread wire through it.

It still wasn't right. The shape of the pyramid was off, and I realized that my 3mm wire was probably too thick. After a visit to the hardware store, I tried again with a much thinner copper wire (i.e., only about 1.5 mm) wrapped around the test tube mixture.

My first prototype pyramid was probably about 25 cm high—and a mess. I had so many difficulties cutting and soldering its copper panels that, in the end, it was much more important for me to be able to close the frame and to hold it upright than to consider whether it was proportionally correct. One thing I can say for certain: it wasn't at all like the pyramid that the Dream Visitor held in his hands ... but it was the best I could do.

There were problems inside the pyramid as well as outside. The copper spiral that attached the phial to the pyramid kept falling down. I knew it belonged on the inside of the pyramid so finally I built a wooden circular base to which I could affix the first coil of the spiral and then continue winding the remaining seven coils more securely. The base also provided a support for the test tubes and the magnets. Now all the structures stayed upright reasonably well.

Emilio had seen my determination to build the pyramid. But he was also afraid I was going to hurt myself and his concern expressed itself in an avalanche of gifts: I received "The Little Chemist," a children's chemistry set, followed by "The Little Electrician," "The Little Joiner," and every other relevant set he could find. These toys were the tools I used to build the first prototype.

In the end, I connected one end of the copper windings around the phial and its magnet to the pyramid's frame and the other end (with the other magnet) to the spiral of wire that protruded out of the pyramid's frame. Then I took a piece of quartz (a stone included in my "Little Mineralogist" set), and with very thin copper wire, I connected it to the vertex of the pyramid. I let it dangle a few centimeters from the phial. The aluminum disks were the easiest part since I did not have to make them. Instead, all I had to do was make the hole Dream Visitor had required: a big one in the center of one disk, and smaller ones on the edges of all four disks to hold them on the pyramid.

First prototype connected to a battery voice recorder.

Experiments with the first prototype

To me, the first prototype of the pyramid was beautiful—and I had made it entirely on my own. There was only a small problem: I didn't know how to make it work. But by now, you know that of course, I didn't give up. I tried everything I could think of . . . with sometimes disastrous results.

The first thing I tried was to connect the pyramid with an electric wire and insert the plug (of the device) in the wall socket of my home—and with a *bang*, I blew out the electric lights of not just my home—or even just my apartment building—*but the entire street!* I never confessed to anybody (except, of course, Emilio) that I was the one who caused that power outage. It took a fair number of electric company workers to get it going again.

So clearly, I didn't need to connect it to any other power source. Maybe the device would work on its own? But how could I tell? I didn't want to just stare at it and hope something happened. I wanted to verify it somehow. And then I remembered the famous "Voices of Friedrich Jurgenson" (from the name of the Swedish researcher who first discovered them in 1959). These "voices" were recordings of sounds made by those who have "passed on," presumably to another existential plane. Later, Konstantin Raudive, a Latvian physicist and engineer who settled in Germany, would build on Jurgenson's work by attempting to communicate directly with the dead.

Was that this pyramid's purpose? Was it picking up something from a dimension unseen and unheard by me?

I organized a trip with some friends to an Etruscan ruin near Rome. I figured the ancient home of a civilization that disappeared thousands of years ago, might be a good place to experiment with communicating with the dead.

When we reached the ruins, I connected the pyramid to an old, battery-operated portable tape recorder. It didn't have a built-in microphone and I did *not* connect an external microphone. Instead, I cut the microphone from the cable with a pair of scissors, connected one jack to the recorder, and the other to the pyramid. I placed the whole thing in a box and left it in the grass among the weeds for hours, far from where my friends and I enjoyed a beautiful day. We lit a fire, grilled sausages, and sat in the grass drinking wine and talking.

When I got home, I rewound the tape and patiently prepared to listen to hours of near silence.

But no.

About three quarters of the way through the recording, I could clearly hear a flute being played by someone who was far from expert and trying to learn. A few correct notes, error, repetition of some, them another try. It lasted for about a minute, then stopped.

Perplexed, but excited, I proposed other tests in two other ancient places. I chose those archaeological sites for their density—as I said, people have been living in those regions for thousands of years.

On one recording, for a few seconds, I heard heavy steps as if someone were crossing the floor of a large and empty room wearing heavy boots. But the recorder had been sitting outside on the grass the entire time, so it made no sense that it had captured an indoor sound. On another recording, for a few minutes, I heard someone humming a bit of tune that seemed very old. The sound grew louder and then faded away, as if the "hummer" had walked by the machine and kept going.

I convinced myself that, somehow, the "pyramid" worked. But surely, the Dream Visitor had not meant that this was the device's purpose? He had said that the device would help us "talk better." So, the dialogue I'd generated at the ruins was not particularly helpful—it wasn't even dialogue. The "pyramid" was supposed to be used to improve communications. It didn't seem to me that these strange sounds could guide mankind to anything better at all.

I suspended the trips to the ruins while I waited for my next inspiration and experiment. Life resumed a routine of lunches and dinners, movie work and Emilio... but the mystery of the pyramid was always in the back of my mind. I confess I enjoyed having a problem to mull over in my quiet moments. I preferred engaging with this mystery to worrying over when—or if—I would get another film.

Finally, I decided I needed the advice of someone who knew more about machines than I did, so I took my invention to my television repairman.

I chose him because I knew he was a nice guy—always smiling and a pleasure to deal with. But I'll never forget his expression when I set my project on his counter and explained my problem.

"Could it work, in your opinion?" I asked.

He stared first at me and then at my little pyramid for a long time without saying a word.

"This looks like a conical horn antenna, like the kind we used while I was in the army," he said at last. "But no, it could never work."

"Why?" I asked.

"Because it's used to transmit radio waves. To amplify them for communication in gigahertz. What frequency have you set if for?"

"I don't know," I answered. "I'm not even sure I know what you mean by 'frequency.'"

His brow furrowed with his confusion. "But didn't you say you made it yourself? How did you calculate how much quartz to use and where to place it?"

"Honestly, I didn't calculate it all." I smiled my most winning and innocent smile. "I took some quartz I had at home, rolled the copper wire around the phial and the little magnets until they looked big enough. That's how I did it."

He burst out laughing at my completely unscientific methods. But he was soon serious again. He gave the pyramid some more long, careful consideration and then said, "Well, at first glance, there are two things that are probably causing you problems. The first is that your quartz is so big and crude, you'd probably need a cannon to make it vibrate. The second thing is that your copper wires aren't insulated. The device is short circuiting. You should try it again with insulated copper and an industrial quartz crystal."

"Can you remake it for me?" I asked hopefully.

"No, I've got more work than I can do right now. And even if I had the time, I wouldn't. I don't want anything to do with these kinds of things."

I was disappointed—I would have liked to have the help of someone who knew more than I did about the technical aspects of what I was trying to build—but I was grateful for his suggestions.

My next stop was to an electronics store, where I moved through a crowd of rather heterogeneous-looking males thronged in front of a counter full of small, transparent containers. Each container was full of strange (at least to me!) gadgets. I headed straight for the nearest salesclerk.

"I want to purchase an industrial quartz crystal," I said.

"Which frequency?" he answered. And before I could reply, he pointed to a wall full of small containers similar to the ones at the counter. "Sorted by frequency. Choose what you want," he said and left me standing there.

And that's how I joined the crowd of men considering the containers. I walked casually up to the wall the clerk had indicated and perused the offerings like I knew what I was looking for. Then, faking indifference, I left the shop like I hadn't seen what I needed. But the truth was, I was completely overwhelmed. I didn't know what I was looking for. I did not understand what I was looking at in those containers. I had no idea what to choose or how to use it and I could tell by the clerk's gruff instructions I wasn't going to get much help in that store. I wanted to cry and stomp my feet in frustration like an angry toddler.

Fortunately, things went a little bit better when I went in search of the insulated copper wire. The salesclerk only asked me, "How many meters?"

"I don't know," I replied. "Keep unrolling it until I tell you to stop."

The clerk might have thought that was strange, but he did as I asked.

I didn't try to remake my invention using the insulated copper wire for a long time. I wanted help—I *needed* help—and I spent a good deal of time trying to think of someone I could ask, someone who would understand what I was doing and had better tools and understanding than I had. I didn't dare try to build a second prototype using my "little welder" tool kit. My first aluminum structure was already falling apart. Every time I touched it something would fall off. And the cheap child-sized soldering gun had burnt holes in my best table and a satin dress. I needed better tools—and someone who could use them more competently than I had. And then there was the problem of the quartz. I had no idea what frequency I was hoping to transmit and so I had no idea what size industrial quartz I needed.

While I pondered these issues, I kept the memory of what the strange little man of my dreamhad told me the pyramid device was for. "To talk better with each other," he had said. I added that to what I read about conical horn antennae and new ideas started to bubble in my brain.

Maybe some kind of loudspeaker was necessary?

I detached the speaker from an old record player and connected the wires to the pyramid. I bought many batteries, and when a friend offered, I detached a "variable-speed drive" from her son's electric toy train and I connected that to my device, too. I tried every speed, moving the drive's switch repeatedly until it stopped humming and started hissing. A spark and sudden crackling sound signaled it had burnt out and I had observed no change in the performance of my device.

I then bought a voltage selector. I connected it to the pyramid and the loudspeaker and inserted the plug in the wall socket. But all that happened was a thin wisp of smoke rose from the voltage selector and it was fried, too. Fortunately, I didn't blow out all the electricity in the neighborhood that time—but still my machine failed to work.

Around that time, I had made a new acquaintance—an aerospace engineer who was vice president of the Aerospace Research Center in Rome. Before that job, he had worked many years with Luigi Broglio of the Italian Space Agency (ASI). He was around sixty years old and a full-bodied gentleman with thick white hair and a beautiful bass voice. My new friend was also incredibly smart and fortunately also open-minded and curious. At that time, he was working with an Anglo-Indian archeologist and Asian languages expert, David Davenport. Among Davenport's projects was a translation of the *Vymanica Shastra*, an ancient Sanskrit text which describes a machine called the Vimana, an ancient aircraft capable of transporting goods and people. The *Vymanica*, together with *Rig Veda*, *Ramajana*, and *Mahabharata* are the books that form the basis of the Hindu religion. This new acquaintance of mine was trying to bring (almost officially) this ancient Indian knowledge into the Aerospace Center.

Unfortunately, Davenport's premature death interrupted his translation. Only one of his books was left to us in Italian, *2000 BC: Atomic Destruction,* which theorized that the destruction of the ancient civilization of Mohenjo Daro in what is now the country of Pakistan was not a massacre as previously believed, but the result of something similar to an atomic bomb. Davenport and other scientists had reached this conclusion after analyzing samples taken from the site.

One evening, I invited my new friend to my home to talk with him about the pyramid. I wanted to know his opinion and to ask if he was available to help. Even though he was about thirty years older than me and a relatively new acquaintance, I felt comfortable having him over and talking to him about all my strange ideas. Perhaps the engineer had hopes of a different kind about my invitation, but when I showed him the pyramid and told him about its inspiration, his expression grew serious. He stared at me for a very long time with the same puzzled expression I recognized from my friend the TV repairman. Finally, I pressed him to say something—anything. He'd been quiet for so very long.

"So? What do you think?" I asked.

"I am truly and sincerely shocked," he answered at last. "How did you get this idea?"

"I told you. I had a dream. In my dream, this being appeared. He told me to do it," I repeated. "I kept telling him I couldn't do it—that I didn't have the skills—but he said, 'Don't worry, it is easy.' So, I tried."

"It is not so easy," my new friend said. "I know that you do not have the necessary knowledge to invent this sort of thing, or to build it. During dreams, sometimes knowledge surfaces from the subconscious … but you couldn't have constructed this just from your subconscious."

"I don't really care where the knowledge came from," I interrupted. "I just want to make this gadget *work*. And that's what I want to know from you. In your opinion, could it work? And how? I'm supposed to place three small mirrors in each corner of the pyramid's base, but at the moment, I don't know how to assemble that. Will that make a difference? Where do the mirrors go?"

My engineer friend looked a little upset that I had rejected his theories and analysis about the inadequacies of my subconscious mind.

"So," he started again, "in this pyramid, I see ideas realized in the same way that you might think about pizza. Anyone can make a pizza, but it takes specialized skills and practice to make good one. You have all the ingredients, let's say. The quartz for the frequency, the magnets and the insulated copper to create an electromagnetic field, the aluminum plates to contain the field and bounce it back within the container, the small mirrors to amplify it. Did you know that these are the same principles used in lasers? And the hole in the aluminum plate is used to discharge the wave created by the frequency. Even your spiral has a logical function, though the way you've placed it is unlikely to have the necessary effect. The only thing I don't understand is the phial. Why is it there?"

"The phial should glow," I said. "In the dream, I had been told that the mercury and salt should be combined in a vacuum. Both the phial and the pyramid (inside) should be vacuums, but I don't know how to do it."

"If you want it to glow, why not use an LED?" And when I asked, he continued, "A LED (Light Emitting Diode) is the little thing that lights up when the device is working."

"No," I replied. "I don't need a LED light in there. The reaction created between the components in the phial is what glows. That's a part of how it works."

"Are you sure? You might not have understood—"

"Yes, I'm sure," I told him. "I understood that, but there was more. I didn't understand it all. It was an upsetting experience and when I woke up, I knew there was a lot that I either missed or that I didn't understand at all."

My new friend stayed with me a little bit longer. He explained concepts I do not recall and made sketches on a piece of paper with calculations I did not understand. But when he looked at me, I perceived in his expression that he wasn't interested in my invention. What interested him was how I'd known to put these elements together and where that information had come from. Perhaps the story of the dream and the strange being who presented the information to me had been too much for him.

Over the following months, I called him a few more times, hoping to arrange another meeting. But he always pretended not to be in, signaling that he didn't want to help me refine the device or figure out how to make the next prototype. Perhaps he'd chalked me up as a crazy actress? I don't know, but I took the hint and stopped approaching him.

CHAPTER TWENTY-FIVE
EXPERIMENTS WITH THE SECOND PROTOTYPE

It was several years later before I attempted a second prototype—1985, to be exact.

Emilio and I worked on our clipping service every month but acting roles had slowed considerably—so much so that I no longer expected that I'd be doing much more work in film. Although my father occasionally helped me financially, I was coming to the realization that sooner rather than later, I was going to have to make big changes in how I earned my living. Ultimately, fate decided the matter for me—but I won't get ahead of myself.

In the meantime, however, following a booming interest in Egyptology all over the world, pyramids had become fashionable. I saw them everywhere in Italy, in all shapes and sizes. One day, I saw one in a store window and I realized it would be an excellent container for my device, if it could be constructed as a vacuum. It was about the same size as the one the Dream Visitor had held in his hands. But the shape wasn't quite right. The one in the store window was a scale model of the pyramid of Cheops, but the one I had been instructed to build should have been taller and more pointed at the top. I bought it, hoping (wrongly as it turned out) that it would work. With the purchase, once again my mind started turning on how to reconstruct the communication device my Dream Visitor had told me to build.

The new pyramid I had purchased was also made of plexiglass but had a square base with a cylindrical column in the center. The cylinder could be used as a pedestal to place little objects (e.g., razor blades, samples of meat, etc.). I had heard about "pyramid power" or "pyramidology" in which objects placed inside a pyramid regenerated, mummified, or dehydrated under the influence of the pyramid's energy. In my small experiments, this phenomenon really occurred—which was interesting—but I quickly left this exploration and went on with my real purpose: trying to figure out how to use this new pyramid to make the communication device I had been instructed to build.

I thought the outer casing of this pyramid would work, but the center cylinder was a problem. That problem was solved when I had a company that specialized in producing billboards, banners, and other outdoor signs cut me a new plexiglass base that was cylinder-free. Now I could attach the other components of my device on this smooth base and let the rest of the pyramid cover them, like a hat.

Now it was time to rebuild the inner workings of the device. Fortunately, I had made another new friend, an electrical engineer, without whose help I would never have been able to complete this work. I explained to him what I needed—giving him the instructions I was given my dream. He followed those guidelines, but there were some substantial changes. For example, the phial was re-made, but this time, instead of buying a premade container, it was custom-made by a glazier who blew glass around a copper wire so that the phial had two poles. Moreover, now that we had a steady base, we were able to place the three mirrors on each corner of the pyramid's base. The quartz was replaced with a smaller and purer stone. It did not dangle from the rest of the workings as it had before. Instead, it was fastened with two thin copper wires to both copper extremities of the phial. Of course, conceptually, the pyramid was the same, but the workmanship and the electrical connections were greatly improved.

But even with the contribution of my electrical engineer's knowledge, the pyramid didn't work. Unfortunately, we were never able to make the inside of the pyramid a true vacuum. Even using a silicone tube, air came into both the phial and the pyramid's interior from somewhere. The only positive result we got from the second prototype came when we connected the pyramid to a piezo-electric lighter I used in the kitchen. It brought back the memory of my early readings about piezoelectricity and it was the only time I saw the phial light up. It wasn't the same clear white light I had seen my dream—it was more of violet-greenish color—but I was happy to see it, all the same.

It was a long while before I had the chance to think about these experiments again. Fate, as I have said, intervened and threw me a curve that changed much about the life I had been living—and set me on an entirely different course.

Second prototype—closed.

Second prototype—open.

PART THREE

THE THIRD LIFE
PALERMO AGAIN

CHAPTER TWENTY-SIX
HOME AGAIN

I got sick. Very sick.

The doctors did not know what was wrong with me. My symptoms were various and didn't seem to add up to any specific diagnosis. I saw several different specialists, none of whom could figure out what was wrong, despite all kinds of tests and questions. They determined that I was basically in good health and having no other diagnosis for my symptoms of extreme fatigue, dizziness, and weakness—and given my profession as an actress—they decided that I was having a serious nervous breakdown. Probably, at least according to them, my condition was brought on by the stress of being without work due to the economic crisis that plagued Italy during that time.

It was true that there were financial stresses: I had no film roles and the hard work of putting out the UFO clipping service barely paid its expenses. But as the months passed, my physical symptoms got worse and worse. Emilio watched me decline with increasing concern. He knew me very well—better than anyone, I think—and he doubted that I was having a mental breakdown. He knew something else was wrong with me, but unable to get any assistance from the medical profession, he made a desperate decision to save my life.

He loaded me on a plane and took me home to my mother in Palermo.

My mother called the family doctor, who had known me since I was fourteen. He came immediately. He looked at the inside of my eyes, opened my mouth to look at my throat, listened to my chest, and then touched the skin of my thighs, which made me deeply uncomfortable. I was sick and weak and dizzy. I hadn't been well enough to go out for months and I felt like a shadow of my usual self. The last thing I needed was a lewd, old doctor taking advantage of me. His touch plunged me into a dark despair. I started sobbing quietly. He stopped after squeezing the muscles from my thighs down to my ankles. Then he turned to my mother and said in Sicilian dialect, "*A stapicciotta ci manca u ferru.*" This girl lacks the iron.

He patted me gently, sympathetically. "You must be very patient. The absorption of iron in the blood is a very long thing. It will take some time."

I felt awful for thinking such bad thoughts about him when all he was doing was completing his examination. He was checking my legs to verify if the lack of oxygen provided by proper iron levels had already become visible in my skin, and for the tightness of leg cramps, another sign of an iron deficiency. And he was absolutely right: I spent almost a year and a half recovering from severe anemia, caused by decades of eating a poor diet. By the time I was well again, I urgently needed two things: a home and a job.

I no longer had a home in Rome and was forced to give up the apartment in the Cassia where I had lived for so long. But with my health in the balance I could no longer keep it. And my economic autonomy had abruptly ended when I moved back to Palermo and there was no means to continue to pay for it. For a while I had some hope of returning to Rome and resuming my acting career. But things were tough throughout Italy during that time, and the film industry had suffered so greatly that even my talent agent had been forced into a new occupation. And then there was the fact that I was now in my forties—too old to play the young love interest and too young to play her mother—and roles for me had been steadily declining. I gave some thought to trying the stage again, but when I remembered how much I disliked the work of live theater I had second thoughts. Transitioning from film to the stage would be difficult and I had to accept that, even though I felt better, my health still wasn't strong. I wasn't physically well enough to face the uncertainties and challenges of an actor's life: bronchitis and flu from long hours and chaotic schedules, intestinal infections from different food abroad, dangerous situations due to the incompetence or ignorance of the producers. And I still wanted my independence; I didn't want to marry. That was for later.

It was hard to let go of my career and my life in Rome. I believe that the mental scream of despair that I sent to the sky was heard all the way to Epsilon Eridani, a star 10.5 light-years distant from our solar system. I didn't want to let any of it go, but Fate had dealt its hand and I had little choice.

After a difficult and brief period as a guest at my mother's apartment, I moved into my grandmother's old house. It was my decision to leave; I couldn't stand another day of arguments and rebukes. I don't believe she ever agreed with any decision I ever made in my life: she wanted me to marry and have children as she had done and didn't understand how the lives of women were changing dramatically from what she had known. She didn't understand my fierce need to live my life without becoming the property of a man. Our disagreements weren't helping me recover, so I moved out.

So, I had a new place to live, but finding work was much more difficult. Nobody wanted an actress, known or not, working in their offices. I think people had a prejudice against someone who had worked in film. They made all kinds of assumptions about me that weren't accurate or fair because I'd been an actress. And in truth, most offices didn't feel right to me. I had worked in a couple, but only briefly. I had grown used to working in my own ways, on my own schedule, and according to my own interests and inclinations . . . but I knew that would have to change, too.

Ultimately, by networking with some old friends from school I found a job. It was hell but I kept it for eighteen years—until I reached retirement age. It was at a local company that had the concession for billboards in airports in Italy and around the world. Among other tasks, I was in charge of contacting foreign airports (since I was the only one who spoke English) to arrange the installation of advertising for Italian customers. I would then review and sign the English-language contracts for my boss, a man a few years younger than me who didn't know a word of English and didn't want to sign them himself. I also managed and translated the foreign invoices before sending them to the accounting office.

Considering that I had no specialization in these fields, I was lucky to get the opportunity. Had it not been for my resourcefulness and willingness to learn, I probably couldn't have kept that job all those years. I might even have enjoyed the work had my co-workers not assigned me every menial task that no one else wanted to do. In addition to my own work, I was answering phones and making photocopies on behalf of my colleagues who "were busy and had other things to do."

Emilio often wondered how I hadn't bankrupted the business given that I managed quotes and currencies from various countries. Money was never something I was particularly good at—and keeping track of it for a business was an unlikely job for me. Emilio worried that one day I'd make a mistake serious enough to get me in big trouble—just from sheer inattention. Thankfully, though, that never happened.

I had been working for just over a year when two things happened: I was asked to work on a candidate's election campaign and Frank Sinatra toured Italy.

It was 1987, and Sinatra's tour would perform at Palermo's *Stadio della Favorita* on June 13th. Frank Sinatra had been, and still was, my linguistic idol since I was fourteen—in the sense that the American-English lyrics of his songs were easy for me to understand and learn from. As a teenager, I spent my free time listening to his music, which I liked a lot, and writing out the words I was listening to. Then, I looked up the meanings of those words, which wasn't always easy because the phonetics of the English language does not always correspond to the spoken word. However, a little by intuition, a little because I was a good guesser, I always managed to learn some English from Sinatra's music. Oh, how I had hoped he would one day come to Palermo! I even wrote him a fan letter, addressed to "Mr. Frank Sinatra, Hollywood, USA."

You can imagine how thrilled I was to learn that, many years later, Frank Sinatra was finally coming to Palermo! In spite of the passage of time, I liked to think that my adolescent request many years before had something to do with it. And you can imagine my excitement when, in return for my work on the election, I was given two free tickets for the show.

My excitement quickly turned to disappointment and irritation, however, when I learned that my tickets were not for seats in the amphitheater but for a spot in the grass where the football (or soccer, as you call it in America) players raced up and down. I was angry. It felt like the hard work I'd done on the campaign had been rewarded with a "thank you" gift not much better than a couple of coffees at the local café. As much as I loved Sinatra, I couldn't imagine myself—a woman in her forties—sitting cross-legged in the humid-wet grass like a child. I couldn't do it. Not even for Sinatra. I gave the tickets to a colleague.

After a couple of years of working for the airport concession company in Palermo, I asked to be switched from full-time to part-time. My request was granted but I soon realized I'd given myself "the hoe on my foot" as the farmers say. Now I had to do eight or nine hours of work in only five hours.

In the meantime, I relieved the stress of work by spoiling myself with little things. I had discovered that the coffee bar below the office sold small bottles of Moet & Chandon champagne—just enough for two small glasses. So, around eleven a.m.—the hour when almost everyone in the office ordered a lunch delivery—I ordered my champagne and a plate of appetizers. It drove my co-workers crazy to see me sipping champagne and eating *hors d'ouvres* for lunch.

When I started working part-time, I began another habit that drove the people I worked with insane with jealousy. In summer, the climate in Palermo is very hot—scorching hot. It is so hot at lunchtime that the asphalt becomes soft and your shoes leave prints in it that will remain there for posterity—or until the road is resurfaced. Almost everyone prefers to spend the lunch break in the office rather than going out, getting into a hot car, and waiting for the air conditioning to reach its maximum just to be able to breathe. And worse, the garage closest to the office wasn't exactly nearby. During the midday hours it was a long, hot, and unpleasant walk. But, as a part-timer, I could leave at two p.m., which meant that in the summer, I had to face that scorching walk to my car at some of the hottest hours of the day. It felt even hotter after five hours working in the building where the air conditioning was cranking at maximum cool. The disparity between the inside temperature and the outside temperature destroyed me every time.

I was friendly with some members of the ANSA (National Associated Press Agency) that had its Palermo headquarters in the same office building. They knew I was writing articles for various newspapers, and often I stopped by their offices to chat—and complain. Their office was the environment that I preferred, and the life of a journalist still suited how I wanted to work and think. When I could, I sought out the conversation with those other curious minds and appreciated the things I could learn from them. Then one day, one of my friends at ANSA gave me one of the most thoughtful and beautiful gifts I have ever received:

A parking pass for the Port of Palermo garage!

It was only 150 meters away from the office (a little less than 500 feet in English measures). It was a small lot with only space for the journalists, a few of the executives who worked in the building, and of course the port white collar workers ... and now, one harried actress turned jack-of-all-trades could park there, too. This gift saved many a long hot walk to my car in the afternoons. Not that the walk itself was dangerous, although, I suppose that since at that time of day there weren't many pedestrians and I might have been something of a target. But that never worried me. I just hated facing the terrible heat.

It was a wonderful gift and I appreciated it greatly. But of course, I still had to walk several long, hot city blocks to the garage, and then hundreds of meters more to my car during the hottest hours of the day. I soon found a solution to that walk as well.

Right in front of the office, there was a large space where horse-drawn carriages often parked, waiting for tourist fares. The seats of those carriages were lined with velvet, now worn out, but which once must have been the pride of some old coachman. The horses waited near a decorated area with dozens of small bows tied to the lattice work. The carriage drivers parked there every day, waiting to transport the tourists who visited when the large cruise ships docked—usually at a premium price for the experience of traveling downtown Palermo in an old-style horse and carriage.

One day, as I stood at the front of my office building, trying to build up my courage and stamina to step out into the heat, I discovered by chance that the horse-drawn carriages could enter into the port through the main entrance. I wasn't sure it would work, but it was two p.m. and the air was so hot and still it burned my lungs when I inhaled. There wasn't even the slightest breeze off the sea. Nothing but hot, hot air. I figured it was worth a shot so . . .

Then I looked up and found one of the coachmen staring at me. He was about sixty, a man who looked like he'd lived a hard life with his thin frame and droopy long mustache. His coach was the closest to the door where I stood and he sat on the box, eating something from a small metal pot that his wife certainly prepared for him. I could tell by the way he looked at me that he understood what I was thinking.

"Do you want me to take you somewhere?"

"No, thanks," I replied. "I see you are having lunch . . ."

"Don't worry about it. Do you have to go far?"

"Actually, I just have to get to the port to get my car. It's in the parking lot there. But this heat . . . it really bothers me," I replied, smiling what I hoped was one of my best and most appealing smiles.

He finished eating, put away his little pot, and told me, "Jump in. I'll take you."

"How much?" I asked. I was pretty sure I would pay it, but I needed to at least know what his expectations were.

"Whatever you want to give," he replied and lifted the reins to get his horse's attention.

I offered him a little tip—an amount equal to a few coffees—and with this agreement, I avoided walking in the heat all summer long.

When my colleagues discovered my "anti-heat" solution, instead of finding it funny, they responded the same way they did to my champagne brunches. They didn't like it at all. They didn't like having a former actress—and one still very well-known on the island—as a colleague. Even my boss was uncomfortable with me. We did not understand each other. Sometimes he said words in Sicilian dialect, and I could not recall their meaning. Often my answers to his questions were not in accord with his logic and he was convinced I was making fun of him, which made him furious. According to him, I wasn't stupid enough to give such an answer innocently, and therefore, I was playing little games and teasing him. In reality, I was too naive to play power games. I genuinely didn't know what he was talking about. I had no experience in business and honestly didn't know the difference between profits and earnings. I didn't know how to read a budget. After all, I had never fought for my money. I had agents for that.

I might have quit a thousand times were it not for the fact that there was so little work on the island. Whatever problems I had with him as an individual, my boss had created a nice little niche business in Sicily—a place where doing business can be difficult if you're not very smart and a little sneaky. Compared to him, I was naive in every sense of the word, and I do not think he ever understood this. He thought I was the clever one.

I must admit, however, there was something in my character that might have contributed to my boss' impression of me. While the others lowered their heads if reprimanded—whether the reprimand was deserved or undeserved—I expressed my opinion whether it irritated him or not. The concepts of his "importance" or the idea that he deserved any special "respect" or "adulation" wasn't something I ever experienced or practiced. Still, he hired me (and I had no particular skills) and I owed him for that. I was grateful to have a job. But I found working in Palermo to be very different from what I had known in Rome. It might have been the local economy and it might have been because of the peculiarities of island culture, but it was quite an adjustment.

I found it necessary to distract myself with other things.

CHAPTER TWENTY-SEVEN
STRANGE OCCURENCES AT CASTRONOVO OF SICILY

One day in 1987, the local paper carried a story about a UFO sighting on the island of Sicily at Castronovo di Sicilia about 76 kilometers from Palermo (an hour and half's drive). The piece, written by a local journalist, seemed like a promising investigation to me, so Emilio and I decided to take a trip there over a weekend to see if we could find out more.

Castronovo is a town of 5,000 inhabitants at 660 meters above sea level, in the Sicani Mountains. The Platani river flows beneath it, cutting through the valley below. It is small and picturesque and otherwise pretty much unremarkable. When we arrived, Emilio and I met Franco Landolina, an experienced journalist and the author of the piece I had read in the newspaper, *Giornale di Sicilia*. He reported that a mysterious luminous object appeared in the sky above Castronovo every night for a week, causing inexplicable telekinetic phenomena throughout the city.

According to Landolina, at about one a.m., a thirty-one-year-old auto repair garage owner was suddenly awakened by his wife. The bed, the windows, and the whole house vibrated violently, and a very loud noise, like the sound of a "pneumatic hammer," tore through the silence of the night. The witness told Landolina that his first thought was that the mafia was storming the house. He rounded up his family—his wife and five children—to hide behind a wall of reinforced concrete along the perimeter of the building. After a while, however, he began to doubt that the sound was the sound of gunfire and, suddenly fearless, went to search. Once in the dining room, he could see a very brightwhite light flooding the kitchen skylight through the open door. All the while, the noise and vibration continued, as strong as ever. He described the light as very intense and very white, almost blinding. He had never seen anything like it before, but he was not afraid of it. He knew immediately that it wasn't a plane or a helicopter, even though the noise was similar.

The coachmaker left his house, hoping to catch a glimpse of what was making the noise and causing the bright light. From the street, he could see a cylindrical object with two flashing red lights on its sides and another bluish light flashing somewhat higher up hovering about ten to fifteen meters above his house. The rest of the object was less clear, seeming to fade into the darkness of the night. After about half an hour of hovering there, the object suddenly disappeared.

Many other witnesses in Castronovo corroborated the garage owner's sighting, and even Landolina, our journalist, said he heard the loud noise.

A couple of nights later, late in the evening, the witness was driving home with his wife and children. At a curve in the road, his headlights swept over what he thought were two luminous cylinders resting on the ground. Before he could process what he'd seen, the driver's side door—which he was certain had been locked—swung open suddenly and every object inside the vehicle was suddenly sucked out as if some unseen hand had attached a giant vacuum hose.

The man immediately pulled over, in fear for his family, afraid they too would be sucked out of the moving car. Once he had assured himself that they were safe, he got out of the car and walked back to where his family's belongings and his work tools lay in the street. He gathered them quickly, looking around for some sign of what had caused the door to jerk open like that. But it was a dark and quiet night. Dark and quiet in the way that only very small towns can be. But the UFO was once again spotted in the night sky on that night and on several of the following nights.

Because of our prior work on the subject of UFO sightings, Emilio and I knew that the Carabinieri would have taken a report. We went to the local Carabinieri barracks, hoping to get more information. The station's huge wooden door was closed. After we knocked, a square-shaped peephole opened and a gruff voice with a strong local accent asked, "What do you want?"

I introduced myself as a journalist with the *Journal of Mysteries*, a publication that focused on paranormal and other mysterious phenomena and for which I had really written occasionally. I told him I was doing a story and hoped to get some information. He made me repeat it twice, then finally opened the door.

The middle-age man who stood before us in his uniform demanded, "Documents."

I was surprised. I had expected to be refused completely from the way he'd acted, peering through the peephole and having me repeat myself. But we both produced our identification. Emilio's looked like it had been issued during World War I—it was old and faded from constantly being stuffed in the pocket of his jeans. I pulled mine from the bag on my shoulder and handed it to him. Without a word, he closed the door and left us there in the street, presumably, to wait.

It was late morning, but there was no one on the street—not a soul. It was like being in the desert or some abandoned town in a western movie. He made us wait a good quarter of an hour, before leaning out of the doorway to hand us back our documents.

"We have nothing to do with this, but if you want, you can contact the Lercara Carabinieri Station, eight kilometers from here." And he closed the door in our faces.

Accustomed to Roman cordiality, this reception left us shocked. But undaunted, we drove the eight kilometers to the town of Lercara.

We found the square here empty and the station practically lifeless. We were met by a lieutenant who was very kind at first. He asked for our identification . . . and then told us he couldn't give us any information about the sighting at all. The way he said it made it clear: he knew about the sighting. He just wasn't going to tell *us* anything about it.

"But can you tell us the name of the witness?" I asked, even though I already knew.

"No, I'm sorry. It is classified."

"But you can tell us if it's a reliable witness? You all know each other here."

"Yes, as far as we know, it's a pretty reliable witness," he said, smiling.

"And can you tell us if you've done any investigation in the area where the object was seen?"

"No, I'm sorry, it was not possible because we have only one truck, and it's broken at the moment."

I had to choke back a giggle over that. It was obvious by then that we weren't going to get much more information, so we left. In Palermo, I really did write up an article about the encounter for the *Journal of Mysteries* with the information I already had. Something mysterious was indeed going on in the skies of Italy ... but when we'll ever know the truth, I don't know.

CHAPTER TWENTY-EIGHT
NEW EXPERIMENTS WITH THE PYRAMID

It was perhaps around 1988 when I decided to introduce a group of my friends to my electro-encephalaudio ("EEA" rather than an EEG, as I call it) bio-feedback machine.

I had not used it in a while—not since my experiments with the plant in my apartment in Rome. On this occasion, a group of friends had gathered in my apartment in Palermo for the evening, and we decided to conduct a very different kind of experiment: we wanted to see if each of us could enter an alpha state at will, verified by the EEA. We did this for a while until everyone was tired of it. I unplugged the cables and electrodes from the device and brought out the pyramid instead. My friends passed it from hand to hand, while I explained what I believed it was supposed to do, then I put it down near the EEA. The conversation continued about the infinite possibilities that might be realized if I could ever get it working.

We were all stunned when, suddenly, we heard a sound from the EEA. We were more perplexed than excited because the EEA couldn't have been making any noises: the wires and electrodes were not connected.

We listened to that sound for about ten minutes. When I finally removed the pyramid from the EEA machine, the sound stopped. By this time, it was very late, and we decided to suspend our continued experimentation for another day. A few days later, we repeated the experiment. But we discovered, to my great dismay, that the EEA no longer worked. It wouldn't work with the pyramid and it wouldn't work on its own as a bio-feedback device. Somehow it had broken and unfortunately, because many years had passed since I had purchased it, the manufacturer was no longer in business. I didn't know who else to contact to attempt a repair. My only consolation in the face of this loss was knowing that, in some strange way, the pyramid resting on the biofeedback machine had produced a sound independent from its connection to any power source. That meant that something in the pyramid had triggered the biofeedback of the device. Something in the pyramid was working, somehow.

In 1990, when I still thought that making the pyramid work would be simple, I was introduced to a new acquaintance who worked for a company that made security systems. But in addition to that, he was passionate about his hobby: using infrared cameras in buildings and homes alleged to be haunted to see if they could pick up images the naked eye could not.

His research interested me less than the fact that he had some technical knowledge, a laboratory to work in, an oscilloscope[8], and maybe, an interest in helping me discover how to make my pyramid work. But I wanted to make a connection with him first before jumping into talking about the pyramid, so I suggested that he could try using his infrared technology on animals. I recounted to him how many times I had noticed a dog or a cat, especially domestic ones, suddenly follow something invisible to us humans. The tension of their bodies, the attentiveness of their eyes and the way they turned their heads as if they were seeing something had always made me crazy with curiosity—especially when there was no one else in the room but me and the animal.

It was the right trigger. The conversation became more intimate (from the "technological" point of view), and I managed to introduce the topic of the communication device I'd been instructed to build in my dream. I left out the part about the Dream Visitor; I wanted, I said, technical advice. One Sunday not too long after our conversation, he invited me to the laboratory where he worked.

It wasn't easy for me to get up early on a Sunday and get myself ready to make the appointment on time, but I did it. I brought the pyramid in a bag and Emilio with me, too. I began by explaining the strange event with the bio feedback machine, but I left the pyramid in the bag and didn't mention the shape of the device. When I could

---

8 An oscilloscope makes a graph of varying voltage or power signals.

tell that his interest was fully cooked, I pulled out our pyramid like a magician pulling a rabbit out of a hat.

I had expected him to be fascinated and excited . . . but instead, there was a long silence and not the slightest reaction.

I immediately feared that he regretted inviting me. After all, he was still a technician, still a scientist of a kind. Perhaps I had hoped too much from his open discussion of ghosts and spirits?

But after a pause that seemed incredibly long, he silently reached out his hands for the pyramid and took it to his work area. He connected it to the oscilloscope and started turning one of the knobs.

Probably with very different expectations, we all focused our attention on the oscilloscope's screen of wavy greenish lines set on a black background. I did not understand what the lines meant, and my host did not help me. He just kept turning the knob and changing the way he connected the pyramid to the oscilloscope. He didn't say anything at all. Not a single word.

It went on like that for a while. I could feel his irritation rising. I waited until I figured he'd had enough time to determine if the pyramid was something that could work or not, then I urged him to tell me his thoughts, at least as a courtesy so I wouldn't have to guess at them.

"I'm baffled," he told me.

"Why?" I asked hopefully.

"Because this *thing*"—he pointed at the pyramid—"cannot work in theory or in practice. It does not make any technical sense . . ."

"But . . ." I pressed him.

"But . . . it emits something or receives something. It doesn't last long, but there is something there. What I see here"—he pointed at the oscilloscope's screen—"are not the frequencies of household appliances like a washing machine or refrigerator. I know those frequencies well. There are other common ones that I also know well. And the laboratory is shielded so we're not picking up something from outside. There is definitely something emitting from your pyramid, but I don't know what it could be. I've never seen anything like it."

"Great!" I said, trying to contain my excitement long enough to ask the right follow-up questions. "How do we find out more?" I thought

I was on the brink of finding the partner I had long needed in the development of the Dream Visitor's device.

"Well, more study and experimentation, I guess," he replied.

"And you could do it?" I asked. I was sure that his own curiosity would push him to agree.

"No," he replied. His tone suddenly changed. He sounded dismissive and mocking as he continued. "I cannot use my boss's lab equipment for this. And even if I could, I wouldn't. I don't have time for this kind of thing."

I was very disappointed but not particularly surprised. By now, I knew well the reaction some people have to things they cannot easily explain. For them, curiosity quickly turns to unease. I was already looking for the words to make a hasty exit (without being rude, of course) when I realized he had not finished.

"You know," he began hesitantly, "I too dreamed of a pyramid..."

As soon as he said the words, I collapsed onto a work stool in astonishment.

"Really?" I exclaimed. "When? There were the same elements? Did you make it? Does it work?" I shot questions at him one after the other, eager for his answers.

"Wait," he told me. He left the lab and started toward the office, where there was a modern shelving unit storing tools and supplies. He moved something, and a part of the bookcase rotated to reveal a wall safe. He opened the safe and brought me four thick copper rods, four porcelain insulators (like the kind used in the old-style streetlights), and a "little pebble" which he told me was industrial quartz.

He put them on the counter. He arranged the square porcelain insulators and inserted the four copper rods into the holes in the centers. Holding the rods together at their tips, he said, "This is what I did."

"But you didn't place the industrial quartz. Why?" I asked.

"Because it won't work. It *can't* work. It makes no sense," he answered dryly. "I dreamed of it in 1986... but nothing specific, not like yours. And I had a strong impulse to build it. But then I let it go. Because it cannot work," he repeated stubbornly.

I pleaded with him to try again but was no use. He wouldn't attempt again with my ideas combined with his because his knowledge and beliefs about what could work and could not work blinded him. And, in my opinion, he was also a little afraid of what it would mean if it *did* work.

He told me nothing else about his dream and was evasive about any more details.

We have not met again.

CHAPTER TWENTY-NINE
THE PYRAMID ATTRACTS SOME UNWANTED ATTENTION

After another period of "pyramidal calm," on December 30th, 1990, Emilio and I decided to take a trip. I was on holiday from my office, the weather was beautiful—sunny and warm—and the idea of spending a day outdoors with the pyramid had me quite excited. I wanted to find a deserted place, possibly another ruin or an archaeological site, and connect the pyramid to a portable, battery-operated radio tuned to a "white space" signal. A "white space" refers to a frequency that has been allocated to a local broadcasting service but is unused. My theory was that perhaps, when the radio was connected to the pyramid, we would hear something through it on the open channel.

But finding anything close to a deserted place in Sicily is almost impossible. The island is small and fairly well-populated and certainly most ruins and historic sites are of interest enough that people travel to experience them. Still, I got out my map and started looking for a place that might be isolated enough to have few visitors. My attention settled on the Magnisi Peninsula in the Gulf of Augusta, on the eastern coast of Sicily between Catania and Syracuse.

Emilio and I were in good spirits as we faced the three-hour drive from Palermo. The actual distance is only about 200 kilometers (about 125 miles) and I'm sure some people could have travelled it faster, but we were in no hurry and I prefer not to drive like I'm on a racetrack, so we took our time. The Magnisi Peninsula is actually an island, two kilometers long, and 700 meters wide, welded to the mainland by a sandy, narrow isthmus of less than 100 meters. A lighthouse sits on the island and not far away lies Thapsos, a huge necropolis that dates back to the Bronze Age (fourteenth century BC), with over 400 graves dug into the limestone. We explored the entire area. The land is completely flat and seems to just barely rise out of the surrounding water. There was also an ancient tower still standing there, perhaps built by the Saracens, with a narrow stone staircase inside that led to the top. It was accessible, but full of trash. We climbed anyway and were enchanted by a marvelous view of the sea. Except for a fisherman in the distance, we were completely alone: the island was deserted.

I pulled the pyramid out of the plastic bag I had brought it in, connected it to the radio antenna and tuned it to a white frequency. There was a little rustling noise that indicated that it was active, but no other sound. We waited, hoping to hear something . . .

And we did.

The radio emitted a constant, steady "beeping" like Morse code. The sound was so regular that we assumed might be some signal from the nearby electronic lighthouse (or some smuggler off at sea, signaling an illegal rendezvous since cigarettes and other goods are frequently snuck in this way in an attempt to avoid the various port authorities). However, as soon as I detached the pyramid from the radio antenna, we couldn't hear it anymore.

"Maybe your pyramid is just an antenna that amplifies signals," Emilio said.

"Could be," I agreed. "But it's also supposed to transmit something. The little blue man said so."

"How can you be so sure?" Emilio asked. "It hasn't done it yet."

"I don't know," I replied, shrugging. "Usually when things get difficult, I get discouraged and give up. But this is different. All these years it's been like this strong impulse inside me, pushing to try to figure it out—pushing me to act. The problem is I don't know what to do anymore."

As we talked, a helicopter droned over to our left. It was flying very high in the sky, heading toward Syracuse, a town only about thirteen kilometers away. Emilio and I glanced at it but didn't pay it very much attention. After all, a helicopter in the sky isn't a particularly extraordinary sight on the island. All kinds of aircraft crossed over it, usually from the east: police and Carabinieri helicopters, medical choppers, military airplanes, NATO crafts heading to a nearby base, etc.

The helicopter passed over us . . . and then suddenly circled back in the opposite direction, dropping lower in the sky. We watched as it passed us then turned again, coming over us a third time, dropping even lower.

Emilio and I stopped talking, watching the helicopter in curiosity as it circled back again and began lowering toward us.

Emilio said, "Disconnect the pyramid and put it away.

"Why?"

"I tell you: disconnect it!" he urged in a tone that surprised me. He sounded worried.

Meanwhile, the helicopter had dropped lower still—low enough for whoever was inside to see us: a man and woman on the roof of an ancient tower arguing vigorously.

"Look, he's landing here," Emilio went on. "Let's leave."

"I cannot believe it," I marveled. Emilio stood up, preparing to leave, but I still didn't move, staring at the helicopter in amazement. Was it possible the helicopter was landing on this little strip of deserted island because of the pyramid? "You think he's landing for us? And if he is, so what? What's the problem?"

Meanwhile, the helicopter hovered near the ancient tower, only a few meters from the ground. The rotors swirled the air around us violently. I was surprised to see it wasn't a police or medical helicopter at all. This craft was very dark gray, almost black. The glass of the cockpit was not transparent; it was shaded and opaque, like the black glass windows of some skyscrapers. The pilot was invisible to us. The helicopter's body had no signs, no flags, or identification numbers anywhere on the body or tail. Nothing. It did not even have the usual skid tube landing gear. Instead there were thick black pontoons, similar to what you typically see on seaplanes. The side hatch was much larger than usual, too. Two Italian cars could have driven inside it side by side. In short, it was the biggest helicopter I had ever seen except in American war movies—and even those had a few numbers or letters on their hulls.

It clearly was not a local helicopter, but of course there was a NATO base nearby. I wondered if that was where this craft had come from.

"Listen," my husband said, trying to convince me that it was time to leave. "It's here because it picked up something with its sensors."

"Beautiful," I said. "Perhaps the pilot can tell us something useful. If we knew what he heard, maybe I could figure out how to make it work better."

"Things are not like that," my husband insisted. "What are you going to tell them when they ask you how and why you built the pyramid? That you dreamed of a little alien man who gave you directions? They're military; they would never believe you. Would you like to spend New Year's Eve being interrogated?"

Now I understood . . . and the possibility of a ruined New Year's celebration convinced me. I moved.

By now, the helicopter had almost landed next to the tower. It was probably only about one meter from the ground and twenty to twenty-five meters away. I turned off the radio, unplugged the pyramid, and stuffed everything back into the plastic bag. Then we hurried down the stairs and, without looking back, left like a pair of lovers without a care in the world, hugging and chatting as we walked slowly and deliberately toward the car. We heard the helicopter lifting back up into the sky behind us.

We were uneasy as we left Magnisi Peninsula, but nobody stopped us, not even on the highway as we made our way back home.

CHAPTER THIRTY
THE UNDERSTANDING

Sometimes the most obvious things are also the most difficult. Take, for example, language—that cluster of sounds that comes from the mouth to express the brain's thoughts or the heart's feelings. In Italy, those sounds are very often accompanied by gestures to capture even more attention. Italians, you know, listen very little. We prefer to talk.

I have no difficulty expressing myself, and yet, very often others find it difficult to understand me. For years, I thought it was just me. That I was saying something wrong. But then, after working abroad, travelling to other countries, and having experiences with other people who had difficulty communicating, I've learned that it's far more complicated than just knowing the right words. In order for there to be true understanding between people, there must be willingness and a real *desire* to communicate—and that is far more complex than words, accents, or linguistic barriers.

The problem is most people are mentally inflexible. They are stuck in habits of thought that prevent understanding rather than fostering it. We have the expression, "We do not speak the same language" but it refers not to actual sounds and speech patterns but to the thoughts, emotions, reasoning, and sometimes moral values that prevent people from truly "hearing" each other. When someone communicates an idea that seems completely foreign to our way of thinking or sounds totally outside of our experience, it feels like they are speaking a language unknown to us. The fear and shock of this unexpected point of view raises alarms and shuts minds so completely that it is difficult, if not impossible, to find common accord afterward.

When I was fourteen years old, a university student (a friend of some friends) tutored me in mathematics over the summer. Math was never my subject and I always needed a little help. Because I was a bit behind, my parents arranged for me to have some tutoring over the summer to be prepared for the next school year. Many, many years later, I found out my childhood tutor was living in Rome after having worked for twenty years as an aerospace engineer. He'd spent ten years working for NASA and another ten years doing similar work for a company in Germany. When I found him again, he was working at Contraves, an electronic manufacturing company in Rome.

Of course, once reconnected to him I had to tell him about the pyramid. How could I not try to see if he could help me? I told him everything and showed him what I'd done, hoping to convince him to join me in trying to figure out how to make it work—or at least to help me understand the glass vacuum and the interaction of the mercury, salt, magnets, and quartz. But to him, an aerospace engineer, the pyramid made no sense. He was certain it could never work. Since it defied what he'd been taught, it *couldn't* work. Yet NASA had given him a plaque for a radar array he had built—an array that had been mounted on a satellite and sent into space—something that, just a few decades before, would have been impossible. I expected him to have more creativity.

Someone like me—someone who writes and thinks about things that are off the traditional path—runs into this inflexible (and frustrating) mindset often. I consider myself lucky that most people only think of me as being "a little bit strange" and not too outrageous because of the things that I am interested in. But it's also why, in my journey into the so-called impossible, when I find something that appears to answer my questions, I dive into it completely and do my best to link it to the other theories and explanations I've found. Linking these various ideas may not be an entirely integrated process—and I'm aware that there may be many missing links in my logical chain—but at least I can relate them chronologically and hope that, in time and with more understanding—more communication—it will become easier for me to complete the analysis or decide to abandon it all together.

More often, however, I find no answers at all. This is even more frustrating. I am always very disappointed when I feel close to an explanation—a new understanding—only to see it evaporate into thin air. Since, according to current norms, my goals are almost always unusual and quirky, I have met this disappointment more than once.

When I met David W. Davenport, who co-authored the 1979 book *2000 BC: Atomic Destruction* with Ettore Vincenti, I felt very close to a major breakthrough and a fresh understanding of the pyramid. He was introduced to me by the aerospace engineer, Franco Piccari, who had told me, in confidence, that they were working together to attempt to reconstruct an aircraft described in ancient Sanskrit texts. Davenport, I thought, might be the only person able to understand how the pyramid could work—especially if something about its mechanism recalled the technology of the ancient world. He had the skills and the right background of experiences. Perhaps he had come across something in his Sanskrit readings would be relevant to the workings of my device? Unfortunately, his sudden and premature death prevented the realization of his ambitions and dreams, and those of many others—including mine.

His work was extraordinary. Davenport was born in India to English parents and was an expert in archeology and oriental languages. In *2000 BC: Atomic Destruction*, he wrote about his work comparing the original Sanskrit texts, *Rg Veda, Mahabarata, Ramaiana*, and dozens of other ancient texts, after having found what appeared to be an "aeronautics manual" in the Indus Valley. Davenport and his co-author theorized that the city of Mohenjo-Daro (now in modern-day Pakistan) was destroyed 4000 years ago by an explosion powerful enough to raze the city, incinerate its inhabitants, and vitrify bricks and pottery. Upon examination of their findings, an Italian laboratory found that samples from Mohenjo-Daro did show evidence of having been exposed to a shockwave of brief and extreme heat of many thousands of degrees centigrade. According to our current knowledge of matter, the only force capable of producing such an effect would have been a nuclear explosion.

Among the other ideas discussed in his book, Davenport dedicated considerable space to the possible technical/technological translation of the ancient aeronautical manual, the *Vymanika-Shastra* or *Aeronautica del Maharashi Bharadwaja*, which briefly describes the operation of the Vimanas, an ancient aircraft that sailed the skies around 4,000 years ago, and the equipment that aircraft used. His exhaustive study led Davenport to conclude that this text should be integrated with other Sanskrit manuscripts, little known even in India and never translated into the West. The *Vymanika-Shastra*, however, could not be considered a true treatise of aeronautical engineering, if only because of its extreme brevity. The entire manuscript is only 124 pages and much of it concentrates on instructions for pilots: what they should eat and wear; what types of metals to be used to build the Vimanas; geological information on finding these metals; instructions on the use of furnaces, bellows, and crucibles to prepare the metals for construction; the description of the three types of Vimana and their equipment, electric generators, and electric motors. There are many different ideas included in too few pages and unfortunately, the text lacks the precise instructions needed to attempt to rebuild the machines today. More than anything else, the book suggests a kind of scientific summary written to allow non-scientists to get a general idea about the subject.

Among the translated passages of the *Vymanika-Shastra* that Davenport quotes in *2000 BC Atomic Destruction*, the one below particularly struck me. Take, for example, the electric motor. It is described as follows:

"The electric motor consists of a thin metal wire wound in turns with a thin wire cage in the middle. The current is brought from the generator to the engine through a glass tube. Appropriate wheels are fixed to the wire cage to connect it with the rotating device of the generator or the pinion shaft."

"Whoever wrote these lines," Davenport explained in *2000 BC*, "certainly knew the electric motor, because he accurately cited the three fundamental elements: the winding (or 'solenoid' to use more technical language); the central rotating part (it is curious to note that in modern three-phase motors, this rotating part is called 'squirrel cage') and the insulator ('glass,' says the text and we immediately imagine the tubes used today, but nothing prevents the use of actual glass, which is excellent insulation, little used today because of its high cost). Furthermore, it is said that the mobile part must be connected on one side to the pole of a generator and on the other side to a pinion, which transmits the movement to the machine in question. It does, however, make only vague reference to basic physical principles, and is confused as regards to the links. The result is that the reader must have good knowledge of electrical engineering in order to interpret what is written, otherwise, even with the best will, all he can get, following the instructions to the letter, will be a 'proto-motor': a contraption that looks like an electric motor, but does not work. It is a description that fits with our notion of scientific vulgarization. It seems more like how an electrical engineer might explain to a layman how, in very general terms, an engine works."

Once again, we run into the difficulty of *language* and the problem of communicating complex ideas. Davenport also struggled with the difficulties of translation from a strange, ancient language to the terms of our modern technological era. To this, we must add that G.R. Josyer, the director of the International Academy of Sanskrit Research in Mysore, completed the initial translation of the *Vimanika-Shastra* that Davenport worked from. Although Mr. Josyer was a distinguished Sanskritist and an expert in ancient Indian culture, he wasn't a scientist and certainly did not have the vocabulary for the most modern aeronautical, electronic, chemical, and metallurgical techniques that would have enabled Davenport to create a more complete scientific understanding of the craft described in the text.

Davenport offered an analogy for the communication difficulty in this passage:

"In a very distant future, a scholar of our civilization could have difficulty understanding what a tiger's eye necklace could be. Everyone knows perfectly well that it is a necklace formed by a particular type of iridescent hard stone, yellow and brown. If, however, between several centuries, a hypothetical scholar came across the same sentence and translated it to the letter, and by 'tiger's eyes' we really meant the eyeballs of the big cat, he would certainly have strange ideas about the habits of twentieth-century women.

"Or he might have difficulty figuring out what the 'gooseneck' could be (the jointed shaft that transmits movement to the pistons).

Or decode the 'whiskers,' the very long and thin crystals, obtained in the laboratory, which are used as non-metallic aircraft components because of their very high resistance to heat and stress. These carbon crystals have been named 'Whiskers' (cat whiskers). But translating the term to the letter would not help the scholar to understand why our planes are built with cat whiskers.

"There are hundreds of examples in today's terminology that can be understood only if we live in the time when these terms are used."

When I describe the construction of the pyramid, I relate it with the terms I know and the knowledge I have. To the scientist, my description inevitably translates as "pizza"—or at least that's what my Roman aerospace engineer friend told me. Similarly, I imagine that if a scholar of the future explained something "technological" to us, something that works on different principles than we know today, what would we understand at first glance? I believe very little.

CHAPTER THIRTY-ONE
ENTHUSIASM WANES

When my father died while undergoing pacemaker surgery, all my enthusiasm and efforts on the pyramid seemed suddenly silly and useless. His loss left me desolate and empty, and worse, I was alone with my pain. Emilio was in Rome tending to his mother, who was also ill. He comforted me as best he could by telephone, but it wasn't enough.

My younger brother disappeared from my life after my father's death. I didn't see him for a long time. Everyone must process their pain in their own way, I suppose; his was to distance himself from his remaining family. My mother, on the other hand, seemed far away. She never spoke of my father's death; she treated it like it hadn't happened. Perhaps she had never forgiven my father for letting me go away to live in Rome all those years ago? But perhaps that wasn't it. She hadn't exactly rejoiced when I came back in 1986, either.

Losing my father shifted the ground beneath my feet and set it rolling. I felt lost and unsure. I never realized how much I had counted on my father's presence: just knowing he was *there* no matter how near or far away he was had grounded me and allowed me to move forward in the directions that interested me. Now that I could no longer count on his guiding presence in my life, I felt fearful and uncertain. Even though I had never leaned heavily on him, I had depended on the knowledge of his existence for security, determination, and the willingness to dare. He was the one who taught me about the solar system, and who fostered my independent spirit and championed my curiosity. Even though we didn't talk often, even though I didn't confide with him about many aspects of my life, I had somehow expected him to always be there. It had never occurred to me how fragile his life was—how fragile all of our lives are—and that he could be gone in just a blink. Suddenly, there were so many things I wanted to ask him, to tell him, to share ... but the opportunity was gone.

The pain of a loss does not disappear with the passing of the years; it just finds a corner of your heart to hide in. It waits there, covering itself with oblivion, trying not to make you suffer continuously. And then, like a child playing hide-and-seek, it pops out and overwhelms you all over again. Writing these few words about my father has reopened wounds that I mistakenly thought had healed with the passage of so many years. But they have not. I miss him as much today as I did on the day he died.

It was many years before my enthusiasm for the pyramid and my mission to get it working returned. But when it did, I found a new ally—and unexpected support.

CHAPTER THIRTY-TWO
NEW MEETINGS, NEW FRIENDS

The first time I saw Dr. Jan Pajak's name was in 1994, in an article published by a New Zealand newspaper. Dr. Pajak was Polish born (but now a naturalized New Zealander) and taught mechanical engineering at the University of Dunedin. His name appeared in one of the clippings in Lucius Farish's UFO News Clipping Service which was still a part of my life, even though by then, Emilio and I were no longer publishing a European edition. Jan Pajak had written something about one of his research projects and though I no longer remember exactly what the article was about, I remember well the feeling I got when reading about his work. Everything he was doing suggested his mind was open to all kinds of unexplained phenomena. Maybe he was the right man to help me with the pyramid? Maybe he was the right combination of curiosity and scientific understanding to finally figure out how to make the device work, I thought. I immediately sent him a letter about my dream and the related pyramid. I didn't have a computer yet, but the article listed his address under his byline. I wonder what he would have done if he had known when he read my letter how many technical problems I hoped to transfer onto his shoulders.

Jan expressed sincere interest in my story and even wanted to work together on a paper about it (I could not believe it!). But he was a bit cautious. After all, I could be a crazy woman with a lot of weird ideas and nothing better to do but waste his time. But he *was* curious. It turned out that my story resonated with some of his own research, but I didn't know that at the time. As we wrote letters back and forth, I invited Jan to Palermo as our guest repeatedly, encouraging him to spend some time with me and Emilio and consider the pyramid firsthand. Finally, in May 1995, Jan arrived in Palermo to meet us and see the pyramid for himself.

Those were four days of intense conversation. For me, it was a full immersion in the English language as I struggled to communicate all of my efforts and attempts with the pyramid in a foreign language. But in spite of these difficulties, I liked talking with Jan very much. From my point of view, his English was fantastic—partly, I suspect because neither of us is a native speaker and the Polish construction of English sentences is very similar to the Italian. But the most fantastic thing was that he understood me. Even when my English was a big mess, he understood what I wanted to say and followed the tracks my thoughts took.

Apart from this selfish consideration, I considered Jan a brilliant mind and an attentive researcher and, at the time, a good friend. It had been a long and difficult road to find an open-minded scientist who listened to me attentively when I spoke about an alleged advanced technology device that came to me in a dream in 1978. And not only that, he'd come all the way from New Zealand to Sicily just to talk to me about it.

During his four-day visit, I introduced Jan to the technician who had built the second prototype. Other friends joined us, and we spent an afternoon showing Jan the experiments we had done with the pyramid. But when I connected the pyramid's phial to the kitchen piezoelectric gas lighter and the phial glowed, Jan's eyes lit up. That was the moment I knew Jan was hooked—and I wasn't a crazy lady foolishly pursuing a foolish dream.

The Endeavor

Jan proposed we write a paper on my strange "dream visitation" and explained that my experience complemented some other research he was doing. He believed that adding my story to the others he had collected would make his findings appear more solid when it came time to publishing his research, and perhaps help in finding funding resources for further work.

"Great. Let's write a paper," I said.

Only it was not that easy. First, I needed a computer ... and second, I needed to learn how to use it. The office I was working in still didn't have computers—most of the offices in Palermo didn't have them. Perhaps you might feel we were technologically a bit behind the times, but in 1995 computers were not as common as they are now. But I wanted to work with Jan, so I was determined to get a computer and begin to use it.

I bought an old PC second-hand. It had very little memory and, I discovered too late, could not run the software that Jan mailed me. And learning to use it was filled with difficulties—not at all an easy task. But I was determined to master it, and I slowly succeeded, teaching myself as I worked. In the end, I was able to write my part of the treatise in Italian, and then translate it into English, a very boring job that takes a lot of time and which was nothing less than amazing given the problems I had with that old computer. After I finished the translation, I sent my text to Jan to correct/edit my terrible English. Later, Jan sent me his part to translate it into Italian. Meanwhile, Jan was translating the English version into Polish, too. And of course, when I say "send" I mean we were conducting all of this correspondence by mail. There were no Internet connections in Sicily yet—and a letter sent via air mail from Italy to New Zealand can take up to three months to arrive, if it arrives at all.

After obtaining the appropriate copyrights and registrations for our document in both New Zealand and Poland, we printed the final treatise at our expense—each of us in our language—and made photocopies for dissemination. It was an incredible amount of work, but we were both proud of the result and willing to labor for something that we both believed in.

After a few years of partnership, and another treatise by Jan, however, my relationship with Jan Pajak was interrupted. As often happens, our interests and ways of thinking diverged and that made it harder for us to work collaboratively. Jan's ideas had become too much "advanced" or "out there" for me. I guess there's a limit to my madness. But whether Jan's ideas are madness or genius, there came a time when I did not share them. Our collaboration ended, and, sadly, I was still no closer to developing a working pyramid.

CHAPTER THIRTY-THREE
REACHING BACK TO THE ANCIENTS

I could not shake the feeling that my current difficulty in figuring how to make the pyramid correctly was the result of my own obstinacy. I had repeatedly interrupted the pale, bald, blue-eyed dream visitor, and because of that, I had lost important information I needed in order to construct the pyramid properly. The results of what I'd done, the things I'd read and the reactions and comments of people who understood more about engines and science than I did had solidified my belief that what I was attempting wasn't nonsense. But it still didn't work, and no one had yet been able to help me figure out what was missing.

A new idea occurred to me. If what I had been told during that short "dream" was somehow real—or at least, had enabled me to tap into another sphere of my own understanding, why couldn't I try to come into contact with the Dream Visitor again, only this time, deliberately? If I could reconnect to my visitor in another dream, perhaps I could ask him directly for more detail? Maybe I could even ask him to repeat the instructions?

It's true: it had now been many years since that dream. Perhaps the telephone lines between me and the blue-eyed man had long since decayed or been destroyed. But I figured it wouldn't cost me anything to try.

I tried and tried. But despite my persistence night after night, I had no success. Only once in all my nocturnal attempts to "dream" of him did anything unusual happen . . . and even then, the visitor failed to appear.

What happened was this: I fell asleep and then suddenly, just like the time I'd dreamed of the visitor, whatever I was dreaming about before just stopped. Like a close-up shot in an action film, I saw a pair of male hands only about 30 cm (twelve inches or so, English) from my nose. The hands were normal human hands, and even a little tanned as they reached toward opening a little black door—about the size of the electrical fuse box in a home. The door was cut into something larger, something apparently made of black metal. My vantage point was extremely close. I could not, unfortunately, get a larger view of what that little black door was attached to, but when the door opened, I saw a small empty rectangle inside. It looked like it was missing something, something that was supposed to fit into the empty rectangular space.

Then the hands grabbed something vaguely similar to a transformer—about the size of the one on the lights of a Christmas tree. I watched the hands turn it between the fingers as if to make sure everything was in order, observing every detail. It was a cube made up of several layers of rectangular material the color of anthracite. Each layer was separated from the ones above and below by small black cubes placed at the corners. Then, the transformer shifted from one of the hands to the other and was inserted into the empty space and the little door closed.

When I awoke, I thought for a long time about what I had seen. Everything about it reminded me of how I had inserted batteries into my tape recorder: the casual way the hands inserted the power into a familiar device and shut them inside. The tiny black separator cubes had looked like little magnets but that dark gray material, so dark it looked almost black, I had never seen that before. What could it be?

I used my encyclopedia and any books and photographs I could find, but it took me about a month to finally discover that this material existed and was called mica.

But did this odd dream of a mica power cube have any connection to the pyramid? Was it something that would make it work? And if so, where did it go in the design the visitor had given me? Or was this new information completely unrelated—just a simple dream—and I was suffering from such a monomaniacal fixation on trying to make the pyramid work that I made things matter when they didn't?

I dismantled my iron because someone had told me that there was mica inside. That turned out to be true, but it was not the type or the color that I was looking for. So of course, it goes without saying that I decided to buy some mica. It took six months of intense research to learn that the type of mica I "saw" is only produced in Germany (or at least in Europe that is the only source) by Dupont Chemical and is not sold at all to retail customers. The company mainly sells that kind of mica to government space programs for use as a coating for shuttles and rockets.

It was clear that I wasn't going to be able to attempt to make the power source I'd seen in this dream. I had to abandon any hope of obtaining the material for my own experiments, interesting though I'm sure they would have been. However, in 1997, I got another piece of information that connected the pyramid dream to the mica dream and made me believe that the two were inextricably related. In fact, my heart skipped a beat and my hands tightened harder on the book I was reading. I read the same words over and over with my heart pounding. I kept asking myself "Is this real?" and all of the other questions you ask when you discover that what you think might be just your own delusional fantasy suddenly might have a real foundation.

The chapter was entitled "The Sun, The Moon and the Avenue of the Dead," and the book was called *Fingerprints of the Gods*, by Graham Hancock. I do not dare try to translate back into English from Italian. Instead, I used the Internet to first attempt to contact the author directly, and when that failed, I found a "fan page" for the book. I contacted the owner of that site, explained my problem, and asked for the original text in English. So, with much thanks to Robert Speight, of Twickenham, Middlesex, England, for the following pages in English, here is what I read in *Fingerprints of the Gods* by Graham Hancock:

> Some archaeological discoveries are heralded with much fanfare; others, for various reasons, are not. Among this latter category must be included the thick and extensive layer of sheet mica found sandwiched between two of the upper levels of the Teotihuacan Pyramid of the Sun when it was being probed for restoration in 1906.

The lack of interest which greeted this discovery and the absence of any follow-up studies to determine its possible function is quite understandable because the mica, which had considerable commercial value, was removed and sold as soon as it had been excavated. The culprit was apparently Leopoldo Bartres, who had been commissioned to restore the time-worn pyramid by the Mexican government.

There has been a much more recent discovery of mica at Teotihuacan (in the "Mica Temple"), and this, too, has passed almost without notice. Here the reason is harder to explain because there has been no looting, and the mica remains on site.

One of a group of buildings, the Mica Temple, is situated around a patio about 1000 feet south of the west face of the Pyramid of the Sun. Directly under a floor paved with heavy rock slabs, archaeologists financed by the Viking Foundation excavated two **massive sheets of mica** which had been carefully and purposively installed at some extremely remote date by a people who must have been skilled in cutting and handling this material. The sheets are ninety feet square and form two layers; one laid directly on top of the other.

Mica is not a uniform substance but contains trace elements of different metals depending on the kind of rock formation in which it is found. Typically, these metals include potassium and aluminum and also, in varying quantities, ferrous and ferric iron, magnesium, lithium, manganese, and titanium. The trace elements in Teotihuacan's Mica Temple indicate that underfloor sheets belong to a type that occurs only in Brazil, some 2000 miles away. Clearly, therefore, the builders of the Temple must have a specific need for this particular kind of mica and were prepared to go to considerable lengths to obtain it; otherwise, they could have used the locally available variety more cheaply and simply.

Mica does not leap to mind as an obvious general-purpose flooring material. Its use to form layers underneath a floor, and thus completely out of sight, seems especially bizarre when we remember that no other ancient structure in America, or anywhere else in the world, has been found to contain a feature like this.

It is frustrating that we will never be able to establish the exact position, let alone the purpose of the large sheet that Bartres excavated and removed from the Pyramid of the Sun in 1906. The two intact layers in The Mica Temple, on the other hand, resting as they do in a place where they had no decorative function, look as though they were designed to do a particular job. Let us note in passing that mica possesses characteristics which suit it especially well for a range of technological applications. In the modern industry, it is used in the construction of capacitors and is valued as a thermal and electric insulator. It is also opaque to fast neutrons and can act as a moderator in nuclear reactions.[9]

Just a few months before I read Hancock's book, Jan had urged me to include my "mica dream" in the paper we were working on together. Initially, I refused. As much as I hoped it was relevant, I felt the mica dream didn't have a solid enough foundation or logical connection to the pyramid dream. But, after reading Graham Hancock's *Fingerprints of the Gods (Impronte degli Dei,* in Italian*)*, I changed my mind because, although I still do not understand the relationship between the mica dream and what I was told to build, it seems I have I found another clue to support my "madness."

One other little note—just to share another piece of relevant information that came into my hands.

---

9 From *Fingerprint of the Gods*, Graham Hancock, pp.

In the book *The Mystery of the 13 Skulls* by Chris Morton and Ceri Louise Thomas, the authors (husband and wife) recount their investigations into the origins and purposes of the quartz crystal skulls alleged to have been found at archeological sites all over North and South America. The most famous crystal skull is the Mitchell-Hedges crystal skull, discovered by the daughter of archaeologist F.A. Mitchell-Hedges on an excavation in Belize in 1926. According to Native American legends, these crystal skulls were used to enter into mental contact with the gods to receive knowledge and wisdom.

During their investigations, Morton and Thomas met and interviewed Frank Dorland, a specialist in crystallography. According to him, there are likely many other frequencies of energy around us not yet discovered by science. He suggests that we should imagine the human body and mind as a radio-system capable of transmitting and receiving these still unknown electromagnetic waves. He theorized that when humans come into contact with a quartz piezoelectric crystal (like the skulls), our electromagnetic energy waves are received by the quartz, and the crystal begins to oscillate, amplifying those signals and re-transmitting them, sending out into the atmosphere where they are absorbed by the cells of our body. This is scientifically sound since quartz crystals do modify and amplify electromagnetic waves and transmit them back. During this process, these waves become stronger and clearer. As we know, natural piezoelectric quartz is commonly used as an oscillator, as a natural resonant circuit or as an amplifier. But Dorland believed that this process only occurs when the crystal has been "set in motion." The best way to do that is to simply touch it or hold it in your hands. (My Dream Visitor held the pyramid with both hands as if to close a circuit.) Dorland believed that the radiation emitted by the crystal skull was received by our hypothalamus, the gland that regulates the electrical and chemical processes of our body.

And in the course of many interviews with Native Americans, the authors were told that in very distant times, the crystal skulls were originally placed inside the pyramids scattered throughout Mexico, Central and South America. Some were even installed on the tops of the pyramids, like beacons.

If this is true, no further commentary is really necessary—except to say that our ancestors knew something we are still trying to rediscover. And it also maybe someone, here and now—someone high in the government, perhaps—who knows how these pyramids worked. It seems likely, since it's hard to believe that no one else has put all this information together yet.

CHAPTER THIRTY-FOUR
THE BATTLEFIELD OF EXPERIENCE

I am aware that my point of view isn't supported by mainstream scientific study or academic specializations. But the experiences lived directly on the "battlefield" are the ones that sharpen one's skills and help a soldier to survive, so to speak. I've had many years to read, to reflect, and to learn about various theories in many different fields of knowledge, fields so far from each other that, logically, it might seem that there is no connection. The pyramid, for example, drove me to tackle all kinds of topics that were difficult for me. But I had to keep searching, so I dove in and gathered as much information as I could. In addition to hoping that the things I learned would prove useful in my own effort to get the pyramid to work, I hoped that by my continued learning, my continued attempts and writings, one day someone might be exposed to what I was doing and be able to continue with it, perhaps developing what I have not and probably will never be able to do.

My sin was pride: I hoped I could build the pyramid communication device myself—even knowing I hadn't heard all the details of the instructions and had little technical knowledge. In fact, instead of wasting so many years "pushing the air" and looking for allies to help me build a communication device, I probably should have communicated in a different way right from the start: I should have written this book sooner and got it out into the world. On the other hand, through the attempt, I learned many things. I enjoyed an intellectual and spiritual growth that no school could have ever given me. I guess God loves sinners, too.

As I write this, it is 2019, more than forty years since I had that dream in 1978, little for me has changed. I still feel the same drive to talk about the pyramid. I still feel the need to spread this information. I still feel the urgency. I still believe that whatever knowledge that might be gained from the Dream Visitor's communication device, mankind needs it. We need it very badly.

Research, money, and espionage

While the orthodox scientific community both in Italy and around the world still refuse to consider the possibility that humans have unexplained abilities, commerce embraces it whole-heartedly. There are products on the market that claim to strengthen PSI energies, to tap into them and to direct them. American universities have researched these topics and have confirmed the reality of the phenomena. The Air Force today has a helmet that hooks potential targets using the brain waves of the pilot. Thought waves that guide missiles. And yet, there are still people and scientists who still deny the existence of powers of mind, simply because they don't yet understand how to access them.

In ancient cultures, Native Americans or shamans practiced remote viewing for the protection of the tribe. This practice is known and documented, although as of 2019, our orthodox science still has great difficulty accepting its truth—or any of the truths of parapsychology. Or at least, that's what they tell us. These same abilities, remember, have been practiced since the 1970s by the American CIA for psychic spying on the former Soviet Union and other enemies.

For all the doubt and disbelief that our institutions profess to have about psychic phenomena, their actions suggest that they too believe some of us have unusual skills.

I reference that here because I believe that the pyramid's function is to increase PSI energy to enable its greater use, specifically for telepathy. As we understand it now, telepathy, like other PSI phenomena that paranormal scientists have observed, appears to work sporadically and for short moments. Perhaps telepathic communication could be strengthened with some kind of carrier wave. But in order to create such a wave, we would first need to know the frequency at which one mind can communicate with another. Indeed, telepathy may not exist on a single frequency but a band of frequencies that vary from individual to individual.

Remember, in my search for someone to help me build the pyramid, how many times I was asked, "What frequency are you using?" If you know the frequency you're trying to receive or transmit, you'll know what quartz to use. And quartz, you'll recall, is fundamental for the functioning of my visitor's pyramid.

While searching the Internet recently, I learned that Dr. Andrija Puharich, the scientist who had discovered Uri Geller and conducted numerous experiments to verify his abilities, had died in 1995. Dr. Puharich was also famous for his inventions in electronic medicine, neurophysiology, and biocybernetics. As a pioneer in electrobiology, he also hoped to discover the extrasensory abilities of the brain. Back in the 1960s, while working with Dr. John Taylor, he had reached the conclusion that the brain activated extrasensory abilities at "8 cycles per second" since this was the frequency he observed to correspond with remote viewing, telepathy, telekinesis, etc.

If that is accurate, what size quartz would activate the pyramid and connect our minds like never before?

Of course, knowing what size quartz to use wouldn't be enough to make my pyramid work. I made other errors in its design that I'm sure have inhibited its operation. For example, the shape is wrong. The pyramid I saw in my dream was not the shape of the pyramid I then built. I used a pyramid with the dimensions of the pyramid of Cheops, but this was purely circumstantial. In fact, I bought that pyramid because it was the only one on sale—not because it corresponded to what the Dream Visitor required me to build. The truth was, I did not know how to build an original pyramid according to the ratios he described. It was just too complicated for me, so when I saw that Pyramid of Cheops on sale, I thought, "It's close enough to try!"

Coincidentally, a few years ago, while shopping at the supermarket, I saw the shape of the "original" pyramid in the detergent aisle.

It was a pyramid-shaped air freshener by Glade. You pull the top away from the bottom to let out the scent. But when this pyramid is closed, it's very close to the shape of the pyramid held in my Dream Visitor.

Room air freshener shaped like a small pyramid by Glade

These clarifications and refinements could be more important than I initially realized. The shape corresponds to a certain gradient of the base corners. And the corners relate to the harmony of the other elements inside the pyramid.

Along with his words, the blue-eyed Dream Visitor sent me important concepts. Unfortunately, I didn't understand much about those concepts, but I absorbed at least some of his knowledge, perhaps through a kind of "mental contagion." For example, the matter of "harmony" or the relationship between each element of the apparatus to every other element, would be relevant to angles of the corners of the pyramid's base. Those ratios are probably subject to some law of geometry that I don't know—as I've said, math was never my subject. But to illustrate it to myself, I could draw the pyramid I made, then outline the pyramid I should have made and compare the angles at the base with a protractor.

This difference in shape could be a critical flaw. Perhaps, in order to transmit, the pyramid must be the exact same shape as the receiver is (wherever that might be). Or perhaps its operation depends on the angle multiplied by two? Perhaps with the appropriate ratios, it doesn't matter if one pyramid is my hand and the other is on the other side of the world, they can still communicate.

Or perhaps not.

I know that the pyramid I made was intended as a tool for communication and felt indirectly validated by Graham Hancock's *Fingerprint of the Gods*. Acting on an impulse, Hancock recounted in the book how he lay down inside the stone sarcophagus of the great pyramid of Cheops and felt an intense sensation: "It was like being inside the harmonic case of a gigantic, resonant musical instrument built to emit a single reverberated note forever. The sound was intense and very disturbing."

Sometimes I wonder, what if all the ancient pyramids we have in the world were nothing more than the remnants of sophisticated communication structures? Not once, but several times Graham Hancock wrote in *Fingerprints of the Gods* that being inside the great pyramid gave him the feeling of being "inside some huge instrument" that had a specific function. After all, we have electricity pylons (you might call them "transmission towers") scattered all over the world. If, a million years from now, long after our civilization has disappeared and other energies have been discovered, scientists unearthed what remained of them, they would certainly wonder what they were for.

When I think about what I've read about the interiors of the pyramids, what if the holes, the wells, the improbable and absurd uphill and downhill paths inside were nothing more than the stone reproduction of a strange, printed circuit? Then Hancock's hypothesis of an ancient civilization, much older than any previously dated by archaeologists, could begin to make sense.

Personally, I believe that my pyramid is an appliance that exploits two components: one known to us, electrical or electronic, and another one that is psycho-bioelectric—and almost completely unknown to us. The psycho-bioelectric component includes the potential to tap into the undeveloped psychic abilities of mankind. And in my opinion, telepathy is one of them. But unless we conduct the experiments that will accurately determine the frequency at which these "telepathic waves" operate and whether they are the same for everyone, I strongly doubt we will ever find the right quartz to transmit or receive.

Speaking of quartz, did you know that, in its natural crystalline state, quartz almost always looks like a pyramid? The scientists say its crystals are "prismatic and end in two rhombohedrons that simulate a hexagonal bi-pyramid." To me, that means that quartz and pyramids are naturally in harmony, in line with what my Dream Visitor had told me.

Reading here and there, I also discovered that our brain cells contain magnetite crystals (a hexacisoctahedral cubic mineral). Salt (NaCl—another hexacisoctaedric cubic mineral) is itself a crystal and, according to some geophysicists:

> The earth's core would consist of a single iron crystal. They came to this conclusion after studying seismic waves. The waves that pass through the center of the Earth in a north-south direction take 4 seconds less to travel the globe's diameter than the waves moving from east to west. There is a single crystal structure that can explain this variation of physical properties as a function of direction: the crystalline structure of iron in the form of hexagonal prisms. (TVNews, 1995)

I don't have a great deal of knowledge about crystallography or geophysics. The chemical specifications I have indicated are reported directly as I read them, but they support my theory that the pyramid structure, the crystalline nature of quartz, the composition of our brains and the Earth's core may all ultimately contribute in the construction of a device that enables telepathy. I can't say that I know how they all work together, and in what relationship, but I wonder: if all these crystals, including those in our brain cells, are electric conductors, couldn't they be used to receive or transmit? After all, my Dream Visitor held the pyramid between the two hands, as if to close a circuit. It is therefore possible that our *brains*—and the magnetite crystals that are part of their composition—are critical ingredients. Perhaps, our *brains* resonate with quartz, salt, and the two small iron magnets. If so, we are not separate from the pyramid communicator, but an integral component of it.

CHAPTER THIRTY-FIVE
HARMONY, SHAPE, AND FREQUENCY

My dream visitor emphasized that the individual elements of the pyramid should be in "harmony," as he put it. I have some thoughts about this, but I lack the scientific words to explain it, so I'll use the stories that illustrate the point best in my mind: crop circles.

Authentic crop circles have a certain harmony. By "authentic," I'm referring to those crop circles that have defied manmade explanation, the ones that remain a mystery to scientific explanation and which are fantastically beautiful in a strict, mathematical sense. After years of inferences and hypotheses, we are just beginning to understand that crop circles could be scientific "communications," using complex mathematical equations. In fact, there are two well-known crop circles, the "Mandelbrot Set" or the "Julia set" crops, named for the scientists Benoît Mandelbrot and Gaston Julia, because their designs echo those mathematical theories. Mandelbrot is known for founding the study of fractal geometry which he developed by plotting the equations of mathematician Gaston Julia on a graph and giving them a two-dimensional representation. To me, the use of mathematics, chemistry, and astronomy make sense as the basis of information exchanges between worlds. What better communication tool could there be?

Learning about mathematical "harmony" led me to the concept of "Phi," also known as the "Golden Ratio." It's a mathematical equation that involves a ratio between two numbers and their sum. Perhaps that equation was what my dream visitor meant when he referred to "harmony" between in the pyramid's dimensions and substances? Perhaps the diameter of the copper rods needed to be in Golden Ratio to the length of the spiral? That ratio in turn would inform the height of the pyramid and the amount of "energy" passing through the whole structure (what electrical engineer's call "impedance"). The phial, in turn, would also have to be mathematically proportional and in ratio to everything else.

In addition to mathematics, the study of cymatics might be relevant to solving some of the questions related to constructing the pyramid. Cymatics, a branch of modal phenomena founded by Hans Jenny, considers the relationship between frequency and wave form. In short, cymatics is the study of visible sound waves. Thin coatings of particles, pastes, or liquids are subjected to specific sound frequencies. They assume specific modules and forms, and these modules and forms occur only at those specific frequencies. No one can yet say why or how these forms are related to the frequencies that produce them. But the fact that the form and frequency are intimately linked is currently irrefutable—or at least that's what I read in John Anthony West's *Serpent in the Sky*. It made me wonder if the sound of speech itself affected the frequency of liquid mercury inside the pyramid's vial. Was there a relationship between sound and how the pyramid is used for communication?

In the Hindu tradition, for example, sound has always been understood as the creative force from which matter is born. Although many scientists dismiss that as religious dogma, some modern physicists have begun to realize that, at the subatomic level, all matter is in a state of constant movement. That means, on some fundamental level, all matter is really *vibration*. If you extrapolate that out to its ultimate level, that means that if we learn to change the ratio of vibrations, we can change the structure of matter itself.

Dr. Hans Jenny, the Swiss doctor and scientist who developed cymatics, captured sound vibrations in visual form. The results were often quite beautiful. More recently Dr. P.G. Manners developed a Cymatic Wave Therapy which he describes as "a medical transplant of harmonic frequencies into the structure of the human body." This therapy is based on the idea that, because the body is in continuous vibration and continuously emitting frequencies, scientific instruments that duplicate the body's ideal frequencies can heal and reinforce the body.

This research suggests that, in time, sound waves may be used more extensively and in different ways than we currently imagine—and perhaps those waves will lead to advances that make my ideas about my pyramid seem not so strange after all.

Coincidence or Serendipity?

A question that I have never fully answered satisfactorily: When is something a "coincidence" and when is it something more?

In 1995, I saw Roland Emmerich's movie *Stargate* in a theater in Palermo. Starring Kurt Russell and James Spader, *Stargate* is about a mysterious "gate" discovered during an archaeological dig that opens the door to a distant planet, reminiscent of Earth's ancient Egypt. I won't relate the whole plot here—you probably have seen it—and it's not relevant except for being highly entertaining. What *was* relevant for me, was one scene that might have been a coincidence . . . but maybe not.

At a certain point in the movie, our heroes exit the "star gate"—the means of travel to this distant world—and look back at it from the outside as they try to understand where they are. They realize that the "gate" is located inside a huge pyramid lying in ancient sand. In the sky above it three planets are visible[10]. The image was nearly identical to a painting I had painted in 1986—nine years before the film was released—and printed on the cover of the paper Jan Pajak and I did together, *History of a Pyramid.*

Coincidence?

Perhaps. If, as Jan Pajak says, some ideas are sown in the minds of many disparate people simultaneously, it makes sense that creative minds (actors, set designers, writers, etc.) can receive them and incorporate those images or concepts into their work—even if those ideas are far outside our immediate reality and those artists have no connection to each other.

---

10 https://www.cinematerial.com/movies/stargate-i111282/p/rfbaohxr

My painting on the cover of the Treatise Jan Pajac and I authored in 1986.

CHAPTER THIRTY-SIX
HELPERS GOOD—AND BAD

I continued to search for the right partner to help me develop the pyramid into a working device. I had some luck with Nicholas Reiter, a technical engineer who worked at a solar energy research laboratory in Ohio (U.S.A.). His specialty was vacuum micromanipulation, which, of course, was one of the components my Dream Visitor had told me I needed for the pyramid's inner workings.

Nick had been interested in electro-engineering since he was very young. He'd researched the effects of the Tesla coil on anomalous electrostatic phenomena and bio-electric and bio-magnetic interactions. I don't know a lot about that, but he did agree to attempt the mercury/salt combination of my phial, with some extraordinary results.

We corresponded by letter. I had sent the paper Jan Pajak and I had written on the pyramid to Don Worley, another United States-based researcher with whom I had an acquaintance and asked if he knew someone who might be interested in tackling some of the ideas and difficulties related to the pyramid's construction. At the same time, I wrote to Nick after reading a short article in a US newspaper about some research he'd done that nothing had to do with anything involving the pyramid. The article just suggested to me that he might be the kind of open-minded scientist I needed.

To my surprise, he not only replied to me, but he told me that he already had a copy of my paper. He'd been sent it by a friend of his who also thought my pyramid was the kind of thing he might be interested in. That friend was Don Worley. I had no idea they were connected, but it was perhaps just another happy coincidence.

Nick undertook the experiment of creating the vacuum of mercury and salt, following the instructions I'd been given by my dream visitor. His entire report is included at the end of this book, but I've included some key excerpts here.

Upon reading the testimony of Ms. Giordano, I spent considerable time pondering the best approach that an experimentalist like myself could take to help the cause of examining, duplicating, and proving at least some of the concepts disclosed.

It seems to be a common trend that, often, both the original recipient of the information and those who later join in the project become wrapped up in "theory." While in the right measure, theoretical modelling at some point becomes very important, it is my feeling that until any unusual aspects of the disclosed invention are repeatable consistently, a very strict "hardcore" EMPIRICAL approach should be taken.

Make no assumptions whatsoever about why or how the device works. Simply follow the instructions to the letter, and use currently accepted materials, instruments, and components to do this. If no results are seen, try again with better quality materials. If still no results, then focus on one portion of the system at a time very carefully, again being strictly empirical.

With this in mind, I decided to start by examining what seemed to me to be the most explicitly defined component of the pyramid appliance, the evacuated ampoule containing equal amounts of liquid mercury and salt (NaCl). I chose this component because it seemed to be the most "non-standard"; without an easy corollary to current technology. Pyramids and crystals have been experimented with by many investigators for years, and represent an interesting field of study with plenty of prior art.

I have to interject here to say he is only partially correct. When I "received" the instructions and information about the contents of the phial, the Internet did not exist, and the epochal movement we call "New Age" wasn't in existence yet, either. Back to Nick's report:

As it has turned out, I have now spent nearly half a year, with many large gaps due to other commitments, examining this fascinating component. As the reader will see, I have seen some surprising results! It is now September of 1996, and I have still not moved on to other device components, other than having built the basic copper pyramid/coil/mirror housing requested by Ms. Giordano's informant. This is due, in part, to the fact that the mercury/salt tube has shown such interesting effects.

Essentially, I have found that the Hg-NaCl evacuated tube appears to act as a novel and unusual piezo-electric generator. When properly built, one of these tubes will spontaneously glow in the dark, emit flashes and flickers of dim light from plasma emission, when mechanically activated, and produce accompanying radio frequency EM "noise." All of these actions appear to be the result of the liquid Hg flowing over, moving across, or jostling the crystal lattices of the NaCl. Further on in this paper, I will summarize the necessary technical considerations needed to produce a tube that works well. To date, I have built twelve tubes. Four of these did not work, for reasons which were later confirmed experimentally and which may be easily avoided.

To display the chronology of my work, I, as a result of this, provide sequential excerpts from my notes. I have edited these only slightly . . .

To summarize his next section simply: Reiter carried out experiments from March 1996 to September 1996, building twelve tubes over that time with different variables (e.g., better compounds, different balance of quantities, etc.). Incidentally, in this section he calls the mercury-salt combination a "coherer," the word I had found so many years ago on in my encyclopedia and which, in many ways, led me to believe that my Dream Visitor was telling me something that might indeed be real. Another coincidence?

Eventually, after many attempts that didn't seem to work, Reiter discovers that:

> By the end of May 1996, several evacuated tubes had been built which did NOT seem to work, even though the integrity of the vacuum on the tubes was confirmed. Eventually, the problem was found to be in hydration of the rock salt (NaCl). Small quantities of water within the tube apparently kill our effect! It was found in two subsequent tubes that good performance would return if the NaCl were thoroughly dehydrated before sealing into the ampoule with the Hg.
>
> The suggested operation to achieve this would be to dehydrate the rock salt in a Pyrex beaker at 200 degrees C in air for two hours before sealing into the quartz tube. This seems to work quite well . . ."

CONCLUSION

Research into a new field, or system, which may contain important new concepts, is often irritatingly slow. The researcher is often tempted to rush headlong into fascinating phenomena, but such temptations are to be resisted. At the time of this writing, I find that I have still not been able to move into the hoped-for second phase of this work, the incorporation of the Hg-NaCl tube into the balance of the pyramid appliance. Such experiments will simply have to come in their own time. For now, my near-term plans include running some experiments to examine any possible psychotronic interactions from the tube fields.

In summation, I would state the following as being major observations to date:

A. When properly constructed, a sealed and evacuated Pyrex or quartz tube containing crystalline anhydrous NaCl, and liquid Hg appears to act as a unique piezo-electric device.

B. When mechanically activated, the contents of the tube produce a visible light-emitting plasma, the characteristics of which are strongly dependent on the composition and pressure of the ambient gas within the tube.

C. The plasma developed within the sealed tube produce strong RF emissions, which may be easily picked up by an AM band radio. The strongest emission appears to be between 500 kHz and 1.0 MHz

D. The appearance of the tube plasma, and the property of RF emission, corroborate Ms. Giordano's own early experiences.

This document is, therefore, only the first of what will hopefully be a series of technical updates. The reader is encouraged to take hold of the data presented herein and continue independent work with the pyramid appliance concept.

In closing, I would like to thank Mr. Don Worley for introducing me to this project, Dr. Pajac, for his theoretical and technical work, and, most of all, Ms. Daniela Giordano for her dream of new horizons in communication for all peoples and creatures everywhere.

To say that I was happy with Nick Reiter's results is, an understatement. I was extremely excited. Unfortunately, Reiter did not have the opportunity to continue working with the pyramid. As sometimes happens, life overwhelms us with unexpected episodes that lead to roads different from those taken. Nick became ill and his untimely death left many people with a void in their hearts. He certainly left one in mine.

The Physics Teacher

Many years passed. I was always looking for partners and getting the pyramid working remained a priority, but no major new developments advanced the project until I met Professor Vittorio Marchi, a physics teacher and researcher in Rome, in 2005. I had sent him the photo of my pyramid model and he had read both the paper Jan Pajak and I had written, and Nick Reiter's summary of his results. When he came to Palermo to give a lecture, we arranged to meet so he could see the pyramid for himself.

He seemed quite interested in what I showed him but didn't offer any thoughts during our meeting. He promised that he would think about it and let me know his opinions after he had returned to Rome. He was true to his word. He wrote me an e-mail that both encouraged me and disappointed me at the same time. Here it is, in its entirety:

> Daniela,
>
> The mica layer, which acts as insulation when placed at the base at a certain depth of the structure, we have already discussed. What had escaped me in my initial hypothesis was the alternating layers of magnetic material. Then, I remembered the example of the energy flow in particle accelerators. In a particle accelerator, energy is concentrated and harnessed by "magnetic confinement." A "tubular" magnetic field is created by magnetic rings arranged transversely to their circular path.
>
> It may well be that the men of the time had already noticed that cosmic ray energies from space could be intercepted and collected magnetically, instead of dispersed into the ground. This is, of course, a hypothesis, but it suggests your device is not entirely far-fetched. This hypothesis serves as the basis of my further investigation.
>
> I thank you for the bringing this information to my attention.
>
> Cordial greetings.
> Vittorio Marchi

That was all.

The dismissive tone of his email made me angry. I had provided him with information he clearly understood was probably valid. He took it, said "thank you" and, in my reading, indicated that my role was finished. Whatever additional research he planned to do I clearly would be excluded from now that I had "brought it to his attention." Clearly, he thought I had nothing more to contribute, as a woman and as a non-scientist. But if I have no role in future studies of the device, why did my dream visitor come to *me*—and not to some hotshot physics professor?

I never answered him or tried to continue this relationship—I didn't hear anything else from him again.

CHAPTER THIRTY-SEVEN
DARK TIMES

After the experience with the physics professor, my research and exploration with the pyramid stopped for quite a while. Not because the project was no longer important to me, but because Fate tossed me deep into the raw reality of the transience of man.

My brother died in 2007 and with his loss, a great deal of my enthusiasm for life died, too. It was like having a piece of my heart torn out—worse, if possible, than the pain of the loss of my father because while my father was, of course, older than me, my brother was nine years younger than me. I had rocked him to sleep, changed his diapers, played with him. I had taken care of him when he ran away from home and biked almost three hundred miles to join me in Rome. He died while sipping coffee at his favorite café. It made no sense at all. He'd been perfectly healthy as far as we knew. I was devastated and so was Emilio, who had loved him like a son. In fact, after our father's death, my brother had looked to Emilio to fill that role.

I don't know if the loss of my brother contributed or not, but my mother died only a few short years later, following surgery on her hip after a fall. All of my birth family were gone. I was alone. Thankfully, I still had Emilio. I still had a husband who, somehow, slowly helped me rebuild my confidence and find the passion for the goals I had always pursued. But it took time to recover that passion.

After all, it had been so many years since my dream visitor gave his instructions. In spite of all the difficulties of exploring the device, researching it, learning about the concepts involved, studying its components, and attempting to effectively construct, I confess, I have loved every minute of it. Working on this project has been, for me, like the salt on a delicious dish: it flavored my life with an interest and purpose that I doubt I would have had otherwise. But after the loss of my brother and mother, I began to feel like my crusade to create this unique communication device was reaching an end. Little did I know, my story was far from over.

As I began to retreat from my project, research and inquiry into these mental energies began to rise around the world. For example, in 2014, a group of scientists used brain waves to transmit a message to colleagues 5000 miles away. They converted the electrical activity of the words "hola" and "hello" from India to Strasbourg. A computer translated the message directly into the mind of a human "receiver" through electrical stimulation, who reported "seeing" them as flashes of light.

Don't believe it? Here are the links[11].

While not exactly like what I have been trying to accomplish, these reports indicated to me that science is beginning to treat ideas like mine more seriously. The use of binary code is a different universe than my own efforts, which did not require computerized translation, but it's a step in the direction of telepathy.

Around this time, as well, I had made the acquaintance of Dr. Horace Drew.

Dr. Horace Drew holds a PhD in Chemistry from the California Institute of Technology and spent many years researching DNA chromosomes in the United States before moving to Australia in 1987. In 2002, however, he became interested in crop circles after speaking at a conference in England and visiting several of the most well-known crop circle sites there. I discovered him in 2012, after reading some of his works on the Internet. I admired the way he analyzed the crop circle phenomenon and that he was open to possible explanations for them beyond the general scientific belief that they had to be a hoax. Since he was a chemist, I thought he might be interested in my device, but he was difficult to locate. I knew he lived in Australia, but after that, I couldn't find any contact information for him.

---

11 http://www.dailymail.co.uk/sciencetech/article-2737532/Could-soon-send-emails-telepathically-Scientist-transmits-message-mind-colleague-5-000-miles-away-using-brain-waves.html. https://nexusnewsfeed.com/article/consciousness/cia-document-claims-cosmonauts-used-telepathy-to-back-up-their-electronic-equipment-in-space

I made calls to Australia, which required me to use my English-speaking skills, which is always a bit of a challenge—and even more so when one is trying to correctly obtain an email address—but eventually, I was successful. I reached out to Dr. Drew to tell him about the device, its components, and what I had done so far. He analyzed it carefully and wrote it up for CropCircleConnector.com, sending me a copy in an email, as well. His report is long, and there are parts that will be familiar, but his conclusions are interesting. Below is an excerpt, but you can find the full report at the end of the book.

> Fluid waves in a liquid mercury-salt mixture, under vacuum and in the presence of an external magnetic field, may be capable of detecting weak bio magnetic energies (a strange message from a paranormal source) by Red Collie (Dr. Horace R. Drew, Caltech 1976-81, MRC LMB 1982-86, CSIRO Australia 1987-2010)
>
> As a result of doing serious research on the paranormal from a scientific perspective, I have been contacted by many people over the years who wish to present me with unconventional ideas. The story which you are about to read may be one of the strangest, yet it seems to make sense in scientific terms. If this story turns out to be true, then we would have apparently been informed by psychic means (and in crop pictures) how to detect weak, low frequency, bio magnetic energies through a new method. Some people have speculated that those energies lie in the realm of telepathy or might even permit contact with another spiritual dimension.
>
> The main feature of this new device is its use of a liquid mercury-salt cell, under vacuum, in the presence of an external magnetic field, to change weak electrical signals from a wire antenna into fluid mechanical waves. Those mechanical waves can then excite a quartz crystal by the phenomenon of piezoelectricity. This general idea seems obvious, but no one on Earth has implemented it

before. Liquid mercury is a good conductor of electricity, especially when mixed with salt. It moves in low-frequency fluid waves when an electric current is passed through it, so long as a permanent magnet is placed nearby.

~~~

Electrical currents running through magnetized liquid mercury may create fluid waves or even torque.

To summarize in plain English, running an electric current through a pool of liquid mercury, in the presence of an external magnetic field, not only transfers electricity but also causes those heavy mercury atoms to move in a wave-like fashion. The transverse, low-frequency electrical wave becomes associated with a transverse, low-frequency, fluid or mechanical wave. This is somewhat akin to sound waves moving through air.

Now here is the important point: those low-frequency electrical waves, after having become associated with fluid or mechanical waves, may in principle become easily *detectable* by various piezoelectric substances, which can convert mechanical motion into electricity (see http://en.wikipedia.org/wiki/Piezoelectricity):

The novel device which we are about to describe uses mostly standard components except for one: a liquid mercury-salt mixture under vacuum, with two permanent magnets placed above or below (or perhaps on either side). When weak electric currents from a spiral wire antenna pass through that mercury-salt mixture, they apparently cause some of the gaseous mercury atoms (in a vacuum) to luminesce or glow, just like for a low-pressure mercury-vapour lamp (see www.edisontechcenter.org/MercuryVaporLamps.html or www.light-sources.com/germicidal-uvc-lamps/products/low-pressure-mercury-lamps).

Yet that does not seem to be its main purpose. The main purpose of such a device seems to be converting a weak, low-frequency electrical signal into fluid waves of mechanical energy, which can then be detected using a piezoelectric quartz crystal. Here is a summary of how the entire device seems to work: low-frequency magnetic energies, which are present naturally in a human body, may first induce low-frequency electrical currents in a spiral wire coil. When those low-frequency electrical currents pass through a liquid mercury-salt mixture under vacuum, with permanent magnets located above or below, they may create fluid waves of energy, just like for ripples moving through the water, or sound waves moving through air. Finally, such fluid waves may impinge on a quartz crystal which has piezoelectric properties. Various piezoelectric substances have been used as "microphones" to convert sound waves into electricity, or as "pick-ups" on the wooden bodies of resonating guitars (see http://en.wikipedia.org/wiki/Piezoelectric_sensor or http://en.wikipedia.org/wiki/Piezoelectricity).

A properly chosen quartz crystal should be able to detect mercury fluid waves at a frequency of 10 to 1000 Hz and convert them into electricity. I cannot tell, from the description given why salt (NaCl) needs to be mixed with liquid mercury in this device, unless it gives better electrical conductance or performance? No one on Earth seems to have tested a mercury-salt mixture before. It should behave something like "liquid copper." Also, I cannot tell whether fluid waves, produced by that liquid mercury-salt cell, are meant to induce a piezoelectric response in the quartz crystal by direct physical contact (i.e. gluing the two objects together), or whether such fluid waves ought to be transmitted to the quartz crystal by an electrical connection (i.e. a copper wire)? Certainly, the quartz crystal needs to be part of the spiral antenna, if part of its role is to transmit such energies to the outside world, after their conversion from very-low-frequency to kilohertz or megahertz waves as higher harmonics.

Analogy to a "coherer" for detecting radio signals.

The liquid mercury-salt cell under vacuum, in an external magnetic field, supposedly acts like a "coherer" (see http://en.wikipedia.org/wiki/Coherer or http://www.youtube.com/watch?v=Q1ohAfCdKvM).

Radio energy from an antenna can change the structure of a current junction containing iron or copper filings, by making them cohere to one another in a paramagnetic fashion. Such cohesion then allows electric current to flow.

This was the first efficient radio-wave detector used for telegraphy. Bose used liquid mercury mixed with iron filings to decohere any junction after a current had passed through, but not as an essential part of the detector itself. In this new device, weak electrical currents from a spiral antenna may change the structure of fluids in a mercury-salt cell, thereby allowing current to flow through the cell more easily. The most likely mechanism would be by inducing fluid Alfvén waves with mechanical energy (like for sound waves in air). Those waves could then be detected as vibrations by a nearby quartz crystal, whether directly or as part of a circuit:

"In devices such as hearing aids, quartz crystals convert *weak sound waves into electric currents*. Some phonographs use quartz crystals to convert vibrations of the stylus into electric impulses."

The mercury-salt mixture could itself have piezoelectric properties, in the presence of an external magnetic field. This is because the electrical currents which pass through it will be linked to a fluid motion of its fluid substances. It is hard to predict how two different piezoelectric substances, the liquid mercury-salt cell and the quartz crystal, might behave when joined to one another.

The human body should emit a weak, low-frequency magnetism around 3-50 Hz, consistent with human EEG frequencies. Quartz crystal radios use a wire antenna to detect weak electromagnetic signals from a distant transmitter. Those signals contain enough power to convert the messages directly into "sound", without requiring any extra power source (see http://en.wikipedia.org/wiki/Crystal_radio#Use_as_a_power_source).

This new device uses the natural energy of human-body emissions to create a weak electrical signal in a coil antenna, which is then transduced into fluid waves by liquid mercury-salt (placed in a vacuum) between two magnets. Next, we may see the emission of kilohertz or megahertz radio waves, when those fluid waves impinge upon a piezoelectric quartz crystal (especially if that crystal forms part of the antenna circuit). In other words, you should not have to "plug it in"!

There must be some kind of frequency resonance which relates all three parts of the device: the spiral antenna coil, the liquid mercury-salt cell, and the quartz crystal, but I do not understand this subject well enough h to give advice. Where is Nicola Tesla when you need him?

Was this device already known long ago on planet Earth?

How could two English crop pictures, from 2007 or 2009, resemble the basic features of that pyramid-shaped transmitter? Instructions were apparently given psychically to only one person on Earth, who has no relation to the crop circle phenomenon. This dilemma puzzled me until I saw an interesting video by Klaus Dona. Here he shows two stone-carved images of a hand-held "pyramid transmitter" from Earth's distant past. One of those ancient carvings also shows an eighteen-ray, oval-shaped UFO, which was recently drawn in crops at Santena, Italy during June of 2012. Again, there seems to be no obvious relation between that ancient carving and the modern crop picture.

This is not the place to discuss "pyramids", although the subject is interesting. A need for resonance in receiving or emitting low-frequency, low-energy waves The major new aspect of this invention seems to be a liquid mercury-salt cell, placed in a vacuum and in an external magnetic field, which by conventional science should convert extremely-low or very-low-frequency electrical currents into fluid mechanical waves of a similarly low frequency. Those mechanical waves can then be detected by a piezoelectric quartz crystal, just like for the musical; vibrations from a guitar. Hardly anyone studies VLF or ELF waves today because of the high technical difficulties. [Citations omitted]

The faint, white glow within that liquid mercury-salt cell could perhaps act like a "spark gap transmitter" as used in early radios (see http://en.wikipedia.org/wiki/Spark-gap_transmitter). Hopefully, some professional engineers will understand how to put these complex ideas into practice, from the approximate descriptions given here.

Summary and conclusions: who will be the first to put this new invention into practice? To conclude, studying the properties of a liquid mercury-salt cell, under vacuum and in the presence of an external magnetic field, while weak, low-frequency electrical currents flow through it, could be a worthwhile pursuit for biomedical researchers as well as for mobile phone companies. Engineers at Apple, Samsung, IBM, Bell Labs, Nokia or Hewlett-Packard, please take note! If you can obtain a patent on this device, by being the first to put it into practice, you might make billions of dollars, just like Hoffman-La Roche did on PCR (Polymerase Chain Reaction).

Nevertheless, human stupidity and inertia remain powerful psychological factors. Most people are afraid to try anything new. For example, any good, experienced molecular biologist could have invented PCR in 1983, rather than a novice. Kary Mullis wrote in his Nobel Prize lecture.

"Not one of my friends or colleagues would get excited about the potential for such a process. Most everyone who could take a moment to talk about it with me felt compelled to come up with some reason why it wouldn't work." No further comments seem necessary here. If any private inventors would like to get in on the ground floor, please feel free to proceed with early experiments, and contact this author by the CCC website if you wish. Once the unique properties of this unknown device are put into practice by thousands of professional engineers worldwide (if it really works), then we may see great advances in "energy medicine" for human health, as well as breakthroughs in human psychology or spirituality. It will not take too much effort and is worth a try.

What excited me most about Dr. Drew's analysis was that he, like Nick Reiter, understood the potentials of my dream visitor's device. But like many of us who are pushing the boundaries of what is considered "accepted science," many of his colleagues still do not appreciate his open-mindedness. Ideas that touch on parapsychology, on Ufology and on the possibilities beyond on our current understanding are still largely met with skepticism and doubt.

Telepathy

In Dr. Drew's analysis—and I've discovered it again and again in my own—you will see the links between parapsychological and UFO research. Why?

Energy.

Both parapsychology and Ufology are about researching energy—and to my mind, that makes them on the cutting edge of the most advanced research in science. The data from the empirical experiments to date indicate the energy readings received from both phenomena behave with substantial similarities and have characteristics that make them very different from all other kinds of energies. To understand them requires a willingness to explore beyond conventional ways of thinking. At the same time, the tests and instruments currently in use are not calibrated to detect these previously unknown energy fields. The tests we have measure the energy we already know, and it is difficult to devise the right tools to measure processes we can barely imagine. We have to know more before we can build the right tools to fully access and understand these energies.

Meanwhile, Ufology continues to have a tremendous impact on our society and the acceptance of the theory that "we are not alone" is becoming more and more widespread. With every passing year, greater numbers of people show a deep interest in space, in psychic phenomena, and in the possibility of the connection between the two.

Jacques Vallée, a physicist, computer scientist, venture capitalist, author, ufologist, and former French astronomer who currently resides in San Francisco, California, suggests "something is happening in the human mind and the same powerful force that has influenced the human race in the past is again influencing it to the present day." I believe he is correct: we are coming out of a "dark age" and are remembering something about our past connections beyond this planet. We are remembering a time when the human mind accessed far more than our "dark age" had previously allowed us to believe.

Like the smallest microscopic cells of raw matter—to the most intelligent forms of life—mankind is evolving. And our evolution means we are on the brink of accepting that there is an infinite world, populated with all kinds of other beings and life forms—separated from us by only the very thinnest of borders. It's true that most average people are not yet ready to accept that truth. And it's true that most of our conventional scientists (especially Italian ones!) still refuse to even consider that telepathy and other PSI phenomena are normal, natural and present in all of us. Not only are they normal, PSI phenomena might be the gateways to the solutions of some of the most pernicious problems in our modern world. If science is reluctant to explore them, my guess is that industry will—and one of these days, not too far in the future, you'll see PSI energies harnessed for all kinds of commercial applications. When the market is flooded with PSI products, perhaps then the scientific "intelligentsia" will finally take these faculties seriously.

I say all of this as a preface to explain the basis of my hypotheses about the Dream Visitor's device, which I believe is intended to amplify our brain waves and enable telepathy. In our current experiments, telepathy, like psychokinesis and all of the other innumerable PSI faculties inherent in the human mind, work sporadically and for short moments. If it were any other scientific phenomenon, science would suggest supporting that skill with some kind of amplification or carrier wave. But in order to do that, as I have stated before, you must first know the frequency (or band of frequencies) of telepathic communication.

CHAPTER THIRTY-NINE
THE PYRAMID IN BOSNIA

I'm always curious, even now when time seems to be going faster than ever and the years pass me by with increasing speed. As I get older, however, I think of my goals differently. They vary more now, and I find I'm less focused on finding someone to help me move the pyramid forward. Instead, I have the attitude that the right person will come. If and when I meet him or her, it will because they have been drawn to the energy—the telepathic signal, perhaps—that I've been sending out with my mental and physical efforts over the years.

For the curious, like me, the Internet has been a tremendous gift. My old *Encyclopedia Treccani*, which once got so much use, now sits dusty and abandoned. I hardly ever reach for it anymore. I say hardly ever because from time to time, when I'm looking for information concerning the past, I find the Internet doesn't always satisfy and I return to my trusty books. While I am hardly the most computer literate person—and I'm certainly not entirely computer-dependent like many young people are—I enjoy following national and international news through the many newspapers and information sources easily accessed through the world wide web. I read with amusement the difference between how news is reported in Italy compared to how it is reinterpreted in English in international sources, and vice versa. It also amuses me when I notice how sometimes uncomfortable news disappears at the speed of light. As usual, however, adrenaline rushes through me when I read news about the subjects that particularly interest me and that was exactly what I felt when I read a piece on the Internet about a pyramid-shaped hill in Visocica, Bosnia that emitted radio signals.

The article was written by a reporter named Riccardo Galli and I found it in *Stampa di Torino* on October 24, 2012. Visocica, is apparently not too far from Bosnia's capital, Sarajevo. Semir Osmanagic discovered the radio signals and theorized that the "hill" was not formed by Nature but "created." Osmanagic supported his theory by excavating the hill and finding portions of ancient paved tunnels moving through it, as though it had once been a working building.

Nor was this pyramid the only one in the area. Named the Bosnian Pyramid of the Sun after a similar structure in Mexico, it is the largest of a group of pyramids clustered in the region. If Osmanagic's hypothesis proves to be correct, he has discovered the first European pyramids, joining the well-known ones in Africa and the Americas. It may also be one of the largest. Estimated to be at least 12,000 years old and standing 220 meters, the Bosnian Pyramid of the Sun far surpasses the famous pyramid at Cheops, which is only 147 meters.

The top of the Bosnian Pyramid of the Sun emits a mysterious and powerful electromagnetic beam. "The phenomenon" as reporter Galli wrote in *La Stampa*, "was investigated by the SB Research Group, an Italian-Croatian-Finnish research group specializing in archaeo-acoustics and based at the University of Trieste. The Croatian physicist Slobodan Mizdrak, after placing a transmitter on top, sent ultrasounds and radio waves to the base of the pyramid and recorded the answer. 'The experiment lasted 39 hours and not 48 as intended, because the generator ran out of gasoline,' says Paolo Debertolis, head of the expedition. The collected data have been verified by three independent centers: the Belgrade Statistical Institute, the Zagreb Institute and the Advanced Mathematics Institute of Vienna. It turned out that the beam is continuous and is generated by a source placed angled toward the vertex of the pyramid from a depth of about 2.44 kilometers (about 1.5 miles) below it."

In short, based on the article, these investigators recorded the "voice" of the pyramid: a sound which was similar to bees buzzing in a beehive. The sound came from an electromagnetic beam born in the bowels of the earth and amplified through the layers of quartz in the Earth's crust. Whether the Bosnian Pyramid is considered one of the great pyramids of an ancient civilization, or whether it's simply a hill, it is intriguing that it contains an electromagnetic beam similar to a beacon that might guide ships and airplanes, or to a transmission antenna similar to our satellite antennas, only much larger. Or perhaps the "belly" of the hill holds a meteorite, even if, usually, meteorites that fall to earth cause craters and not pyramids. Perhaps, buried under rocks, earth and vegetation lies the remains of a UFO that crashed or landed here millennia ago.

Many are skeptical about Osmanagic's thesis. But from the peak of Visocica, an electromagnetic beam with a radius of about 4.5 meters was recorded. That much is a fact. The true nature, origin, and purpose of the beam remains a mystery.

That was as far as the newspaper article took me. Hungry for more information, and curious about both this new pyramid and its electromagnetic beam, I dug deeper. It came as no surprise to learn that Osmanagic's discovery had given rise to an incredible amount of controversy in the media. Initially, the orthodox scientific community immediately disqualified his discovery and even attacked not only his finding, but also his credentials as a scientist. I looked back at the initial article I had read in the *La Stampa* and was surprised to find no mention of Osmanagic's background or qualifications at all. Further searching quickly revealed that Dr. Semir Osmanagic, Ph.D., was an author, researcher, and businessman. Born in Bosnia, he had immigrated to the United States and currently resided in Houston, Texas (USA). He taught at the American University in Bosnia and Herzegovina as a professor of anthropology and served as the director of the Institute for Anthropology at the same university. In 2008, his university hosted a conference on the study of pyramids which was attended by fifty-five leading experts from ten countries—including China. His bestseller *Pyramids Around the World* has been published in the United States, Turkey, Slovenia, Serbia, Estonia, Croatia, Hungary, Czech Republic, Germany, France, Spain, Kuwait, Italy, and Bosnia Herzegovina. He had been interviewed on American TV channels like the National Geographic Channel, and dozens of others in the Moscovite and European broadcast regions.

That was his reputation when I read about him in 2012, but he'd had to struggle to achieve that acceptance and those accolades. In 2004-2005, he had a faced a firestorm of disapproval as many scientists attacked his research. Some even called him a cheat, alleging that he exploited a natural formation for financial gain. But he did not give up. He continued to advance his theories until he found financial support for excavation of the area. Finally, in March 2015, a new Lidar laser scanner mounted on a satellite and focused on the Bosnian pyramids provided detailed topographic photographs that confirmed his theory. The pyramids weren't "just hills" but were truly ancient artificial structures. [12]

I learned about the Stone of La Manà around the same time.

The Stone of La Manà, Ecuador

The stone is an OOPArt, an acronym derived from the English words "Out of Place Artifacts." Numerous archaeological finds around the world could be classified as exactly that. OOPArt are objects that are problematic because they don't seem to coincide with the historical period to which our scientific dating methods correlate them. Finding, for example, a steel bolt in a sealed five-thousand-year-old tomb would be a problem for any archaeologist. OOPArts are also a very slippery scientific endeavor. Orthodox archaeologists prefer not to deal with these unusual findings because OOPArts seem to suggest that they haven't managed their sites with the necessary professional rigor and may expose them to some controversy or ridicule from their colleagues. That sort of criticism would, of course, be damaging for any archaeologist—especially if the criticisms are covered by the media.

Laying those difficulties aside for the time being, OOPArt is also called mysterious archeology. Proponents of it as a legitimate phenomenon exist all over the world, believing that these out of place artifacts are evidence that a more technologically advanced civilization than ours existed millions of years ago and either died out or was destroyed. In some of these claims, there's a bit of the "buffalo" (i.e., exaggeration or fake news). But those are often obvious with only a slight amount of research. Look a little deeper, and you might wonder, as I do, if there might be something more to be concluded from some

---

12 https://www.smithsonianmag.com/history/the-mystery-of-bosnias-ancient-pyramids-148990462/

of the unusual objects found on archeological digs at sites around the world.

I was led to OOPArt after reading Dr. Drew's (Red Collie) thoughts about my pyramid. He referenced "Klaus Dona" in his article, and I had to find out who this Klaus Dona was. I quickly discovered that Dona was a Viennese-born art curator at the Habsburg Haus in Austria and that he was known for organizing exhibitions of OOPArt all over the world. His passion for these objects is so great that he even joins archaeological expeditions with the intention of finding interesting objects that, from his point of view, represent OOPArt. When possible, he acquires these objects and organizes opportunities for them to be shown to the public. He is well-known in the field, and many archaeologists and museums lend him finds or artifacts that they determine to be of uncertain historical attribution. He's even been the subject of a documentary film, *The Klaus Dona Chronicles: Secret World* (2011). The film is interesting, but one extraordinary section of it left me breathless.

The film revealed that more than three-hundred artifacts were found in 1984 by an engineer named Sotomayor, in La Manà, Ecuador. The discovery was accidental: workers set off dynamite while building a road, opening a sealed underground tunnel they hadn't known existed. Exploration of the tunnel led to yet another discovery: the ruins of an ancient pyramid that originally must have been more than 70 meters tall. Some of the artifacts found there matched items found in other archeological digs and included stone objects with fluorescent inlays visible only under black light. In the proper light, however, these inlays revealed recognizable representations of the constellations Orion and the Pleiades. One black stone contained inlays of the planet Earth—but with two additional continents—etched in quartz.

All of that was fascinating, but what left me breathless was another dark stone that contained the engraving of a man sitting on a pedestal, *holding a small pyramid with both hands*! On his head, he wore a sort of helmet with a kind of antenna sticking out of the top of it. From the man's eyes, horizontal lines are directed towards two men. Above this "scene" floats an oval object surrounded by rays—very similar to the illustrations of flying saucers and sometimes seen in crop circles around the world.

According to archaeologists, none of these inlay artifacts fit the style or ideology of Pre-Columbian culture. These objects seem even older.[13]

La Manà stone found in Ecuador by Klaus Dona

I was so stunned and amazed, I hardly knew what to think! The pyramid I had dreamed of had not involved helmets or antennas . . . but to see something so similar engraved on a stone found in an Ecuadorean tunnel, seemed too much of a coincidence. Although the stone was "dated" as from the Pre-Columbian period, I agree with Klaus Dona: the engraving seems very ancient. Perhaps my Dream Visitor was showing me a refinement in the workings of the device?

Klaus Dona theorized that the man in the engraving illustrates how the pyramid works through the lines coming from his eyes; but Dona doesn't follow the kinds of psychokinetic experiments that have always captured my interest. From my point of view, the three lines emanating from the seated figure illustrate the transmission of *thought* to the other figures. The small pyramid between his hands is the medium through which that transmission occurs. It fit perfectly with what my Dream Visitor had said: the pyramid was a means "To talk better to each other."

One last thing about the Stone of La Manà. The image engraved at the top of the stone bears an incredible resemblance to a crop circle that appeared in Santena, in the province of Turin, Italy on 17 June 2012. The massive circle is incredibly intricate and extends for over 100 meters.

---

13 https://www.bibliotecapleyades.net/ciencia/esp_ciencia_life48.htm

CHAPTER FORTY
FUNDING AND FINANCING

Fueled by these new images and ideas, I continued to search for someone to work with me to develop my pyramid, but it is not easy to find people with the combination of knowledge in engineering, chemistry, and physics—as well as an openness to theories and ideas like mine, which to many may seem unorthodox. As difficult as it has been, one thing is certain: it is easier to find them abroad than in Italy.

I had begun thinking of new ways I could reach a larger audience and share the pyramid and all my ideas about it. Finally, I realized that the next logical step would be to write a book. A book could more easily travel the world and reach the right hands—hands with the ability and a mind with the curiosity to finally build what I have worked on for most of my adult life.

And obviously, I thought as I considered my new plan, my new book had to be written (and published) in English. Of course, I first had to write it in Italian. Then I had to translate it into English ... and then, I'd have to find an editor who, having read my translation, could take my thoughts from my semi-literate knowledge of the language and turn it into something elegant and fluent to present to an American publisher.

Of course, as usual, I did things my own way. I bypassed all the usual practices of the publishing world, like searching for a literary agent. Of course, representation is important—I had learned that in my years working in film. But finding the right agent takes time. I'm getting older and doing the book the "long way" seemed to me to be too cumbersome, too time-consuming and too complicated for a woman at my time of life. Instead, I got to work writing. I wrote, first in Italian, then translated the best and most salient parts, then switched back to Italian to write the next part. Simultaneously, I started looking for a good editor—someone with some technical and scientific knowledge, solid literary preparation, intellectual curiosity, experience in telling stories, and, above all, a sense of humor. I had no idea how difficult that process would be—or how expensive—until I started searching and learned that the cost for the translation of a book in the United States was outrageously high, especially for me in this chapter of my life. I continued writing myself while looking for someone to help me.

It seems to me that sometimes I get my best ideas when I don't get exactly what I want. Sometimes those ideas that come when I'm trying to get through an obstacle are better than the original goal itself. And other times . . . well, I'll be the first to admit, sometimes my ideas are just a little weird.

I was thinking about how to hire someone to help me write my book when I remembered that once, years ago, I saw a TV interview with Robert Bigelow, the American billionaire who founded Bigelow Aerospace. Always interested in UFOs, Bigelow also founded the National Institute for Discovery Science in 1995, an organization set up to research paranormal phenomena. Like most of us who have embarked on this research, he quickly discovered that the transition from UFO research to paranormal research to be smooth and nearly automatic. In 2017, the *New York Times* reported that over many years, Bigelow Aerospace had also conducted a very secret study on UFOs—on behalf of the Pentagon.[14]

So, to overcome my seemingly insurmountable economic problem, I commissioned someone in the US to translate my biography, the synopsis of my book, and a letter to Mr. Bigelow, in which I asked for financial sponsorship for the completion and translation of my manuscript, then to reach out to Mr. Bigelow on my behalf. I figured it would be easier for a native English speaker to get around the various gatekeepers and find the best physical address and email address for me to introduce Mr. Bigelow to my research, theories and efforts exploring the pyramid. I figured that, since Bigelow had an interest in these kinds of subjects, perhaps he might consider funding my further work? And

---

14 https://www.nytimes.com/2017/12/16/us/politics/pentagon-program-ufo-harry-reid.html

if he accepted, Bigelow's financial contributions would have not only paid for the completion and translation of my book, but also advanced work in both the paranormal and Ufology. Having a sponsor would have been a great solution for me—and for Robert T. Bigelow, the cost of my little project would have amounted to just pennies of his fortune.

Oh well. It was worth a shot and I enjoyed hypothesizing all the possible scenarios I could explore with Robert Bigelow's money! Too bad it didn't work.

I continued to write and translate on my own.

Mercury tanks under a pyramid in Mexico!

I love the Web. In the process of writing this book, so often I have discovered things that surprised me—and it's so much easier and cheaper to learn on the Internet than by buying books!

On April 25, 2015, I had another experience of surprise and amazement when I found an article published both in *The Guardian*. and on *Smithsonian.com* that once again made me realize my pyramid ideas might have links to a distant past.

Apparently, during the excavation of the Pyramid of the Feathered Serpent (Quetzalcoatl), close to the Pyramid of the Sun (where, you'll recall, the layers of mica were found), Dr. Sergio Gomez, an archaeologist with the National Institute of Anthropology of Mexico, discovered three large rooms at the end of a tunnel. One of these rooms contained significant amounts of liquid mercury.

The Maya used a mercury by-product, cinnabar, as an element of decoration in art and on the body, like tattoos. But as Rosemary Joyce, a professor of anthropology at the University of California (Berkeley) commented, the Aztec/Mesoamericans theorized to have built these pyramids did not use liquid mercury. It appears to have had no practical purpose in those ancient societies. Yet archaeologists have found mercury in three other Aztec/Mesoamerican sites. Furthermore, Dr. Gomez said there was evidence that something large and heavy was pulled out of the tunnel at some point in history. Archaeologists have long assumed that it might have been some kind of grave or tomb, they don't know for certain. Perhaps it was a container for liquid mercury?

The Pyramids of the Feathered Serpent and the Pyramid of the Sun are both located near Teotihuaca, the "place where the Gods live" or "City of the Gods," in the language of the Aztecs. It is believed to have been in active existence between 150 BC. and 250 AD. This small "city" of about 54 square kilometers (about twenty square miles) was the home of about 200,000 people. During the excavations, thousands of ritual objects were found including many made with reflective mica(!), a sparkling mineral probably imported into the region. Among these ritual objects were four almost perfectly preserved greenstone statues, three females and one male, lying near the entrance to one of the rooms. The female statues were adorned with necklaces and earrings and wore "backpacks" full of symbolic objects, including, several small mirrors (!) which were believed to aid in communicating with the future and the past.[15]

All this contributes to our present-day understanding of the city's origin and daily life, but for archaeologists and scholars, including Annabeth Headreck, a professor at Denver University, there are still many mysteries to be solved, since the ruins of Teotihuaca show no royal tombs and no palaces or seats of power.[16]

> ScienceDaily (Jan. 7, 2010) – Researchers from the Helmholtz-Zentrum Berlin für Materialien und Energie (HZB), in cooperation with colleagues from Oxford and Bristol Universities, as well as the Rutherford Appleton Laboratory, UK, have for the first time observed a nanoscale symmetry hidden in solid state matter. They have measured the signatures of a symmetry showing the same attributes as the golden ratio, famous from art and architecture.

---

15 https://www.theguardian.com/world/2015/apr/24/liquid-mercury-mexican-pyramid-teotihuacan
16 https://www.smithsonianmag.com/history/discovery-secret-tunnel-mexico-solve-mysteries-teotihuacan-180959070/

I added the highlight to the clip from *ScienceDaily* reproduced above. I had suggested the use of the golden ratio for the construction of my small pyramid many years before this article was published. Like the liquid mercury, the mica sheets, the La Manà stone and so many other pieces of information that have come to me over the years, it was yet another confirmation.

MORE CONNECTIONS: Style, Crop Circles, Science and Finance

I have discussed crop circles before briefly. These elaborate designs that appear every year at the beginning of summer, mostly in the south of England—but since 1996 also in the United States, Canada, Germany, Italy, France, Australia, Brazil, Japan, and recently also in Indonesia. The authentic ones, which incorporate particular characteristics such as chemical, biological, and electromagnetic effects in the soil, are of enormous beauty and harmony. When they first began appearing in 1975, they were simple circles. Now, they are often stunning works of art, increasingly complex and often representing intricate mathematical equations (I mentioned the Mandelbrot Set crop circle or the spectacular one of the Julia set crop, earlier). Creating in this style reveals a great deal about the creator, just as an artist's painting reveals the painter, a writer's words reveal the writer and a singer's song reveals the singer.

If indeed these images were created by some non-human force, how better to communicate with us than with mathematics? We may not yet understand the message, but the excitement is in the challenge of figuring it out.

If it is possible that some crop circles are "messages" to us from other beings, then the responsibility for continuing the dialogue falls on us. Apparently, the Earth is rising to the challenge. In September 2010, the United Nations recognized the importance of preparation for dialogue with extraterrestrials by appointing Dr. Mazlan Othman, a little-known Malaysian astrophysicist as director of UNOOSA, United Nations Office for External Space Affairs. UNOOSA is a division of the United Nations task force that promotes international cooperation on the peaceful use of outer space. But Dr. Othman's unique title and role has caused her to be referred to in the media as the Alien Ambassador![17] Her appointment brings the possibility of alien contact to the forefront of international awareness. Had it not been for the media attention surrounding her, her speech at the prestigious British Royal Society in London entitled "The Detection of Extra-Terrestrial Life and the Consequences for Science and Society" would have been attended by only the smallest handful of the scientific elite—and I would have never read about it.

Professor Othman's speech at the seminar highlighted her views about how to respond to alien contact. She believes that the United Nations Office and the United Nations Committee on the Use of Outer Space (COPUOS)—rather than individual nations—should manage a global response to the discovery of extraterrestrial life. Extraterrestrial encounters require a global response in order to face the scientific, social, legal, and ethical problems that will surely arise, Dr. Othman told the attendees. But, as is evident from the topics of some of the other speakers—and their qualifications—when it comes to responding to "contact" with "different" beings, humanity has no idea yet what it will do.

Here, as an example, are some of the topics discussed at the Royal British Society conference:

> *The Evolution of Organic Matter in Space,* Professor Pascale Ehrenfreund, George Washington University and University of Leiden, The Netherlands (Netherlands).
>
> *Predicting How The Extra-Terrestrials Will Be—And Preparing For The Worst,* Professor Simon Conway Morris FRS, University of Cambridge, U.K. Professor Conway is convinced that "if the phone rings, it is better not to answer"—a proposed response in line with the views of Stephen Hawking, one of the most brilliant theoretical physicists of our time.

---

17 https://www.cbsnews.com/news/united-nations-appointing-ambassador-to-alien-world/

Extra-Terrestrial Life in The Cosmic Vision and Beyond the European Space Agency, Dr. Malcolm Fridlund, European Space Agency (ESA), Astrophysics Mission Division, The Netherlands (Netherlands).

The Search for Life in Our Solar System and The Implications for Science and Society, Dr. Christopher P. McKay, NASA Ames, Space Science Division, USA.

The Search for Extra-Terrestrial Intelligence, Dr. Frank Drake, SETI Institute, USA.

The Implications of The Discovery of Extra-Terrestrial Life for Religion, Professor Ted Peters, Pacific Lutheran Theological Seminary, USA.

Fear, Pandemonium, Equanimity, And Delight: Human Response to Extra-Terrestrial Life, Professor Albert A. Harrison, University of California, Davis, USA.

Discovery of Extraterrestrial Life: Scales of Assessment of Its Importance and Associated Risks. Professor Ivan Almar, Konkoly Observatory of the Hungarian Academy of Sciences, Hungary.

Thanks to Nick Pope, former British Minister of Defense, who was both present at the seminar (along with many other prestigious names) and wrote about the experience. His reports indicate that this gathering of scholars was not free from heated discussion. Perhaps that's what really caused global warming?

The conference at the Royal Society was followed by another meeting, equally important and, in a sense, more disturbing. But most average people are completely unaware of it.

In late January 2011, Riyadh, Saudi Arabia hosted the 5th Annual Global Competitiveness Forum. Although it was attended by former heads of state like Bill Clinton, Tony Blair, and Jean Cretien, former Canadian Prime Minister, the forum was organized for the top executives of the most innovative international organizations and corporations in the world. Italy's own Alberto Pirelli, vice president of the tire company that bears his family name, attended, along with entrepreneurs from around the world. The Forum's goal was to identify global challenges and to seek innovative solutions for them that stimulate economic growth and sustainable market competition.

In this context, the Forum hosted a plenary session of major international UFO experts entitled, *Contact: What We Can Learn from Outer Space?*

Although no one that I would consider to be a true Ufologist spoke, the panel included some big names from the scientific community, including Stanton Friedman, the nuclear physicist, Nick Pope, the former British Minister of Defense, Jacques Vallee, mathematician and astrophysicist, Michio Kaku, astrophysicist, and scientific writer, and the Zaghloul El Naggar, a professor of Earth Sciences. Interestingly, Pope and Vallee attended the Forum in search of investors looking to contribute capital for start-up opportunities in the "extraterrestrial sector." So, it appears the Forum reached far beyond the discussion of UFOs, and into the real connections between science and high finance.

These world and financial leaders were lectured on the fundamental concerns and questions regarding UFO visitations and extraterrestrial life. Various theories were presented about how corporations and other entities could remain economically competitive in response to alien contact. For example, if an alien invasion resulted in an energy shortage (and there were many oil producers at the Forum), investments in alternative propellants and propulsion systems might be key. Clearly, extraterrestrial life and new technologies are closely linked—and these topics were discussed by these serious men and women without any stigma. The scientists were able to state boldly: "We are looking for capital to understand UFOs and be prepared for them—and this effort will in turn make us both competitive and be profitable."

Meanwhile, the rest of us, at the popular level, are still debating whether UFOs exist. We're still watching television shows where "guests" debate the pros and cons for entertainment purposes. Or we're diving into ufology as a leap of faith without evidence.

That these world leaders and entrepreneurs are actively thinking about UFOs and how to make money after alien contact strikes me as good news that can ultimately lead to the transformation of our civilization as we know it. But I hope that whatever technological advances derive from events like the Forum are shared uniformly among the major nations of the world. I can imagine serious conflicts over technologies that are inequitably deployed.

Of course, speaking about venture capital and developing new technologies makes me think about my pyramid "model" lying somewhere in my home, now old and bent. Wouldn't I love to have found an investor interested in helping me experiment with it more fully! And then, as I continued to search the Internet, I came across more powerful images[18]. Do I find these things to stir my imagination? Am I still being led to that one person who has a message for me—a message that will bring my device to life? Or perhaps I'm just fixated on pyramids. Yet, when I look at these crop circle[19] images that have appeared over the years (many years after my dream) I can't help but wonder. Either I've experienced an awful lot of coincidences—or they, too, are a part of the message I need to understand.

---

18 https://www.pinterest.it/pin/44895327505314929/
http://www.cropcircleconnector.com/2016/hackpenhill/hackpenhill2016a.html
http://cropcircleconnector.com/Sorensen/classics/classics.html
https://www.michaelglickmanoncropcircles.com/blog/the-fractal-field/
19 For those interested in the topic of crop circles, here are the best sites:
http://cropcircles.lucypringle.co.uk/
http://www.cropcircleconnector.com/

CHAPTER FORTY-ONE
TELEVISION, COMMUNICATION AND DNA

The 4400 was a television series than ran from 2004 to 2007, starring Julianne Moore. Briefly, it's the story of 4400 people who reappear—sometimes after decades of being missing—all on a single day. The series traced how each of them had changed and explored the theories about what happened to them, including the possibility that they had been taken by aliens or by future versions of mankind. The series was incredibly successful, especially in the United States where it received three Emmy nominations in 2005. And of course, its creators Rene Echevarria and Scott Peters delved deep into some aspects of UFO phenomenology.

It's fascinating to me how much you can learn about what's really happening with American scientific research into ufology by watching films and television shows. Behind every script (well, those that are well done), there is not only imagination but also careful *research* into the most advanced ufological investigations. The idea that "they," (the aliens in the show) or at least some of them, came from the future or another level/level of reality that represented the evolution of man over God knows how many thousands of years, is among the most advanced hypotheses on the nature of extraterrestrial life. It is present both from the testimonies of those who say they were actually abducted and in the most cutting-edge research of quantum physics.

In one of the episodes of *The 4400*, patients confined in a psychiatric hospital construct a device they believe is the means to return them to the future. The completed apparatus is shaped like a ramshackle tower and composed of cables, I-beams, relays, light bulbs, satellite dishes, and materials recovered here and there. Even the weathervane, taken from the roof of the hospital, stands at the top of their "means of communication" with the future. The director of that episode masterfully created an atmosphere of frenetic urgency and determination as the characters attempted to build the device. The staff at the hospital even become afraid that some kind of "contagion" had infected everyone who approached the tower, their behavior was *that* intense. Although the Tower did not ultimately send the characters to the future, it released a pulsating discharge of energy that "awakened" a fellow patient—a distinguished professor in the field of neurological sciences. Thanks to the electric energy of the tower, he recovers his faculties and resumes his research.

What I described might sound like a nice bit of creative writing, but in 1992, Giacomo Rizzolatti, an Italian neuroscientist, who had been involved with the discovery of mirror neurons, wrote about emotional "contagion." Elaine Hatfield followed up on the term in 1993, with her pioneering research in the field of Relationship Science, defining emotional contagion as: "The tendency to automatically imitate and synchronize expressions, vocalizations, postures and movements with those of another person and consequently, to converge emotionally."[20] Certainly, most of us have experienced emotional contagion in one way or the other. How many times have you found yourself happy and well in the company of cheerful and enthusiastic people and, depressed and unhappy around those who are sad?

Beyond the science fiction, there are three important messages to be gained from that episode:

1) The characters received an "order," perhaps by mental means, to build an apparatus of unknown technology;

2) The characters felt an urgency and determination to build it, even though they had no scientific background; and

3) The entire episode had its foundation in actual neurological science.

This is the *real* information. There are numerous similar cases in the literature of people receiving advanced technologies and ideas from

---

20 https://medium.com/game-of-self/emotional-contagion-why-you-must-be-careful-who-you-surround-yourself-with-a8e2201988c0.

mysterious sources. In fact, it seems that many people receive not only new technical ideas but also innovative philosophical, medical, and scientific concepts as mental impulses or from communications that defy explanation.

A question arises for me, however. If these "gifts" of information are real—if the information I was given is real—why wasn't it given to a physicist, for example, or to someone with greater technological knowledge who would have understood how to implement what the information required? The answer may lie with some people's ability to receive new information without preconceptions. Or perhaps some brains are better wired to accept information from different communication frequencies. Or perhaps it's simply a matter of willing intellectual curiosity.

I believe the screenwriter who drafted that episode of *The 4400* had had some experience similar to the one in the episode. An experience not unlike some I have had here in Italy when I found scientists who became as interested in my device as I have been since 1978. To date, none of the scientists/researchers I have contacted have taken the trouble to verify the feasibility of the device in its *totality*. For better or worse, every scientist I've "worked" with has confirmed the functionality of some elements within it—each within his branch of specialization.

That episode resonated with me, because I too had been "gifted" with a technological insight that I understood would solve a problem. But was it really a gift—something given to me by someone or something yet unknown? Or did I—and people like me—receive this disparate information randomly?

In the book *VernetzteIntelligenz*, Grazyna Fosar and Franz Bludorf, a physicist and a mathematician respectively, wrote about the revolutionary results they and others have obtained in the field of modern genetics. For example, the German biophysicist Fritz Albert Popp has researched the phenomenon of bio-photons, a natural light radiation emitted by every living organism (i.e., the old auras we observed taking pictures with the Kirlian in the seventies) for years.

This bio-photonic radiation is very weak and only becomes visible with substantial strengthening methods in a darkroom. Popp and his research group observed that our body not only emits light but also absorbs light from the environment. When we are kept in the dark, bio-photonic radiation decreases considerably. Further research suggested that something inside our body could store light as energy, regardless of the food we eat. And soon after, it was discovered that the memory of light in our body is found in that part of our DNA called the "silent DNA."

Because of the characteristic shape of this gigantic molecule—the double helix (which when seen from above, looks like a circle) the DNA represents an ideal electromagnetic antenna. But what happens to electromagnetic energy when it is collected by DNA? It is stored, causing the molecule to oscillate. In physics, such a system is called a harmonic oscillator. Over time, however, this oscillator loses energy. If, therefore, the DNA collects the energy of light and/or emits information contained in the electromagnetic oscillation thanks to its radiant emission, could it be an additional organ of communication of our body? And could it be manipulated by electromagnetic radiation? Further research has also shown that, regardless of its function as a protein producer, DNA behaves like a complicated biological electronic chip that communicates with its environment.

In 1990, a stellar group of scientists convened in Moscow to research the human genome. Along with the physicists of the famous Lebedev Institute, molecular biologists, biophysicists, geneticists, embryologists, linguists—experts across all disciplines and study areas—joined the project. The project director was, and still is, Dr. Pjotr Garjajev, biophysicist and molecular biologist and member of the Russian Academy of Sciences and the Academy of Sciences in New York. In the process of their research, the interdisciplinary approach of this Moscovite group revolutionized how we talk about and understand DNA and human genetics.

Today, we talk quite naturally about the genetic code as an information system. Before the project, genetics was the exclusive realm of chemistry rather than including the language of code. We owe these words to the linguistic experts who lent their skills to the research, since linguistics is the science that studies the structure of language. It investigates not only the languages that are developed by individuals from different countries and cultures but also artificial languages such as those, for example, used to program computers.

Examining the semantics (meaning of words) and the regularity of a language, such as the syntax (mutual relationship between words and phrases to construct a sentence or a complete expression of something) is the basis of grammar. Applying that structure to genetic code, it turns out, determined that DNA code follows the same rules as our language. But not the rules of any specific languages, such as Russian or German, but rules that are fundamental to languages as a whole. In essence, all the languages existing on this earth have comparable structures. Thus, it is possible to put together the structure of the genetic code in a manner which follows the structure of every human language on Earth.

Pjotr Garjajev and his collaborators concluded that the structure of DNA does not correspond to the structure of the human language, but it is human languages that follow the rules of the structure of the genetic code! DNA and the genetic code had already existed for a long time before the first human being spoke with articulated words. Thus, every human language has developed from primordial times following basic models already existing in the structure of the genetic code. Given that this code has a structure, even more information can be transported through it. DNA scientists call it "I-communication."

DNA I-communication could explain why the abilities of healers, mediums, or spiritual masters can have an effect on one person and not on another. It could also explain why hypnosis works for some as a medical therapy but not for others. The medical model of psycho-neuro-immunology considers the effect of hypnotic suggestions exclusively as mechanisms within the brain's control, especially in areas that are presupposed to contain the subconscious layers. Now it seems to be much simpler: DNA can react directly to *words*. At the right frequency (there's that word again,"frequency") a word can affect an individual and achieve a certain result. As yet, no one has determined a frequency that is valid for all individuals, but in humans, this phenomenon of hyper-communication—a sudden access to information outside of one's knowledge—is generally called inspiration, intuition, or trance.

This makes me think of *Ali Baba And The 40 Thieves*. The words "Open Sesame" were the magic formula used by Ali Baba in the fairy tale to open the entrance to a cave where the forty bandits had hidden a treasure. Who would have thought that it was only a question of frequency? Who or what gave the author the idea? The phrase appears for the first time in the translation of *The Thousand and One Nights* by Antoine Galland, French Orientalist and archaeologist, sometime between 1704 and 1717. No previous oral or written versions of history are known, or at least so says Wikipedia.

The Moscovite group and their colleagues can already prove experimentally that DNA reacts to modulated laser light and to radio waves. Both, however, must have the correct frequency. Apart from the hundreds of possibilities that these discoveries suggest—everything from treating diseases, slowing down the aging process, correcting genetic errors, etc.—the Russian researchers have also discovered that our DNA can create interference in a vacuum, producing a space tunnel. These tunnels are the microscopic equivalent of the so-called Einstein-Rosen bridges left by the extinct stars near black holes. DNA attracts these pieces of information and transmits them to our consciousness. From the results obtained with experiments on laser-irradiated DNA tissue, the Russian scientists assumed that energy outside space and time continues to pass through these DNA-activated tunnels even when the tissue sample is removed. The most frequent side effects in hyper-communication are magnetic fields close to the people involved. In fact, electronic devices can be interfered with and stop working for hours when hyper-communication is in progress.

Returning to my own interests, this scientific research opens a panorama of possibilities for both ufology and psychokinetic paranormal energy investigation. It could explain why all the young talents, from my "mini Gellers" to the "indigo children," were initially hit by a beam of light of unknown origin. Could someone be making a slow and gradual change in humanity by altering or reshaping the frequencies of our DNA through light or just communicating with us through it? Even the plants, in their own way, have a kind of DNA. Could that explain the appearance of small spheres of light that produce crop circles or why the stems of the plants involved never seem to be broken? Could that explain why the "contacted ones" receive messages in their own language and why, in many cases, the concepts and emotions arrive completely wordlessly. Or why electromagnetic disturbances occur on particular occasions or to some people. Or why some people, under certain conditions, experience significant temporal anomalies. And it could even explain why incredible coincidences occur time and time again to pleasantly surprise us.

And last, but not least, one could explain why disparate people receive or "catch" instructions to build technological devices that never work, or as in my case, a device to "talk better" that doesn't talk at all yet.

It seems that "someone" has already thought of everything—without all the unnecessary and insincere discussions of democracy. They have been talking to us and our environment for a long time. The only thing that bothers me about it is the thought that, all along, all of my interests and actions *could be* not the results of my evolving consciousness but a response to something suggested to my DNA. Oh well. The ego dies hard.

CHAPTER THIRTY-EIGHT
MEMORY OF WAR

We say, history repeats itself and it is strange but true. It's something I've never understood. Why does history have to repeat itself? Why should it? But perhaps the answer lies in the truth that, in spite of our talk of "awakening consciousness" and "spiritual advancement" so far, mankind has never changed its essential nature.

In 2016, Italian news was centered around the instability in Libya—and how, at the forefront of an international peacekeeping mission led by the United States, Italian forces were commanding a mission to bring the North African country out of the chaos that made it a perfect home for the expansion of the Islamic State. As I read these headlines, strange as it might be, I was reminded of something altogether different: the sweet (more or less) stories that my father used to tell me at bedtime to coax me into sleep. Unfortunately for him, then (as now) I was never sleepy until morning. But I would still beg, "Dad, can you tell me a story?"

"And then you promise me that you fall asleep?" he would answer, putting on an expression that was meant to be serious and stern, even though we both knew he loved telling me stories about his life. I was the only one in the family who listened to them with genuine interest.

"Yes, yes, I promise," I would always promise, but of course we both knew that I would probably stay awake long after the story had ended. "Come on, start!"

"Many years ago, when we were at war, and I spent my free day on a little boat that my Libyan adjutant had found. He piloted it and I was very happy to spend the day out of uniform. I didn't have swimming trunks, so I just made some out of a sheet and rolled another one into a kind of turban to protect my head from the sun. I plunged into the clear waters of the Benghazi Gulf and swam for a long time. We had a nice wind in the stern, and the boat flew over the water, taking us far from land. But soon enough, the day was over, and unfortunately, we had to return to the camp that had been set up a few kilometers from the city.

"Back at camp, I threw myself on the cot and fell into a deep sleep, giving the sun and the sea their tribute. I felt as if I had only been asleep for a few minutes when someone grabbed me violently. I opened my eyes, and two things happened: my Libyan adjutant thrust my rifle toward me, and I heard the sound of the grenades and shots. The sounds of combat were loud and close: they seemed to be right in front of my tent. I was immediately frightened for my men: I was the officer in command, and I'd been asleep and unable to lead them. I grabbed the rifle, and, still half-asleep, threw myself onto the sand, shooting wildly all the while. My adjutant yanked me hard and I turned toward him. He was gesticulating violently, his eyes wide with fear. It took more than a few seconds to understand that he was pointing in the true direction of the enemy fire—and that I was firing in the wrong direction. I immediately rolled myself in the opposite direction and fired again. But in the process of somersaulting myself into position, I got sand in my eyes and I was firing blind. At that moment, I felt a searing "smack" in my leg and my thigh throbbed with pain. I'd been shot! The enemy fire had hit me! I was hurt, I was bleeding, and I was angry because I knew the wound was bad and that I'd be sent home to recuperate. I had no desire to go. It felt like I was abandoning the war effort and the people of the area. The Libyan people I had gotten to know were good people, and I felt like they liked me. I knew I liked them, and I liked my responsibilities. And I liked the feeling of fighting for something. I was annoyed and upset that I was hurt, and I would have to go home. But I got a silver medal for my service and I guess that's some consolation."

He stood up."Now go to sleep."

"You have a medal? Still? Can I see it?" I asked. I was even more excited than I had been before his story and feeling even less like sleeping. Hearing his war story galvanized me and set my imagination ablaze.

"It's around here somewhere. I'll show it to you one day. Now, sleep."

Today, I have a small golden shadow box frame, lined with red velvet in which two medals rest, darkened by time: one bronze and another silver. I hung the shadow box on the wall beside my computer. I found it many, many years after my father told me that story, as a grown woman. I cannot tell you the joy I felt in finally being able to take possession of something of my father's. He didn't give a damn about those two pieces of metal, but for me, they are a direct link back to the memories of my father and his tremendous impact on me.

I doubt that the Italian boys or men going to Libya today will approach their task with the same enthusiasm or, let's face it, innocence with which my father faced his experiences there. But I guess that unfortunately, in that part of the world, history repeats itself.

I wonder, if I can ever get my device to work, what difference heartfelt communication, from mind to mind, might make on the shadows and memories of war.

CHAPTER FORTY-TWO
2019—ANNUS HORRIBILIS

This is the part I cannot write without crying.

In 2019, after battling cancer fifteen years, my beloved Emilio passed away. To the end, we lived as though his disease wasn't there; we fought it with our love and enthusiasm for all the projects, travels, arguments, and fun we shared. We continued to talk and work and explore together—like we had done since that first day we met on the set of the movie I was working on and I had found myself telling him about my interest in astronomy.

Every spring, he waited for the swallows to return to Palermo. For him, the arrival of the swallows was the signal that he had fought cancer successfully for yet another year. This year when they came, I watched them alone, feeling like a light around me had gone out.

Emilio hated his visits to the hospital, and to keep his spirits up when we went for his check-ups, I, ever the entertainer, hummed "The Marines' Hymn" in the car on the way. It was our way of gathering strength for the fight, and my silliness amused Emilio endlessly. Between one joke and another—all little personal things that no one else knew about or understood—by the time we reached the gigantic waiting room of the oncology department we were always laughing. The other waiting patients always stared at us in bewilderment: there is nothing funny about cancer. I agree, but we had to laugh about it to keep the fear from consuming us. That worked for many, many years and many, many visits.

But in January 2019, for the first time since his diagnosis—for the first time in our *lives*—I had to call for an ambulance. I knew then we were reaching the end of the line; I was afraid that it might even be that very day. He hung on for three more months, but it still seemed like a speeding race toward death. He was seventy-seven years old when he passed, and our life together was still beautiful. I miss his breath; I miss his love; I miss his thoughts. I miss the sense of confidence he always gave me, and the encouragement that was in every word, every look and every act. I miss our life together more than there will ever be words to capture.

In one of his last lucid moments, he told me, "Finish writing your book." He made me promise. He knew I would give up without him.

And then he told me, "I'm sorry to leave you alone. Forgive me."

I cried then and I cry now when I remember it. He didn't want to leave me; I didn't want to be left. But this was our Fate.

Sometimes, to encourage me as Death drew closer, Emilio would say to me, "Time is the only luxury that remains. Without time, there's nothing but the shapeless quagmire of eternity's monstrous boredom. Time is what gives life meaning. It's too precious to waste."

He was right, of course. What will I do with the time I have left? I don't want to waste it. I've promised to finish this book and after that . . . in Emilio's memory, I'll come up with something.

CHAPTER FORTY-ONE
UNIFICATOR

We are living in a unique moment in time, a time in which almost everyone—both everyday people and scientists—realizes that the health of the globe is in the balance.

For many years now, climate change has been at the forefront of international discussion. In addition, water shortages, energy shortages, geological landslides, and even the possibility of asteroids hitting the Earth—have been areas of concern. There seems to be a sense that the planet is reaching a crisis from which there may be no return. Everyone is infected by the fear that we must act soon or face our extinction. The media, in particular, amplify this fear by raising alarms that, while frightening, very often do not help anyone to understand the problems or their solutions.

According to the astronomers at NASA and European ESA, in 2029, an asteroid will come close enough to the Earth to be visible in the sky. It was named "Apophis" after the Egyptian god of death and destruction, and some scientists theorize that its passage will affect the Earth's magnetic field. According to the Mayan calendar, the current Golden Age (the fifth and last, governed by the god Quetzalcoatl) was due to end in 2012. Maurice Cotterell (a mathematician) and Adrian Gilbert (an engineer) hypothesized in their book *The Mysteries of Orion* (1994) that the cataclysms that brought the end of the Mayan civilization were caused by an inversion of the Earth's magnetic field, due to a shift of the planet's axis. In fact, the Earth does periodically undergo variations of its axial tilt in its orbit around the sun. Based on his studies of sunspot activity and the Maya calendar, Cotterell concluded that the Mayan prophecy concerning the end of the Fifth Age is derived from a calculation of the next inversion of the Earth's magnetic field. Who knows? Perhaps a similar shift in the Earth's axis plunged Atlantis and Lemuria into the sea and caused the Great Flood 10,500 years ago.

For some time, a group of astrophysicists and geophysicists, including some from the United States, have argued that the poles of both the Earth and the Sun will undergo a magnetic inversion. They believe the last time this happened was millions of years ago, in the extinction event that killed the dinosaurs. NASA has recently blunted public fears about this magnetic shift, however. The official word is that the inversion of the poles will make the Earth's magnetic field slightly weaker—nothing to worry about.

Both the warning of an extinction level event, and the reassurance that there is no danger are based on computer models of terrestrial behavior. No one really knows exactly what will happen—even though, in the lifetime of our planet the magnetic field has shifted fourteen times in the last four and a half million years. The only thing we know with certainty is that ancient texts by people all over the world—the Americas, the Middle East, Israel, and India—all report geological catastrophes that happened approximately 3,600 years ago that may have been the cause of the inversion of the poles.

Why is this significant?

The magnetic fields of the Earth affect its core and, consequently, its rotation. Science has confirmed that, right now, the terrestrial magnetic fields have decreased to their lowest value in two thousand years. At the same time, the rotation of the Earth's core is slowing down, and this naturally affects the crust of our planet. The fossils of mammoths discovered through polar ice coring and the extreme climate changes we have been experiencing in recent years, suggest that we are already entering the early stages of pole inversion. Or at least so I read in *Nature* back in April 2002.

But I bet most people haven't heard about the Earth's pole inversion episodes. You have heard about global warming instead. What we know—what theories are advanced, and which are hidden and barely discussed—is handed out in such a piecemeal and limited way. The result is many of these subjects are very hard to understand. But the truth is that there are many branches of science that study potentially catastrophic events: geology, astronomy, meteorology, archeology, history, volcanology, space science, and even geomythology which is a scientific discipline that researches the geological origins of myths and legends. The theory is that a scientific analysis of the folklore of many cultures, even those related to taboos or areas considered dangerous or infested by demons, can expand the current knowledge of what areas have been previously at risk and might be the epicenters of cyclical natural disasters.

When it comes to apocalyptic scenarios, however, Gregg Braden is at least one charismatic scientist who offers some hope. Some call him a visionary because he so eloquently unites science, myth, spiritualism, mysticism, and religion to explain the mysteries and eliminate confusion about phenomena that are still not well understood today.

Braden has many credentials. He designed computer systems for Martin Marietta Aerospace, worked as a computer geologist for Phillips Petroleum and managed Technical Operations for Cisco Systems. He is also a respected researcher in the field of Sacred Geometry and the author of many successful books. Braden's work pioneers the connection between the wisdom of our ancient past with modern day science, as well as the rehabilitation of the Earth and the peace of our future. Born in Alaska, he has lived most of his life in New Mexico. For more than twenty years, however, he traveled far and wide across the world, among ancient mountain villages, remote monasteries, and ancient temples to scour forgotten texts.

According to Braden, the answers to current concerns about our future can be found among the oldest sciences of humanity, each of which suggests that our success or failure as a species is directly related to the relationship we have with Creation. From the finds in the Egyptian temples to the Dead Sea Scrolls, from the Shroud of Turin to the recent discoveries in Quantum Physics that have shaken the foundations of modern science, an increasing amount of evidence suggests that we are directly connected to everything else in our world. Our ability to recognize this relationship provides us with the key to our survival—and if recognized and implemented, will lead humanity to a great era of peace, cooperation, and wisdom.

Through a series of experiments conducted over the past ten years, Braden reveals undeniable evidence of a form of energy that we could call the "Divine Matrix." Everything—from the success or failure of our careers, our personal relationships, world peace—is influenced by how we participate in the events, both personal and global, of our lives. This is because all of creation is permeated and connected by a field of subtle energy. We "speak" directly to this field through emotions, convictions, and prayer. Thanks to this field, we influence the healing of our bodies, the peace in our families, communities, and nations. It can be called by many names: some call it the "Spirit of God," others the "Web of Creation," and there are many other names, based on the faith or beliefs we practice. In any case, thanks to the ancient traditions, we are now aware of the existence of this form of energy and how to apply it in our lives.

Unlike traditional prayer, this prayer technique has no words. Instead this prayer is based on the silent language of human emotions. Through the quality of our feeling, the ancients believed, we are given direct access to the power of creation: The Divine Spirit.

Modern science echoes Braden's work. Science has also rediscovered the spirit of God—as a field of energy that differs from any other form of energy—or a Quantum Force that connects everything. And this field responds to human emotions. In quantum science, the theory is that feeling or emotion is the way we move from one quantum to another. That means that the expression "The faith that moves mountains"—something most of us have heard many times—reaches beyond religious belief. In this context, "faith" is a state of mind, an inner conviction, composed of thought and emotion, which connects to that energy field and allows the realization of many events that might be called strange or "unusual or mysterious.

Remember those experiments with remote viewing that the United States conducted? The ones it attempted to apply as military tools? Well, remote viewing and many other phenomena in the sphere of parapsychology are none other than the result of our inner attitude and our ability to connect to creation through these fields. Braden says there is no reason to wait for catastrophic events; we all have the collective power to change reality. In fact, there is no single reality but many *possible* realities that we alter by our collective emotions. Knowing that this force exists means we can communicate with it and discover that this energy field heals our deepest wounds and creates the peace among nations that will be the key to our survival. So, according to Braden, the more people to become convinced that no cataclysm will hit the Earth, the less chance there will be it will ever happen.

Some people mistakenly believe that Braden recommends we pray our way out of the world's problems. He does not. In fact, as our consciousness swings in this period of extreme and sudden natural calamities, Braden also reminds us of our responsibilities to ourselves and our families. He suggests preparation: basic survival needs at home and in the car for a minimum of four or five days, to plan in advance the possibility of contact with loved ones and their family members, to stay informed and be prepared to help others.

Braden's books are always filled with long and complex arguments, supported with a great deal of research. Naturally, his thought is influenced by the secular background of scientists and American citizens. I only mean to give his ideas a brief explanation. The strength of his work is precisely that, without prejudice or pre-conditioning, Braden scientifically explains to us what each of us, in the depths of our hearts, has always suspected: there is a "field of consciousness" beyond what we can see with our eyes. In difficult moments, each of us, lay people and believers of any faith, instinctively turn to something "out there" to help us. On an instinctive level, each of us knows that something beyond us exists and we ask for its guidance, hoping to be heard and granted help or wisdom. As Max Planck (1858-1947), the father of quantum physics said, "Behind the existence of all matter, there is a conscious and intelligent mind. This mind is the matrix of all matter."

As for me, I do not know if this book will ever see the light of day—and even if it does, whether anyone will find it credible. I have simply recounted the most salient experiences of my life. Although many of those experiences may seem strange, other interests have been completely normal. I love fashion: fabrics like velvet and silk, lipsticks, makeup, and glamour. I love jewelry—everything that glitters and shines. I'm crazy about shoes and lingerie. I loved the lights and attention of working in the film industry, but apart from that, I think of myself as a quiet person, too: one who can spend hours reading and exploring on the Internet. I am very conscious of the unusual combination of talents and weakness I have. I hope I have used the talents well and worked with my limitations as best I could.

It comforts me to know that two other film actresses have taken unusual paths like I have: Hedy Lamar[21] (1914-2000), an Austrian actress who became very famous in America following her emigration. She was known as a great beauty, but she also pioneered wireless communication by developing a communication system to help fight the Nazis during World War II and only now is being fully recognized for her contributions to devices like the cell phone and satellites. She was always inventing and received many patents and awards for her efforts.

And then there was Corinne Calvet (1925-2001). Born as Corinne Dibois, she was a French actress who appeared mostly in American films. In 1983, Corinne retired from the screen and re-invented herself as a therapist, specializing in hypnosis. She studied at the Arica Institute, a school of spiritualism, and built a new career as a hypnotherapist, specializing in hypnotic regressions.

Perhaps, one day my legacy will be similar? Perhaps one day this manuscript and the pyramid that I have invested so much of my efforts in developing, will be as common as the fields of hypnosis and wireless communication are now?

But now I smell something burning. I have become so wrapped up in myself and my story that I've forgotten the vegetables cooking on the kitchen stove again. Lately, it seems I burn more food than I eat. Perhaps it's a signal of something deep in my unconscious? A reminder of how much I hate eating alone. It reminds me of the chilling and very sad scene of Stanley Kubrick's *2001: A Space Odyssey* where the very old and tired protagonist sits at the table in the empty spaceship. There is

---

21 www.women-inventors.com/Hedy-Lammar.asp

no sound except the clang of his spoon against his bowl as he eats his soup. I identify with him, as I close down this computer and await my "Fourth Life," in which, I hope, I at last see the Dream Visitor's device come to life!

APPENDIXES AND SOURCES

FULL REPORT RECEIVED FROM NICK REITER:
Preliminary Analysis of the Pyramidal Appliance Concept

Presented to Daniela Giordano
by
N. A. Reiter
14 September 1996

I. Introduction.

On 29 February 1996, a manuscript was received by me which outlined the summary and technical implications of a rather unusual case of alien contact. The said manuscript was provided courtesy of Mr. Donald Worley, an Indiana UFO investigator. I had previously corresponded my interest to Mr. Worley in alien contact cases which involved unusual technical concepts being given to a human recipient. Mr. Worley felt that the case of Daniela Giordano would be an excellent example for my studies. I am deeply indebted to him.

The manuscript was a privately published work, co-authored by the original experiencer, Ms. Daniela Giordano of Italy, and a scientific correspondent, Dr. Jan Pajac of New Zealand. The bulk of the work is an in-depth analysis of alien contact cases where technological developments are imparted to humans, and the various societal and philosophical implications of this concept. Dr. Pajac, himself, seems to be an avid researcher of new energy and technology concepts with an impressive academic background and portfolio of published papers. The balance of the document is a monograph by Ms. Giordano describing her experience, and subsequent attempts to build a working device from the concepts presented to her by an alien entity.

The work by Giordano and Pajac is, in a sense, a release into the public domain of the technical details of an amazing device demonstrated and claimed to be a telepathic communication aid. The device was observed by Ms. Giordano to provide or facilitate direct mind to mind communication, at least in a short-range mode. Both authors think that analysis and empirical work should continue on the concept by interested independent parties.

The following report is a summary of this researcher's work on the concept given to Ms. Giordano. Like the original, it is being released into the public domain.

II. The Received Information, and What I Have Done.

On a night in 1978, Ms. Daniela Giordano of Palermo was enjoying an average night's sleep when a vivid lucid dream-like state took over. In this state, Daniela was confronted by a white alien with large blue eyes. The alien held a translucent white pyramid in its hands, which flickered and glowed when the entity spoke. The strange being informed Daniela that she was to build "one of these." The pyramid appliance was said to be a mind to mind communicator, or an amplified telepathic link. It was observed that the entity was seemingly speaking Italian right into Ms. Giordano's mind. A long string of verbally related design parameters ensued, and Daniela became frantic because the alien would not stop or slow down its description of the pyramid's workings. The monologue finally ceased and faded to black. The encounter ended with a thoroughly frustrated Daniela awakening with her mind full of jumbled technical concepts, totally out of her background or understanding. Yet through it all, an obsessive desire remained to follow the instructions, and build a device which would revolutionize the field of communications, and benefit humankind at large. The instructions given by the blue-eyed entity detailed a device which would, or at least should, be easily built with currently available materials. Although certain gaps exist in Ms. Giordano's recollections, enough remained for Daniela herself to build a couple of device prototypes over the years. While neither of these appeared to perform the same way as the "shown" device, they did, on two or three occasions produce some peculiar effects which seemed to be the result of a subtle but unusual radio frequency emission. More recent models produced by Dr. Pajac and his associates have failed to work as a telepathic communicator also.

The design provided consists of a copper pyramid frame, with a large internal helix, small reflecting mirrors, a quartz crystal, and a mysterious vacuum tube containing liquid mercury and salt. Aluminum disc faces for the pyramid, as well as an airtight outer sheath, were said to be required. The final step was to be the pumping out, or evacuation, of the final sealed pyramid.

Upon reading the testimony of Ms. Giordano, I spent considerable time pondering the best approach that an experimentalist like myself could take, to help the cause of examining, duplicating and proving at least some of the concepts disclosed. I have, in the past, looked into several other unusual invention disclosures which were said to have come from an "extraterrestrial" source. While it would not be fair to dwell on these other cases at this time, one important lesson learned from these had indeed allowed me to develop what I believe to be a sound methodology for investigation. It seems to be a common trend that, often, both the original recipient of the information and those who later join in the project become wrapped up in "theory". While in the right measure, theoretical modelling at some point becomes very important, it is my feeling that until any unusual aspects of the disclosed invention are repeatable consistently, a very strict "hardcore" EMPIRICAL approach should be taken. Make no assumptions whatsoever about why or how the device works. Simply follow the instructions to the letter, and use currently accepted materials, instruments, and components to do this. If no results are seen, try again with better quality materials. If still no results, then focus on one portion of the system at a time very carefully, again being strictly empirical.

With this in mind, I decided to start by examining what seemed to me to be the most explicitly defined component of the pyramid appliance, the evacuated ampoule containing equal amounts of liquid mercury and salt (NaCl). I chose this component because it seemed to be the most "non-standard"; without an easy corollary to current technology. Pyramids and crystals have been experimented with by many investigators for years, and represent an interesting field of study with plenty of prior art.

As it has turned out, I have now spent nearly half a year, with many large gaps due to other commitments, examining this fascinating component. As the reader will see, I have seen some surprising results! It is now September of 1996, and I have still not moved on to other device components, other than having built the basic copper pyramid/coil/mirror housing requested by Ms. Giordano's informant. This is due, in part, to the fact that the mercury/salt tube has shown such interesting effects.

Essentially, I have found that the Hg - NaCl evacuated tube appears to act as a novel and unusual piezo-electric generator. When properly built, one of these tubes will spontaneously glow in the dark, emit flashes and flickers of dim light from plasma emission, when mechanically activated, and produce accompanying radio frequency EM "noise". All of these actions appear to be the result of the liquid Hg flowing over, moving across, or jostling the crystal lattices of the NaCl. Further on in this paper, I will summarize the necessary technical considerations needed to produce a tube which works well. To date, I have built 12 tubes. Four of these did not work, for reasons which were later confirmed experimentally, and which may be easily avoided.

To display the chronology of my work, I as a result of this provide sequential excerpts from my notes. I have edited these only slightly.

Hg:NaCl "coherer"- 6 March 96

15 mm diam. x 100mm CFQ (clear fused quartz) tube fitted with a rubber stopper at either end. 2mm diam tungsten rod pushed through stopper at either end. Tube filled with about a 50/50 mixture by volume of rock halite and 99.9% purity Hg. Entire volume of the tube filled with the mixture. DC resistance from one tungsten rod to the other = .2 ohms. We connect the tube electrodes to a meter and check for voltage and current. Absolutely nothing noted. No psychotronic effects.

Hg:NaCl vacuum ampoule - 8 March 96

.1 mole of 99.9% Hg (20g) plus .1 mole of halite crystals (5.8g) were placed into a methanol cleaned CFQ ampoule of 10mm ID and

300mm length. The ampoule was evacuated to a pressure of about 20mTorr (air) and sealed with a hydrogen torch.

When excited by a small Tesla coil, or Van De Graaf generator, the ampoule glows with a pearly white light! Streamers of greyish white plasma play over the halite crystals. Even gentle rubbing of the CFQ ampoule with a hand in the dark produces whitish flickers.

When a small transistor AM radio is placed near the excited ampoule, a popping sound is heard. This seems to correspond with the plasma discharges around the halite. The popping sound is picked up most strongly at about 650 to 700 kHz.

We also note that the popping sound is heard when the ampoule is turned upside down or shaken gently by hand. This is confirmed by the darkroom observation of white flickering. The discharging in this mode seems to be occurring as the Hg trickles across or swirls around the halite crystals.

On 11 March, a second ampoule was prepared and tested. It was identical in contents and vacuum, but of a shorter length, about 160mm. This was intended to reduce the "empty volume" of the tube. We observe that the actions of this second ampoule are identical to the previous one.

The ampoule was placed near the head of a Geiger counter and excited by tumbling. No indications of radioactivity were noted.

On 13 March 1996, we examine the emissions from the second ampoule on an oscilloscope; a Sencore SC61. It appears as though the impulsive emissions can be effectively coupled through the quartz ampoule by capacitive means, for initial analysis. A strip of aluminum foil wrapped around a portion of the ampoule was connected to the floating input of the Sencore. The ampoule was tilted and wiggled to produce discharges. We observe that the discharges are indeed erratic non-sinusoidal impulses, with a ramp period of 2 to 5 microseconds, and a decay of 20 to 50 microseconds. We suspect that the coupling through the quartz plays a role in distorting the impulse waveforms. Because of this, an ampoule should indeed be constructed with a sealed end electrode so that that discharges may be coupled directly.

It was also noted that shaking or squeezing the non-evacuated "coherer" tube does not produce any discharges. Thusly it seems that a vacuum is necessary for the overall function of this component.

On 21 March 1996, we construct a pyramidal frame using Cheops proportions, out of copper clad brazing rod. Height = 27 cm.

On 30 March 1996, a third evacuated Hg: NaCl ampoule was built. This piece was roughly 16 cm long, with the seal-off stub at the center. Clear fused quartz of the same diameter as the first two ampoules was again used. At both ends of this ampoule, however, a tungsten rod electrode was fused to provide direct electrical coupling from the ampoule contents. These sealed electrodes were fashioned from an old quartz Kr lamp out of an industrial YAG laser.

The ampoule was again filled with .1 Mole of NaCl, but about .2 Moles of Hg was added to allow greater flow around the crystals. This works well. The luminating effect in a darkened room is striking, with a fluid - like phosphorescence apparent when the ampoule is rocked or shaken gently. Again, the color is a hard - to - describe whitish grey, with perhaps a faint yellow-green overtone. It is a peculiar effect. The audible effect over a small radio is quite intense, with the same spark-like crackle and hiss as noted previously.

By 20 April, I had constructed a fourth tube; however, I replaced the NaCl with small bits of broken quartz rock (quartz beach pebble broke up); SiO2. Our intent here was to replace the NaCl with another well-known piezo-electric mineral. The balance of the tube construction was identical to the previous unit. Results were positive: the tube displays similar luminescence and RF interference. However, we note that the levels of both were noticeably LESS than the NaCl tube. Therefore, we conclude that piezo-electric materials other than NaCl will work with Hg but may not give as good results.

By the end of May 1996, several evacuated tubes had been built which did NOT seem to work, even though the integrity of the vacuum on the tubes was confirmed. Eventually, the problem was found to be in hydration of the rock salt (NaCl). Small quantities of water within the tube apparently kill our effect! It was found in two subsequent tubes that good performance would return if the NaCl were thoroughly dehydrated before sealing into the ampoule with the Hg.

The suggested operation to achieve this would be to dehydrate the rock salt in a Pyrex beaker at 200 degrees C in air for two hours before sealing into the quartz tube. This seems to work quite well.

From June 14 to July 5, 1996, we experiment with optimum vacuum pressures and ambient gas mixtures. The same evacuation/sealing equipment is utilized, but a bleed valve is added to the pumping line, so that various gases may be added at low pressures to the tube before sealing. We try nitrogen, argon, and dried air.

It appears that dried air, ergo the presence of oxygen, produces a slight greenish hue to the luminescence. This is consistent with traditional oxygen plasma observations. Argon produces a bluish white, more diffuse glow. However, the most vivid performance is achieved with nitrogen, at a fill pressure of about 50 to 100 mTorr. The plasma flashes around the NaCl crystals are brightest, with a clear bluish white color.

A spent Bayard Alpert Ion Gauge tube was connected to the vacuum pump via a long flexible vacuum line. A small quantity of Hg and NaCl were placed at the bottom of the tube. A small transistor radio was placed about .5 meter away and tuned to 650 kHz. We swish the Hg and NaCl around in the tube whilst pumping on it and listening at the same time to the level of crackling on the radio. We note the pressure range where the RF emissions from the plasma are strongest. Empirically, we observe that the plasma effect starts at about 1 Torr and dies out at about 10 mTorr. (Pressure dropping) Best results appear to be from 50 to 300 mTorr of N2.

In July, we performed a simple experiment to determine the polarity of electrical fields developed by the action of the Hg over the NaCl crystals. One of our better tubes was wrapped with a strip of aluminum foil to form a sheath. A second layer was formed by wax paper. On top of this, we wrap a final sheath of foil to form a cylindrical capacitor pick-up. Leads from a voltmeter were connected to the two foil cylinders.

When the tube is tilted so that Hg runs back and forth over the NaCl, we observe a buildup of voltage on the foil sheaths, indicating a field gradient around the tube. We likewise observe that the voltage polarity is different depending on whether the Hg is flowing over the NaCl, (crystal compression) or flowing away (crystal expansion). We, therefore, conclude that the electrical field and plasma produced are similar in action to those produced when classical piezo-electric transducers are mechanically actuated.

III. Conclusion.

Research into a new field, or system, which may contain important new concepts, is often irritatingly slow. The researcher is often tempted to rush headlong into fascinating phenomena, but such temptations are to be resisted. At the time of this writing, I find that I have still not been able to move into the hoped-for second phase of this work; the incorporation of the Hg - NaCl tube into the balance of the pyramid appliance. Such experiments will simply have to come in their own time. For now, my near-term plans include running some experiments to examine any possible psychotronic interactions from the tube fields.

In summation, I would state the following as being major observations to date:

A. When properly constructed, a sealed and evacuated Pyrex or quartz tube containing crystalline anhydrous NaCl, and liquid Hg appears to act as a unique piezo-electric device.

B. When mechanically activated, the contents of the tube produce a visible light-emitting plasma, the characteristics of which are strongly dependent on the composition and pressure of the ambient gas within the tube.

C. The plasma developed within the sealed tube produces strong RF emissions which may be easily picked up by an AM band radio. Strongest emission appears to be between 500 kHz and 1.0 MHz

D. The appearance of the tube plasma, and the property of RF emission, corroborate Ms. Giordano's own early experiences.

This document is, therefore, only the first of what will hopefully be a series of technical updates. The reader is encouraged to take hold of the data presented herein and continue independent work with the pyramid appliance concept.

In closing, I would like to thank Mr. Don Worley for introducing me to this project; Dr. Pajak for his theoretical and technical work, and most of all, Ms. Daniela Giordano for her dream of new horizons in communication for all peoples and creatures everywhere.

FULL REPORT FROM HORACE DREW

2012: I have been able to contact another scientist . . . in Australia, Dr. Horace Drew (nickname Red Collie). This below is his comment received by e-mail. Later it has been published online at CropCircleConnector.com.

Appendix 1. Summary of key functional elements or other features art —fluid waves and pyramids—26/10/12
VIA email to Daniela Giordano
Only, not the final form. Any comments?
Best, Collie

Can we find novel technological devices by studying English crop pictures? Part VII. Fluid waves in a liquid mercury-salt mixture, under vacuum and in the presence of an external magnetic field, may be capable of detecting weak bio magnetic energies (a strange message from a paranormal source) As a result of doing serious research on the paranormal from a scientific perspective, many people have contacted me over the years who wish to present me with unconventional ideas. The story which you are about to read may be one of the strangest, yet it seems to make sense in scientific terms. If this story turns out to be true, then we would have apparently been informed by psychic means (and in crop pictures) how to detect weak, low-frequency, bio magnetic energies through a new method. Some people have speculated that those energies lie in the realm of telepathy or might even permit contact with another spiritual dimension. The main feature of this new device is its use of a liquid mercury-salt cell, under vacuum, in the presence of an external magnetic field, to change weak electrical signals from a wire antenna into fluid mechanical waves. Those mechanical waves can then excite a quartz crystal by the phenomenon of piezoelectricity. This general idea seems obvious, but no one on Earth has implemented it before. Liquid mercury is a good conductor of electricity, especially when mixed with salt. It moves in low-frequency fluid waves when an electric current is passed through it, so long as a permanent magnet is placed nearby. At the very least, this device may offer the means for a new kind of biomedical imaging which could assist human health. "How is your life energy doing today?" a doctor in the year 2020 may ask. Look at the great progress made in medicine since the introduction of CAT scanners (using x-rays) or magnetic resonance devices. What if we could detect weak bio magnetic energies as well? We should not discount new scientific ideas, just because they come from a paranormal source: look at the invention of PCR It would be foolish to discount new ideas, just because they come from a paranormal source: look for example at the invention of PCR or "polymerase chain reaction". Kary Mullis, a junior scientist, first conceived of PCR in 1983 while he was driving up to his cabin in Mendocino Country (see www.nobelprize.org/nobel_prizes/chemistry/laureates/1993/mullis-lecture.html): "With two oligonucleotides, DNA polymerase and four nucleoside triphosphates, I could make as much of any DNA sequence as I wished, on a fragment of specific size. I thought the new idea had to be an illusion. It would change DNA chemistry forever. It was too easy!" Two years later in 1985, after driving up to the same cabin in northern California, Kary encountered a "glowing raccoon" which was probably a hologram (see www.cufos.org/IUR_spring99_addendum.html): (please insert "device-crop1.jpg" here) "At the end of the path under a fir tree, something was glowing. I pointed my flashlight at it, which only made it whiter. It seemed to be a raccoon. I wasn't frightened. Later I wondered if it could have been a hologram? The raccoon spoke: 'Good evening, doctor.' I said something back, probably 'Hello.' The next thing I remember, it was early in the morning, and I was walking on a road uphill from my house." Mullis had no idea how he had gotten there but was not wet from the early morning dew. His flashlight was missing. He was never able to find it. He had no signs of injury or bruising. The lights of his cabin were still on, along with groceries on the floor. Six hours had gone by unaccounted for. PCR was one of the most valuable scientific inventions of the 20th century, worth billions of dollars. Based on that known example, I would advise everyone to take this new paranormal story very seriously. Before telling such a story, I would like to recount one other case of Nobel-Prize winning science from the 1950s, to help explain how the new device seems to work. Thus, we will look next at fluid or "Alfvén" waves of liquid mercury, which may be formed in the presence of an external magnetic field. The odd character of Alfvén waves, first discovered in liquid mercury in 1948. Hannes Alfvén was an astronomer, who became interested in how electric or magnetic fields might propagate through deep space, or through hot stars (see http://en.wikipedia.org/wiki/Hannes_Alfven). In 1948 he wrote (see www.catastrophism.com/texts/electricity-in-space): "The electrical phenomena in stars present us with a new problem. We cannot bring those stars into our laboratories, but we can investigate similar electrical behaviors in a medium comparable to the gaseous body of a star. Still, we cannot work with very hot gases or intense pressures in a laboratory. The closest we can come is a liquid. Of all common liquids, mercury is the best conductor of electricity. We conducted some experiments with mercury and observed curious results. Normally if you tap the side of a vessel containing mercury, its surface ripples. Yet when we placed that vessel in a strong magnetic field, the mercury became viscous. When we dipped two ends of a metal wire into the mercury, it was like moving a stick through syrup. When any wire moves across a magnetic field, the motion induces an electric current. Such electric current then induces a secondary magnetic field which opposes the first one, and thereby slows any further motion. (This is 'Lenz's Law', also seen for a neodymium magnet dropped down a copper tube.) Next, we filled a small tank with mercury. In the absence of a magnetic field, stirring mercury at the bottom of the tank did not disturb any mercury on the surface. Yet when a strong magnetic field was applied, stirring mercury at the bottom was quickly communicated in waves to mercury at the top. Once again, when mercury is stirred in a magnetic field, such motion generates electric currents. Those electric currents with their secondary magnetic fields seem to transfer any bottom motion to higher layers of mercury above, by means of magneto-hydrodynamic waves." Electrical currents running through magnetized liquid mercury may create fluid waves or even torque. To summarize in plain English, running an electric current through a pool of liquid mercury, in the presence of an external magnetic field, not only transfers electricity but also causes those heavy mercury atoms to move in a wave-like fashion. The transverse, low-frequency electrical wave becomes associated with a transverse, low-frequency, fluid or mechanical wave. This is somewhat akin to sound waves moving through air (see http://theory.physics.helsinki.fi/~xfiles/plasma/08/lect07/MHD_wavesS.pdf). Now here is the important point: those low-frequency electrical waves, after having become associated with fluid or mechanical waves, may in principle become easily detectable by various piezoelectric substances, which can convert mechanical motion into electricity (see http://en.wikipedia.org/wiki/Piezoelectricity): (please insert "piezo-movie.gif" here) Whereas ordinary electricity or magnetism at such low frequencies might be very hard to detect. In this second video, we can see how liquid mercury near a strong magnet creates the rotary motion of a "homopolar motor", when an electric current runs through it (see www.youtube.com/watch?v=V61ENFlR0S4&feature=fvwrel). The novel device which is about to describe uses a liquid mercury-salt mixture under vacuum, in the presence of an external magnetic field. The novel device which we are about to describe uses mostly standard components except for one: a liquid mercury-salt mixture under vacuum, with two permanent magnets placed above or below (or perhaps on either side). When weak electric currents from a spiral wire antenna pass through that mercury-salt mixture, they apparently cause some of the gaseous mercury atoms (in a vacuum) to luminesce or glow, just like for a low-pressure mercury-vapor lamp (see www.edisontechcenter.org/MercuryVaporLamps.html or www.light-sources.com/germicidal-uvc-lamps/products/low-pressure-mercury-lamps). Yet that does not seem to be its main purpose. The main purpose of such a device seems to be converting a weak, low-frequency electrical signal into fluid waves of mechanical energy, which can then be detected using a piezoelectric quartz crystal. Here is a summary of how the entire device seems to work: low-frequency magnetic energies, which are present naturally in a human body, may first induce low-frequency electrical currents in a spiral wire coil. When those low-frequency electrical currents pass through a liquid mercury-salt mixture under vacuum, with permanent magnets located above or below, they may create fluid waves of energy, just like for ripples moving through the water, or sound waves moving through air. Finally, such fluid waves may impinge on a quartz crystal which has piezoelectric properties. Various piezoelectric substances have been used as "microphones" to convert sound waves into electricity, or as "pick-ups" on the wooden bodies of resonating guitars (see http://en.wikipedia.org/wiki/Piezoelectric_sensor or http://en.wikipedia.org/wiki/Piezoelectricity). A properly chosen quartz crystal should be able to detect mercury fluid waves at a frequency of 10-1000 Hz and convert them into electricity. I cannot tell, from the description given (see below), why salt (NaCl) needs to be mixed with liquid mercury in this device, unless it gives better electrical conductance or performance? No one on Earth seems to have tested a mercury-salt mixture before. It should behave something like "liquid copper". Also, I cannot tell whether fluid waves, produced by that liquid mercury-salt cell, are meant to induce a piezoelectric response in the quartz crystal by direct physical contact (i.e., gluing the two objects together), or whether such fluid waves ought to be transmitted to the quartz crystal by an electrical connection (i.e., a copper wire)? Certainly, the quartz crystal needs to be part of the spiral antenna, if part of its role is to transmit such energies to the outside world, after their conversion from very-low-frequency to kilohertz or megahertz waves as higher harmonics. Brief but factual description of the device from a reliable source who wishes to remain confidential. Recently I asked the person who had received instructions on how to make this device, from a lucid psychic contact, to write down exactly what had been conveyed. This person has little knowledge of professional science and knows nothing of fluid waves in magnetized mercury. Thus, the instructions which you are about to read did not come from the recipient's subconscious mind.

"You must build a pyramid like this one," he said.

"Why?" I asked.

"The better to speak with. Don't worry; it is not difficult" he replied. The pyramid emitted a bright, soft, white light that pulsed as he spoke, following the rhythm of his words.

Here is what you must do. Take a phial and fill it half with mercury and half with salt, then place it in a vacuum. Next, connect the phial to a spiral wire and the spiral wire to a pyramid (frame). Then place a quartz crystal inside of that spiral wire, above the phial. Finally, place an aluminum disk on each of the four faces of the square pyramid. One of the disks must have a hole in its center. The skeleton (edges) of the pyramid and the spiral antenna should both be made of copper. You should connect them. The cap and base of the pyramid may be made of semi-opaque plastic. When you join everything together, remember that you have to follow certain (size?) ratios. A ratio (of sizes?) between the pyramid skeleton and the spiral wire must be the same. The quartz crystal and its (piezoelectric?) frequencies must be harmonics (of those sizes?). Lastly, the inner volume of the pyramid should be kept in a vacuum." Several other technical words, conveyed to the recipient, were "magnets", "coherer", "windings" and "mirrors as a resonator" without any clear context. Inside of the pyramid, there should be two magnets, one placed at each end (or side) or the mercury-salt vial. There was some notion of a "vesica Pisces" from sacred geometry. Images of two early prototypes, as well as similar images shown in English crop pictures. We can see below two early prototypes of this device, which the recipient of the psychic message tried to make without any professional help: (please insert "device-crop2.jpg" here) Above we can also see two "pyramid" shaped crop pictures from southern England on June 7, 2007, or July 22, 2009. Those bear a remarkable resemblance to the early prototypes. How can this be, if the design principles were only given to one person? For a possible answer to this dilemma, please see below. Analogy to a "coherer" for detecting radio signals. The liquid mercury-salt cell under vacuum, in an external magnetic field, supposedly acts like a "coherer" (see http://en.wikipedia.org/wiki/Coherer or http://www.youtube.com/watch?v=Q1ohAfCdKvM). Radio energy from an antenna can change the structure of a current junction containing iron or copper filings, by making them cohere to one another in a paramagnetic fashion. Such cohesion then allows electric current to flow: (please insert "device-crop3.jpg" here). This was the first efficient radio-wave detector used for telegraphy (see www.geojohn.org/Radios/MyRadios/Coherer/Coherer.html). Bose used liquid mercury mixed with iron filings to decohere any junction after a current had passed through, but not as an essential part of the detector itself (see http://web.mit.edu/varun_ag/www/bose_real_inventor.pdf). In this new device, weak electrical currents from a spiral antenna may change the structure of fluids in a mercury-salt cell, thereby allowing current to flow through the cell more easily. The most likely mechanism would be by inducing fluid Alfvén waves with mechanical energy (like for sound waves in air). Those waves could then be detected as vibrations by a nearby quartz crystal, whether directly or as part of a circuit (see http://science.howstuffworks.com/environmental/earth/geology/quartz-info.htm): "In devices such as hearing aids, quartz crystals convert weak sound waves into electric currents. Some phonographs use quartz crystals to convert vibrations of the stylus into electric impulses." The mercury-salt mixture could itself have piezoelectric properties, in the presence of an external magnetic field. This is because the electrical currents which pass through it will be linked to a fluid motion of its fluid substances. It is hard to predict how two different piezoelectric substances, the liquid mercury-salt cell and the quartz crystal, might behave when joined to one another. No need to plug it in! The human body should emit a weak, low-frequency magnetism around 3-50 Hz, consistent with human EEG frequencies. Quartz crystal radios use a wire antenna to detect weak electromagnetic signals from a distant transmitter. Those signals contain enough power to convert the messages directly into "sound", without requiring any extra power source (see http://en.wikipedia.org/wiki/Crystal_radio#Use_as_a_power_source). This new device uses the natural energy of human-body emissions to create a weak electrical signal in a coil antenna, which is then transduced into fluid waves by liquid mercury-salt (placed in a vacuum) between two magnets. Next, we may see the emission of kilohertz or megahertz radio waves when those fluid waves impinge upon a piezoelectric quartz crystal (especially if that crystal forms part of the antenna circuit). In other words, you should not have to "plug it in"! There must be some kind of frequency resonance which relates all three parts of the device: the spiral antenna coil, the liquid mercury-salt cell, and the quartz crystal, but I do not understand this subject well enough to give advice. Where is Nicola Tesla when you need him? Was this device already known long ago on planet Earth? How could two English crop pictures, from 2007 or 2009, resemble the basic features of that pyramid-shaped transmitter? Instructions were apparently given psychically to only one person on Earth, who has no relation to the crop circle phenomenon. This dilemma puzzled me until I saw an interesting video by Klaus Dona. Here he shows two stone-carved images of a hand-held "pyramid transmitter" from Earth's distant past (see www.youtube.com/watch?feature=player_embedded&v=bZJCD_Ox8w4): please insert "device-crop4.jpg" here) One of those ancient carvings also shows an eighteen-ray, oval-shaped UFO, which was recently drawn in crops at Santena, Italy during June of 2012. Again, there seems to be no obvious relation between that ancient carving and the modern crop picture. The central part of the "oval UFO" (as drawn in crops) shows our inner solar system for a date of December 21, 2012. There is apparently a large, underground pyramid in Alaska which has strange electrical properties, and was built long ago by an unknown civilization on Earth (see www.earthfiles.com/news.php?ID =2000&category=Environment or www.earthfiles.com/news.php?ID= 2001&category=Environment). This is not the place to discuss "pyramids", although the subject is interesting. A need for resonance in receiving or emitting low-frequency, low-energy waves. The major new aspect of this invention seems to be a liquid mercury-salt cell, placed in a vacuum and in an external magnetic field, which by conventional science should convert extremely-low or very-low-frequency electrical currents into fluid mechanical waves of a similarly low frequency. Those mechanical waves can then be detected by a piezoelectric quartz crystal, just like for the musical; vibrations from a guitar. Hardly anyone studies VLF or ELF waves today because of the high technical difficulties (see http://en.wikipedia.org/wiki/Extremely_low_frequency or http://en.wikipedia.org/wiki/Very_low_frequency). Clearly, the copper pyramid skeleton, spiral wire antenna and quartz crystal would need to be constructed with some kind of resonance, to detect or emit low-frequency, low-energy waves of such long wavelength, while only being 27.5 cm high (see www.youtube.com/watch?v=fT5_MmeSeDU). The faint, white glow within that liquid mercury-salt cell could perhaps act like a "spark gap transmitter" as used in early radios (see http://en.wikipedia.org/wiki/Spark-gap_transmitter). Hopefully, some professional engineers will understand how to put these complex ideas into practice, from the approximate descriptions given here. Summary and conclusions: who will be the first to put this new invention into practice? To conclude, studying the properties of a liquid mercury-salt cell, under vacuum and in the presence of an external magnetic field, while weak, low-frequency electrical currents flow through it, could be a worthwhile pursuit for biomedical researchers as well as for mobile phone companies. Engineers at Apple, Samsung, IBM, Bell Labs, Nokia or Hewlett-Packard, please take note! If you can obtain a patent on this device, by being the first to put it into practice, you might make billions of dollars, just like Hoffman-La Roche did on PCR. Nevertheless, human stupidity and inertia remain powerful psychological factors. Most people are afraid to try anything new. For example, any good, experienced molecular biologist could have invented PCR in 1983, rather than a novice. Kary Mullis wrote in his Nobel Prize lecture (see www.nobelprize.org/nobel_prizes/chemistry/laureates/1993/mullis-lecture.html): "Not one of my friends or colleagues would get excited over the potential for such a process. Most everyone who could take a moment to talk about it with me felt compelled to come up with some reason why it wouldn't work." No further comments seem necessary here. If any private inventors would like to get in on the ground floor, please feel free to proceed with early experiments, and contact this author by the CCC website if you wish? Once the unique properties of this unknown device are put into practice by thousands of professional engineers worldwide (if it really works), then we may see great advances in "energy medicine" for human health, as well as breakthroughs in human psychology or spirituality. It will not take too much effort and is worth a try.

Red Collie (Dr. Horace R. Drew, Caltech 1976-81, MRC LMB 1982-86, CSIRO Australia 1987-2010).

BIBLIOGRAPHIC SOURCES

Parapsicologiascienza del Futuro. By John White and Stanley Krippner. Armenia Editore, (1978). Chapter by D. Scott Rogo: "Vociparanormaliregistrate: una breccia parafisica" (copyright 1977).

L'universodellaParapsicologia. Edited by Benjamin B. Wolman, Laura A. Dale, Gertrude R. Schmeidler, Montague Ullman. Litton Educational Publishing, Inc. (1979), Armenia Editore, (1979).

Parapsicologia come scienza. By John Gaither Pratt, Armenia Editore (1976).

2000 C.C.: DistruzioneAtomica. By David W. Davenport and Ettore Vincenti, Sugar Co. Edizionis.r.l., v.le Tunisia 41, Milano, Italy (1979). (Note: pages 129 and 130 of this book contain an ancient description of the pyramid).

Psychic Discoveries Behind The Iron Curtain. By Sheila Ostrander and Lynn Schroeder, Prentice-Hall, Inc. (1975). Editrice MEB (Corso Dante, 73, 10126 Torino), (1975). [Note: references in "ScopertePsichicheDietro la Cortina di Ferro". Chapter XXVII, from page 353 to page 362.]

I PoteriSegretidellePiramidi. Bill Schuland Ed Pettit. Fawcett Inc. (1977) and for Italy News Blitz-Eulama S.A./Armenia Editore. (1977.)

I PoteridellePiramidi. Bill Schul and Ed Pettit, Armenia Editore(1989.)

Executive ESP. By Douglas Dean and John Mihalaski and Sheila Ostrander and Lynn Schroeder. Prentice-Hall, Inc. Englewood Cliffs, N.J. (1974.)

The energies of consciousness—explorations in Acupuncture, Auras and Kirlian Photography. By Stanley Krippner and Daniel Rubin (Editors), Gordon and Breach Science Publishers Inc., (1975).

Galassie di Vita—l'auraumananellafotografia Kirlian e nell'agopuntura. Stanley Krippner and Daniel Rubin, Series Ricerched'Avanguardia. Casa Editrice MEB, (1977).

La Vita SegretadellePiante. (The Secret Life of Plants), by Peter Tompkins and Christopher Bird, Penguin Book Australia Ltd.(1973.) Published in Italy by Sugar Co. Edizionis.r.l. (v.le Tunisia 41, Milano, Italia.

Evidence of a Primary Perception in Plant Life. By Cleve Backster:, International Journal of Parapsychology, Vol. X, No. 4, winter 1968.

Evidence of a primary Perception at Cellular Level in Plant and Animal Life. Unpublished work by Backster Research Foundation, Inc. (1973).

Parapsicologia. Dr. Mylan Ryzl, published in Italy by EdizioniMediterranee, Roma, Italy.(1971).

Esperimenti di suggestion mentale. By Leonid L. Vasiljev, M.E.B., Torino, Italy (1972).

Supernatura. By Layall Watson, Hodder and Stoughton, London, (1973) Published in Italy by Rizzoli Editore. (1973).

EsplorazioniPsichiche in Usa (Psychic Exploration). By Edgar D. Mitchell & Associates, Inc., G.P. Putnam's Sons, New York (1973).

Impronte degli Dei (Fingerprints of the Gods). B` y Graham Hancock. Published in Italy by Casa EditriceCorbaccios.r.l., Milano. (1996)

Da dove vengono I mieipoteri? By Matthew Manning, published by Editore Milan, Italy, (1976).

DizionarioEnciclopedicoItaliano, Volumes 1-10. Istitutodell'Enciclopedi aItaliana. (1970).

Psychic Children. By Samuel H. Young, Doubleday & Company Inc. Garden City, New York (1977).

"Sony scientist stirs controversy with research in ESP laboratory." Peter Landers—Associated Press writer—published October 25 1995, *Daily News of Fort Walton Beach*, Florida, U.S.A.

Il Serpentenel Cielo (original title *Serpent in the Sky*). By John Antony West (1979), published by Armenia Editore, (1981).

Il Misterodelle 13 Chiavi. By Chris Morton and Ceri Louise Thomas, copyright 1999 RCS Libri S.p.A., Via Mecenate 91. Milano, first edition by Sonzogno: October 1999. Original title: *The Mystery of the Crystal Skulls: Unlocking the Secrets of the Past, Present and Future*. Thorsons, division of Harper Collins Publishers Ltd (1997).

Dreams of Dragons. By Lyall Watson, Hodder & Stoughton Ltd. London U.K., 1986. Italian title: *Gliultimi Draghi*. EdizioniMediterranee, Rome, Italy, 1992.

L'arte di sognare. By Carlos Castaneda, 1993, RCS Rizzoli Libri S.p.A – Milan, Italy

Il DodicesimoPianeta. By Zacharia Sitchin, Stein And Day Publishers, (1976) by EdizioniMediterranee, Rome, Italy (1983).

La Via dellaImmortalità. By Zacharia Sitchin (1980) by arrangement with EulamaS.r.l., Rome, Italy. 1986 Armenia Editore, Milan, Italy.

La Genesi. (Genesis Rivisited). By Zacharia Sitchin, (1990), Gruppo Futura (1995.)

Il Giorno degli Dei. (The End of Days) By Zacharia Sitchin, 2007, Edizioni PIEMME Spa, 2009.

Esperimenti di Suggestionementale. By Leonid L. Vasiljev, published by MEB 1972.

Extraterrestrial Life. ContemporaryIssues Companion, Greenhaven Press, Inc., San Diego, CA (2001)*I bambini questi sensitivi*. By Jean-Paul Bourre, Armenia Editore, Italy (1980).

Il Codicedella Vita: Le origini divine del DNA (The God Code—The divine origins of DNA). By Greg Braden. Harmony Books (2000), Macro Edizioni, Italy (2005).

Entanglement. By MassimoTeodorani. Macro Edizioni, Italy. (2007).

Teletrasposto. By Massimo Teodorani, Macro Edizioni, Italy. (2007).

La mentefuori dal corpo. By D. Scott Rogo, SiadEdizioni, Italy (1979).

Disegno del destino. By Edward W. Russel, Casa Editrice MEB (1977).

Il Mistero di Orione. By Robert Bauval and Adrian Gilbert, 1997 by Casa EditriceCorbaccio.

Qualcunaltro è sullaluna. By George H. Leonard, 1977 by Armenia Editore, Italy.

Unusual Mars Surface Features. By Vincent Di Pietro, Gregory Molenaar and Dr. John Brandenburg, Mars Research, Fourth Edition, Glenn Dale, Maryland (1988).

Penetration. By Ingo Swann. Published in the United States by Ingo Swann Books, Rapid City, South Dakota, 1998.

Piramidiperdute in Bosnia e piramidinelmondo. By Sam Osmanagich, 2017, Uno Editori, Italy.

Le Coincidenze non esistono. By Jan Cederquist, Rizzoli, Italy. (2010).

Captain of My Ship, Master of my Soul. By F. Holmes Atwater, Hampton Roads Publishing Company, Inc. 1125 Stoney Ridge Road, Charlottesville, VA, 22902. (2001).

Piramidinelmondo. By Sabrina Stoppa, HarmakisEdizioni—Divisione S.E.A. (ServiziEditorialiAvanzati), Montevarchi, Arezzo, Italy (2017.)

The Premonition Code. By Theresa Cheung and Dr. Julia Mossbridge, Watkins Media Limited, London, UK, 2018.

Il SettimoSenso. (The Seventh Sense) By Lyn Buchanan, published by Pocket Books, a division of Simon and Schuster, Inc,, New York (2003). Published in Italy by Edizioni Il Punto d'Incontro s.a.s. in December 2006. Reprinted in November 2010 and 2015.

Real Magic—Ancient Wisdom, Modern Science, And A Guide To The Secret Power Of The Universe. By Dean Radin, PhD. Harmony Books, an imprint of Crown Publishing Group, a division of Penguin Random House LLC, NewYork. (2018).

Supernormal—Science, Yoga, And The Evidence For Extraordinary Abilities. By Dean Radin, PhD., Deepak Chopra Books, an imprint of the Crown Publishing Group, a division of Random House, Inc. New York. (2018)

Daniela Giordano won the Miss Italy contest in 1966 and immediately followed the path of Italian cinema from 1967 to 1983 appearing in about forty films. In addition to various other professional activities including freelance journalist, she has dedicated herself to avant-garde research in the field of subtle energies, looking for solutions to the intellectual stagnation of the time on topics opposed by most of the scientific circles. Her publications include *Io, Daniela* (2018) and *Tre Vite in Una* (2020). Today she continues to work as a freelance writer and paints. Her work is on FineArtAmerica.com.

www.ingramcontent.com/pod-product-compliance
Lightning Source LLC
Chambersburg PA
CBHW031617160426
43196CB00006B/165